EDITORIAL BOARD

SAUL LEVMORE
DIRECTING EDITOR
William B. Graham Distinguished Service Professor of Law and
Former Dean of the Law School
University of Chicago

DANIEL A. FARBER
Sho Sato Professor of Law
University of California at Berkeley

HEATHER K. GERKEN
Dean and the Sol & Lillian Goldman Professor of Law
Yale University

SAMUEL ISSACHAROFF
Bonnie and Richard Reiss Professor of Constitutional Law
New York University

HAROLD HONGJU KOH
Sterling Professor of International Law and
Former Dean of the Law School
Yale University

THOMAS W. MERRILL
Charles Evans Hughes Professor of Law
Columbia University

ROBERT L. RABIN
A. Calder Mackay Professor of Law
Stanford University

HILLARY A. SALE
Professor of Law and Affiliated Faculty
McDonough School of Business, Georgetown University

PATT V. DONNER: A SIMULATED CASEFILE FOR LEARNING CIVIL PROCEDURE

SECOND EDITION

DAVID BENJAMIN OPPENHEIMER
Clinical Professor of Law
Berkeley Law

MOLLY LEIWANT
JD 2013
Berkeley Law

SAM WHEELER
JD 2013
Berkeley Law

FOUNDATION PRESS

The publisher is not engaged in rendering legal or other professional advice, and this publication is not a substitute for the advice of an attorney. If you require legal or other expert advice, you should seek the services of a competent attorney or other professional.

© 2014 LEG, Inc. d/b/a West Academic
© 2019 LEG, Inc. d/b/a West Academic
    444 Cedar Street, Suite 700
    St. Paul, MN 55101
    1-877-888-1330

Printed in the United States of America

ISBN: 978-1-68328-888-6

INTRODUCTION TO THE STUDENT EDITION

My co-authors and I are delighted that you're using our casefile for your civil procedure course. We hope you enjoy using it as much as we enjoyed writing it.

The casefile is intended to introduce you to the world of civil litigation, and to help you apply the cases and rules you're studying in civil procedure to an actual (well, fictional) legal dispute. You will represent the parties—sometimes the plaintiff, sometimes the defendant—as you help draft the pleadings that are intended to move the case toward trial, or settlement, or dismissal, or a decision on the merits without a trial. Thus, you'll be learning by doing.

The casefile includes 9 exercises, most of which present you with a pleading which is largely completed. You will be asked to draft the missing (but critical) portion needed to complete it, using the rules and cases you are studying in class. We call this approach to learning the "90% solution." Our goal is to help civil procedure come to life, and to deepen your understanding by asking you to apply the cases and rules you are studying in the classroom the way lawyers apply them in actual litigation, but without taking too much of your time.

As you will soon learn, the case concerns a graduate student who found an apartment she hoped to rent. When the apartment manager rented it to someone else, she suspected that his reasons were improper. She sought legal advice from a law school clinic. No spoiler alert is required before informing you that this will lead to a lawsuit. Your work at each stage of the pleadings will shape its resolution.

The case draws on my experience as a civil rights litigator and law professor. On the first edition, my co-authors were three of my former teaching assistants, all of whom went on to work in litigation and/or as judicial law clerks. Two of them (Sam Wheeler and Molly Leiwant) have continued to work on the casefile. After law school, Sam worked at the San Francisco office of a large Washington DC law firm, and currently works as a career law clerk at a federal district court. Molly is a litigation associate at Paul Hastings in New York.

In addition to Molly and Sam, we've been assisted by several Berkeley Law students and graduates. On the first edition, Rebecca Schonberg was also a co-author. Rebecca clerked for the United States District Court and then the California Supreme Court, and is now a Staff Attorney at the Habeas Corpus Resource Center. Courtney Whang joined the team as the first edition was going to press, and helped shape the process that led to this new edition. She is now clerking on a United States District Court. Prior to publication, the casefile was road-tested with over 200 Berkeley Law students who provided their valuable input. Since its release, it has been used by over 3,000 law students at law schools throughout the country.

For this second edition, the *Patt v. Donner* team expanded when Cady Sartorius, Thomas Dec, Martha Leticia Camarillo, Sarah Hunter, Aaron Thomas Murphy, Melanie Ramey, Eric Anderson, Jordan Elkin, Kelsey Schuetz, Deniz Irgi, Chris Bowman, Ian Jacobster and Meredith Spoto—all past or current Berkeley Law students and civil procedure teaching assistants—joined me in revising the casefile. With the help of two of the original co-authors, Molly and Sam, the revision team incorporated the suggestions received over the years into this updated edition. Despite the work that each of the 18 collaborators have put into crafting and later honing these materials, we know it can be improved. We hope you will send your suggestions to doppenheimer@berkeley.edu so that the next edition will be even clearer and more helpful to future students.

Civil procedure is more than a set of rules; it shapes the way courts function, the contours of legal strategies, and access to the courts. We hope that this book will provide with you with some firsthand understanding of its importance and a glimpse into some of the work you'll do when you begin your career in a few short years. And, we hope it will be fun to use. Yes, we believe that studying civil procedure can be fun.

DAVID B. OPPENHEIMER
CLINICAL PROFESSOR OF LAW
BERKELEY LAW
BERKELEY, CALIFORNIA
FEBRUARY 2019

TABLE OF CONTENTS

PATT V. DONNER: A SIMULATED CASEFILE FOR LEARNING CIVIL PROCEDURE

SECOND EDITION

CHAPTER 1
DRAFTING THE COMPLAINT

CHAPTER 1 MATERIALS

PAULA PATT INTAKE FORM

Berkeley Legal Clinic
2013 Center Street, Suite 310
Berkeley, CA 94704

Client Intake Form

Date: 8/22

Name: Paula Patt

Age: 23

Address: Road Inn, 1423 University Ave, Oakland, CA

Telephone: 510-806-4849   **Is it OK for us to leave a message at this number?** Yes

Email address: paula.patt.3@gmail.com

Occupation: Graduate Student in Anthropology at UC Berkeley

Income: Stipend of $16,000 per year + $2500 per semester as a research assistant + $8000 for teaching at a summer program

Have you come to this clinic before? No

Please describe the reason for your visit today: I applied to rent an apartment in downtown Berkeley but I was rejected. The landlord said some nasty things to me during the walk-through. I think he may have a problem with my five-year-old daughter. I want to know if there's anything I can do.

How would you like to see this issue resolved? I would really like to rent the apartment—it is perfect for me and my daughter because it is close to campus and very affordable, and it's in a safe neighborhood. On my limited budget, every dollar counts. I would at least like the landlord to recognize that he did something wrong when he was rude to me and denied me the apartment. I don't think he should be able to treat people that way.

CHAPTER 1 MATERIALS

CLIENT RETAINER AGREEMENT

Berkeley Legal Clinic
2013 Center Street, Suite 310
Berkeley, CA 94704

August 22

Client name: Paula Patt

Re: Retainer Agreement for Pro Bono Legal Assistance

Dear Ms. Patt:

This letter is intended to set forth our relationship as required by the California Business and Professions Code section 6148. If the terms of this agreement are acceptable, please countersign one of the duplicate originals of this letter and return it to us. We cannot assist you with any legal matter until we receive this letter.

1. Identification of the Parties. This agreement is made between Berkeley Legal Clinic ("Attorney" or "Clinic") and Paula Patt ("Client").

2. General Nature of Assistance. Berkeley Legal Clinic will assist Client with their housing discrimination claim.

3. Respective Responsibilities of Attorney and Client. Attorney will endeavor to represent Client competently in accordance with the highest legal and ethical standards. Client will be cooperative, responsible and truthful in their relationship with Attorney. However, both parties have the right to withdraw from this relationship at any time.

4. Attorneys' Fees and Payment. Clinic will not charge Client for services. If the case goes to trial, the Clinic will be paid with court-awarded statutory attorneys' fees. If the case settles, the Clinic will have its expenses paid and the remaining settlement will be divided with 70% going to the client and 30% going to the Clinic.

5. Dispute Resolution. Occasionally, attorneys and their clients have disputes arising from their relationship. If this happens between Client and Attorney, both parties agree that the dispute will not be resolved by lawsuit. Instead, if we are unable to work out the dispute among ourselves, then, upon the request of any party, it will be resolved by arbitration conducted by the American Arbitration Association in San Francisco. Judgment upon any reward rendered by the arbitrator may be entered in any court of competent jurisdiction.

6. Miscellaneous.

    (a) This agreement contains the entire agreement between Client and Attorney. This agreement may be modified only by subsequent written agreement between the director of Client and Attorney.

    (b) If any provision of this agreement is held in whole or in part to be unenforceable for any reason, the remainder of that provision and of the entire agreement will remain in effect.

    (c) This agreement shall apply to any additional or subsequent matters that Attorney agrees to undertake on behalf of the Client, unless the parties agree in writing to some different arrangement.

    (d) The California Business and Professions Code requires Attorney to inform Client whether Attorney will maintain errors and omissions insurance coverage applicable to the services to be rendered by Attorney. The Berkeley Legal Clinic will maintain errors and omissions insurance coverage applicable to the services to be rendered by Attorney, as set forth in this agreement.

      Attorney Signature: _____

      Attorney Name: <u>Sam Pellegrino, Berkeley Legal Clinic</u>

The foregoing is agreed to by:

      Client Signature: _____

      Client Name: <u>Paula Patt</u>_____

CHAPTER 1 MATERIALS

PAULA PATT INTERVIEW TRANSCRIPT

A video of Paula Patt's initial interview can be found at http://www.kaltura.com/tiny/92zff

Subject:	Re: Paula Patt Interview
From:	Matt Madison <mmadison@berkeleylegalclinic.org>
To:	Sam Pellegrino <spellegrino@berkeleylegalclinic.org>
Date:	August 23 3:17 PM

Professor Pellegrino,

Here's a transcript of my intake interview yesterday with Paula Patt for your review; it sounds like she might have a solid case for discrimination since the building manager was interested in renting to her until he found out about her daughter. I am looking into the discrimination statute and I look forward to your thoughts at our meeting later this week.

Matt

Matt Madison
Certified Law Student
Berkeley Legal Clinic
www.berkeleylegalclinic.org

<patt-transcript.pdf>

Interview with Paula Patt by Matt Madison
Transcript by Matt Madison

MATT MADISON: Come in. Hi, Paula, right?

PAULA PATT: Hi

MR. MADISON: Hi, I'm Matt. Very nice to meet you.

MS. PATT: Nice to meet you.

MR. MADISON: So glad that you're able to come in. So, I want to tell you right off the bat, I'm actually not a lawyer, despite trying to dress like it and look like it. I'm actually just a second year law student. But we're actually working through the Berkeley Legal Clinic and it's a program where law students who are certified, like I myself, work with people like yourself who are in difficult situations and try to figure out what the legal options are and give advice. But I do want to tell you that there is an attorney working with us; he's my supervising attorney, he's my Professor Pellegrino. Depending on how far this process goes, you'll probably interact with him some because he'll participate and make sure that if he needs to step in, he does so. I also bring that up to say we're actually recording this conversation, and we're recording it because Mr. Pellegrino will actually come back and look at the tape and not only will he give me advice on doing my job well, but he'll also use it to figure out what's going on and if he sees something that I didn't see, he'll use that. Is that okay with you?

MS. PATT: Yeah, that's fine.

MR. MADISON: Okay, great. And also, even though it's being recorded, this conversation is still confidential so we're still under—I'm still acting as your attorney in this situation, so there's still confidentiality for us.

MS. PATT: Confidential, like I can tell you anything and you won't tell?

MR. MADISON: Well, not, not anything. If you were to tell me that you're planning on committing a crime I would have to tell the authorities. But as long as you're not going to do that.

MS. PATT: Okay, that's not happening. No, I'm not planning on doing that.

MR. MADISON: Okay, then I think we'll be in good shape for this conversation. Okay, so I've read your intake form and I've looked over the situation but I find it really helpful to just hear what you have to say first. So why don't you just tell me, first of all, why don't you tell a little about yourself?

MS. PATT: I'm a grad student here, at Berkeley—or I'm about to start, and I just moved here from the Boston area. And I'm going to be an anthropology grad student. And I moved here with my daughter Sally, who is 5—I'm 23.

MR. MADISON: Well, great. Congratulations on moving to California. I hope your daughter is really happy about the weather; it's a lot nicer here.

MS. PATT: I think she's excited.

MR. MADISON: Alright, well wonderful. Let's talk a little bit about the actual situation that happened. You, you said you're looking for an apartment right?

MS. PATT: I'm looking for an apartment. I'm, I'm not even sure if there is a situation exactly—I just was—something happened—and I was kind of upset about it and telling a friend and she thought that it might be some sort of housing discrimination thing and said I might as well get it checked out.

MR. MADISON: Right, absolutely, I'm so glad that you did. So many people don't take advantage of the resources that are available to them to get legal advice when they have situations like this so it's really good that you came in. So tell me a little bit about this particular situation that happened—so was it an apartment that you were looking for?

MS. PATT: Yes. So when I first moved out here we were just staying in a motel, we're actually still in a motel now.

MR. MADISON: I'm very sorry for that.

MS. PATT: And I contacted the grad student housing office to see if they had any resources or ways that they could tell me to try to get an apartment here. And we're trying to live really close to campus because obviously my classes are on campus and Sally is going to go to kindergarten at the Lab School, right on campus also. So they actually said to look at all the online websites, like Gregslist and the other ones because that's pretty much where landlords in Berkeley will post their vacant apartments

MR. MADISON: Okay, so where did you find the information about the particular apartment that you had an issue with?

MS. PATT: So I looked on Gregslist and I saw this one on Telegraph and it looked like it would be perfect for us.

MR. MADISON: And so, how did you get in touch with the people who were renting the apartment?

MS. PATT: So I contacted the—whoever was the contact on the Gregslist ad and we ended up setting up a time for me to see the apartment later that same day.

MR. MADISON: Great. And was that all that you guys corresponded about, just visiting the apartment?

MS. PATT: Well, when we were having the conversation, he mentioned—I think it was the building manager who I was talking to—he said oh, you're a grad student, I really like renting to grad students. So he seemed really positive and then the other thing was that he asked me to bring out a filled, filled-out application with me. So he sent me, he e-mailed me the link to a standard application.

MR. MADISON: At some point we'll probably try to get a copy of that application if you have it. Do you have one, just stored away—

MS. PATT: Uh, yeah. I actually made a photocopy after I filled it out and I have it in my bag that's in the reception area.

MR. MADISON: Great, we'll definitely want to do that. So during that phone call did he ask you any other questions or did you guys discuss anything else?

MS. PATT: No, it was pretty quick. I said I wanted to see it, that I was interested in the one bedroom and he said we could set it up later that day and was positive about me being a grad student.

MR. MADISON: So you felt pretty good about your ability to get this apartment after talking to him on the phone?

MS. PATT: I definitely felt optimistic. It seemed like it would be a really good set up. He liked that I was a grad student and I was able to see it the same day.

MR. MADISON: Well, sounds good okay. So then you went to the apartment later that day; so how did it go when you went to the apartment?

MS. PATT: Well I went a few hours later, with Sally and we showed up and you know, at first I knocked on the door and Mr. Walters—that's who I had talked to earlier—he answered and he seemed really friendly. And then right away, he kind of looked down and saw Sally and that's when his—that's really when everything changed.

MR. MADISON: Had you guys not discussed that you had a daughter before he met her?

MS. PATT: I don't think it came up in the phone conversation, because we were really just setting up a time to see it.

MR. MADISON: So you said he made a face, did he say anything when he saw Sally?

MS. PATT: Well he—so his expression changed. And he asked, "Who is this?" And I obviously wanted him to see that Sally was really well-behaved so I said this is my daughter Sally, "Sally say hi to Mr. Walters." I could tell—you know she said "Hi Mr. Walters" but she was a little nervous and intimidated, she was kind of hanging on me a little, meeting someone new. But she said "Hi Mr. Walters" to him.

MR. MADISON: And so after that, what did Mr. Walters do?

MS. PATT: Well then we went inside the apartment and you know, he just—his whole attitude seemed different and it kind of made me uncomfortable. He seemed like he just wanted to get the visit over with and didn't really want to show me around and he asked a lot of questions I wasn't that comfortable with.

MR. MADISON: If you don't mind me asking, I know it's difficult but what kind of questions did he ask you about?

MS. PATT: Well it was all these personal ones that didn't really seem like they had to do with you know, how long I'd been renting, like where I lived before or what's my credit like. He asked how old Sally was, and I said five. And then he asked how old I was; I don't really like telling my age but he seemed pretty insistent so I said that I was twenty-three.

MR. MADISON: Okay, and did he have any kind of response to that?

MS. PATT: Well, he just seemed—he just said "okay," but he just seemed kind of negative about it, like asking me more and more questions, and it seemed like the more questions he asked me, the less likely he was—or the less interested he was in renting to me.

MR. MADISON: Did he ask you any other questions that particularly bothered you?

MS. PATT: Well I think the most uncomfortable one was that he actually asked how many sexual partners I'd had.

MR. MADISON: And how did you respond to that when he did that?

MS. PATT: Well I was really uncomfortable, and I said "I don't see how that's any of your business."

MR. MADISON: And, and how did he respond after that?

MS. PATT: Well then he said, "Oh you know, you're right you're right don't worry about it." But it was just one more question that he was asking me, and that was after he had already asked about Sally's dad. It just seemed too personal.

MR. MADISON: And so—I really appreciate you being honest about that stuff because I know it's difficult to talk about. Changing to a little more of a positive subject, what did you think of the apartment?

MS. PATT: I thought it was great. I mean that's why I was still going through it, because it seemed perfect. It was a big one bedroom, so I could put Sally to bed at night and then I could work at my desk in the living room to finish my schoolwork. It was really bright and sunny and carpeted—so Sally could run around and I wouldn't have to worry about her making too much noise or getting hurt. It was basically a perfect fit for us.

MR. MADISON: Well that sounds great, but obviously we're here because it didn't work out so I'm really sorry about that. So after the conversation ended, what did you guys—after you visited the apartment what did you guys do? Or what did you do?

MS. PATT: Well, I wasn't getting a good feeling from Mr. Walters anymore; he seemed uncomfortable. But I wanted to try everything I could to get the apartment, so I asked him what else I would need to do. And I gave him that application and then he also said to give him a $35 check to run like a credit check.

MR. MADISON: Okay. And had he told you about this credit check before, before when you had the phone conversation?

MS. PATT: No he hadn't mentioned that.

MR. MADISON: Okay and you did give him a check there?

MS. PATT: Yes, when I went to visit the apartment I gave him the $35 check.

MR. MADISON: And who did you write the check to?

MS. PATT: Just to him, Will Walters.

MR. MADISON: Okay great. And after you took care of writing the check and gave it over to him, did you hear back from him about the apartment?

MS. PATT: I didn't hear anything back from him, so I actually waited almost a week and I was looking for other things, and nothing was good and so then I decided you know, it's worth giving him a call. So I called him and I asked—I said, "Hi, this is Paula Patt, I saw the apartment last week. Is it still available? Did you get my application?" And he just said "the apartment is no longer available" and hung up on me.

MR. MADISON: Wow, well I'm really sorry that he did that. So just judging by what you've told me and the few notes I've taken and looking at your intake form I think there might be a case for discrimination here. There is a law that says you can't discriminate against a person because they have children, and maybe that's applicable in this case. But just before we get to that, I just want to get a sense from you; what are your expectations in coming here and talking with me? What do you hope to get out of this?

MS. PATT: Well, I guess I don't really know how this works. We're still living in the motel, and I just really—I would love to get the apartment if it's still available, and if not, I just—the way that Mr. Walters made me feel, it seems like he shouldn't be able to do that. So I at least want him to know that he can't do that.

MR. MADISON: Absolutely. So I think the first thing you suggested is a possibility—getting into the apartment. Basically, if we proceed with a lawsuit we'd be able to ask for a restraining order or an injunctive order. Essentially, what it would say is that if that building has that apartment available, or a similar apartment in the building then the court could require that it only be rented to you. Does that sound like something that might be interesting to you?

MS. PATT: That sounds good. You said lawsuit—how—what does that—what does everything really mean?

MR. MADISON: So, right now what we're doing today is just getting some information. And what we're going to do is get some information from the other parties and figure out whether there's enough here. And I'm going to go back and do some research and work with my supervising attorney. But if, you know, contacting them hasn't solved the problem—if contacting the other parties hasn't solved the problem, then if you're interested in that—then what the next step would be is to go to court and to make a claim and to ask for some relief. And as I said, one of the options would be that injunctive order to get the apartment, if it hasn't been rented, or possibly another one in the same building.

MS. PATT: Okay, I mean that one is really the best fit for us that I found so far, so that does sound good.

MR. MADISON: And you know, supposing that it has been rented, it doesn't mean you don't have options. Another thing that we can do is that we can sue for damages.

MS. PATT: And what is that?

MR. MADISON: Sure, so what that might look like—it won't be a lot of money. But what it might look like are the costs associated with having to find a new place—you know, playing at the hotel that you have had to live at while you've been trying to get into a new apartment. And if you find an apartment that you really like and it's a little more expensive than the one you saw, maybe they'll pay the difference—that would be another form of damages. Those are all possible. But certainly either by just talking to the other parties or by bringing a suit, certainly we'll look to get some kind of apology from Mr. Walters, to acknowledge that he made a mistake, or from the building acknowledging that they made a mistake and that they discriminated against you.

MS. PATT: Yeah, yeah, I really just—I really at least want that because he just shouldn't be able to do this to anyone else.

MR. MADISON: Right. Absolutely, and I do have to tell you though, there is a possibility that when we go to collect more information we'll find out something that makes it so there's actually not a case here. Obviously we're going to be in contact with you about that and keep you informed. It doesn't mean that you did anything wrong and it doesn't mean that they didn't do anything wrong. But it means there might be some factor that comes up that makes it not possible for us to bring a suit, but we'll keep you informed on that.

MS. PATT: Okay

MR. MADISON: Well, at that I really—I don't have any other questions for you, do you have any other questions for me?

MS. PATT: I don't think so right now.

MR. MADISON: Well great. So then the next step is that I'm going to go back and do a whole bunch of research and make sure that I'm ready to pursue this and I'm going to work with my supervising attorney and we're going to see what we can figure out. It was great to meet you.

MS. PATT: Thank you for your help Matt.

MR. MADISON: I hope things get better, and just please keep us informed if anything changes, okay?

MS. PATT: Okay.

MR. MADISON: Great, thank you so much.

STUDENT NOTES TO FILE AFTER INTERVIEW WITH PAULA PATT

Berkeley Legal Clinic

2013 Center Street, Suite 310

Berkeley, CA 94704

MEMORANDUM

To: File
From: Matt Madison, Certified Law Student
Date: August 23

RE: Interview and Follow-up Call with Paula Patt

Ms. Patt came to the Legal Clinic yesterday morning to seek advice about a housing problem. I spoke to her at the clinic and followed up with her by telephone today. In brief, she applied to rent an apartment in downtown Berkeley and was denied. The landlord made certain unpleasant remarks while giving her a tour of the apartment that led her to believe he may have had a discriminatory motive for denying the apartment. Specifically, she thinks that the apartment was denied because of her status as a single mother.

Ms. Patt is a twenty-three-year-old United States citizen. She has a five-year-old daughter named Sally and has never been married. She was previously living in Boston, Massachusetts, and teaching at a charter school, and she moved out to Berkeley this summer to begin a PhD program in Anthropology at UC Berkeley.

On August 15, she saw an internet ad for an apartment near campus. She called the number listed and spoke with a Mr. Will Walters. He did not identify his relationship to the building. He was very friendly on the phone and even said: "I like renting to grad students." Ms. Patt did not mention Sally at all during this initial phone conversation. At the end of their talk, Mr. Walters invited Ms. Patt to come see the apartment that afternoon.

Ms. Patt and Sally went to view the apartment together. When they entered the apartment, Mr. Walters seemed surprised to see Sally, made an unpleasant face at her, and stopped being friendly once he knew Sally was Ms. Patt's daughter. He asked rude questions throughout the visit about Sally's age, Ms. Patt's age, Ms. Patt's marital status, the whereabouts of Sally's father, the frequency with which Sally and Ms. Patt saw Sally's father, Ms. Patt's sexual history, and the moral implications of having a child out-of-wedlock. His questions made Ms. Patt feel uncomfortable, insulted, and out-of-place. At the end of the tour, she filled out an application and submitted it to Mr. Walters, along with a check for $35.00 for a credit check. After hearing nothing for a week, she called Mr. Walters to ask about the apartment. He said: "It's taken" and then hung up on her.

Ms. Patt came in yesterday wondering whether there is anything she can do to get the apartment. After she found out that she was rejected, she is still looking for a place to rent.

I told her that there might be a case of housing discrimination here, but that we have to do more research to find out. I know that federal law prohibits landlords from denying apartments based on familial status. She gave me a copy of the application she gave to Mr. Walters. I also asked her to bring in any other the documentation she has, including the internet ad and her financial records. I also asked her to bring in any emails she may have written to friends or journal entries or notes she made for herself that document the facts in detail after they happened.

Here's a link to the interview: http://www.kaltura.com/tiny/92zff.

CHAPTER 1 MATERIALS

INTERNET AD FOR APARTMENT

$1,800/1br-1 brm in cozy apt bldng close to campus (berkeley) (map)

Date: 08-15, 8:30AM PDT

Reply to: 123456@gregslist.org

Please call 510-123-4567

Nice 1brm apartment in quiet building. Located within walking distance to UC Berkeley, Downtown Berkeley.

Address: 1357 Telegraph Avenue

One bedroom

Rent: $1,800

Deposit: $1,000

Available: August 15

Remodeled Kitchen

Stove/Range: Gas

New carpet

Owner Pays: Water and Garbage

Lease Term: 10 months or 1 year

1357 Telegraph Avenue (google map) (yahoo map)

- it's NOT ok to contact this poster with services or other commercial interests

PostingID: 123

CHAPTER 1 MATERIALS

EMAIL RE: 1357 TELEGRAPH AVE.

Subject:	Re: Paula Patt Interview
From:	Matt Madison <mmadison@berkeleylegalclinic.org>
To:	Sam Pellegrino <spellegrino@berkeleylegalclinic.org>
Date:	August 24 3:44 PM

Professor,

I checked at the Alameda County Clerk-Recorder's office, and the deed for the property that Paula was turned away from is in the name of a Dan Donner, who lives at 1509 East 11th Street in Brooklyn. Mr. Donner has owned the property since 2007.

My friend Frank called Will Walters, the property manager, and asked if the apartment was still available. He said that it was rented.

As we discussed, I stopped by the building to see if any of the current tenants would be willing to talk about the management and their policies. I didn't get all that much information, but one tenant, a Tara Tenenbaum who has been there for about a year, told me that there are currently no children in the building, and that she would let me know if any other units become available. I should have the memo on the Fair Housing Act ready for you later today. Let me know if there is anything else I can do for this case.

Matt

Matt Madison
Certified Law Student
Berkeley Legal Clinic
www.berkeleylegalclinic.org

On Aug 24 at 10:15 AM, Sam Pellegrino <spellegrino@berkeleylegalclinic.org> wrote:
> Thank you, Matt. It would actually be better if you could have someone else make the call to
> Mr. Walters to inquire about the apartment. It's too early to know, but there is a chance this
> could go to trial and I wouldn't want you to be disqualified from helping to represent Ms. Patt
> because you had to serve as a witness.
>
> It would also be helpful if you could research who owns the building. We may be better off
> naming the owner rather than the manager as a defendant.
>
> There is some other legal and factual research that you could look into as well. Please give
> me a call if you have a chance later today to discuss that.
>
> Sam Pellegrino
> Berkeley Legal Clinic
> spellegrino@berkeleylegalclinic.org
>

> On Aug 24 at 10:04 AM, Matt Madison <mmadison@berkeleylegalclinic.org> wrote:
>> Thanks for your feedback, Professor. I was able to reach Paula this morning and follow up
>> on the subjects you suggested.
>>
>> She and her daughter moved to the area on August 9 and have been staying at the Road Inn
>> since then. She found Mr. Walters' apartment on Gregslist on August 15 and visited the
>> same day. On August 21, she called to inquire about the status of the application and was
>> told the apartment was rented.
>>
>> Paula doesn't remember the exact questions that Mr. Walters asked her. She said that he
>> focused on her age, Sally's age, and Sally's father's location and relationship with Paula. He
>> also said something to the effect of "raising a kid must be a lot of work," and questioned the
>> morality of having a child out of wedlock. According to Paula, he did not ask about other
>> personal matters like her religion or political views. I wrote a memo to the file documenting
>> the initial interview and follow up call.
>>
>> Would you like me to call and check whether the apartment is still available?
>>
>> Matt Madison
>> Certified Law Student
>> Berkeley Legal Clinic
>> www.berkeleylegalclinic.org
>>
>> On Aug 24 at 9:01 AM, Sam Pellegrino <spellegrino@berkeleylegalclinic.org> wrote:
>>> Matt,
>>>
>>> I had a chance this morning to review your interview with Paula Patt. You did a good job of
>>> helping her to feel comfortable telling her story, and you explained the possible next steps
>>> well.
>>>
>>> One thing for you to work on is once the client is comfortable talking to you, you can start to
>>> ask more direct questions to be sure you get the relevant facts. In this case, it would be
>>> helpful to know what the dates were of the events involved, and what specifically the
>>> manager said to Ms. Patt.
>>>
>>> Sam Pellegrino
>>> Berkeley Legal Clinic
>>> spellegrino@berkeleylegalclinic.org

CHAPTER 1 MATERIALS

RENTAL APPLICATION

Rental Application

Applicant(s)

Full Name _Paula Patt_ Age _23_

Driver License Number _X987654321_ Driver License State _Massachusetts_

Phone Number _510-806-4849_ E-mail Address _paula.patt.3@gmail.com_

Prospective Move In Date _ASAP_ Rent Amount _$1,800_

Full Name _Sally Patt_ Age _5_ Relationship _daughter_

Driver License Number _N/A_ Driver License State _N/A_

Phone Number _same_ E-mail Address _same_

Rental History

Previous Address City State ZIP _921 E 7th Street, South Boston, MA 02127_

Landlord's Name _Liza Lingenson_

How Long at This Address _two years_

Landlord's Phone Number _617-111-3578_

Rent and Payment Period _$925/month_

Reason for Leaving _moving to California for graduate school_

Previous Address City State ZIP _23145 Cambridge Street, Cambridge, MA 02139_

Landlord's Name _Lester Lodgedale_

How Long at This Address _one year_

Landlord's Phone Number _857-993-6875_

Rent and Payment Period _$675/month_

Reason for Leaving _finished college and started a new job_

Employment

Current Employer Name and Address _UC Berkeley Anthropology Program_

Supervisor Name _Prof. Alana Albersworth_

Supervisor Phone Number _510-688-2145_

Monthly Salary _$2,417 (includes stipend and research assistant salary)_

Financial Information

Bank Name _First Bicoastal Bank_

Balance _$12,793_

Savings Account # _3129-6125-1247-9126_

Current Balance _$10,041_

Checking Account # _4719-1352-2459-9834_

Current Balance _$2,752_

Attach $35 check for screening expenses made out to: Will Walters

CHAPTER 1 MATERIALS

LEGAL MEMO RE: FAIR HOUSING

Berkeley Legal Clinic
2013 Center Street, Suite 310
Berkeley, CA 94704

MEMORANDUM

To: Sam Pellegrino, Supervising Attorney
From: Matt Madison, Certified Law Student
Date: August 24

RE: Federal Fair Housing Act

The federal Fair Housing Act (FHA) was enacted in 1968 with the goal of providing "within Constitutional limitations, for fair housing throughout the United States." 42 U.S.C. § 3601. The FHA was passed as Title VIII of the Civil Rights Act of 1968 just one week after the assassination of Dr. Martin Luther King, Jr.

In 1988, Congress amended the FHA after finding that racial discrimination was still rampant—it estimated that there were as many as 2 million discriminatory acts nationwide each year. H.R. REP. No. 100–711, at 15 (1988), *reprinted in* 1988 U.S.C.C.A.N. 2173, 2176. The House Judiciary Committee cited the weak public enforcement mechanisms as the cause of the statute's inefficacy, and empowered the Department of Housing and Urban Development (HUD) to bring cases before administrative law judges. *Id.* at 16. The 1988 amendment also added protections for families with children. *Id.* at 19. The Committee cited the importance of the family unit as the most "fundamental social institution of our society" and Congress' broad commitment to "provide a decent home and suitable living environment for every American family" in explaining the motivation for this change. *Id.* In addition, the Committee noted that, since black and Hispanic families often have more children than white families, adults-only housing policies often have a racially discriminatory effect, as well. *Id.* at 20.

Under the FHA, it is unlawful to refuse to sell or rent, or to refuse to negotiate a sale or rental, on the basis of race, color, religion, sex, familial status, or national origin. 42 U.S.C. § 3604(a). The FHA defines "familial status" as one or more individuals under the age of 18 being domiciled with a parent or guardian, or a designee of a parent or guardian. *Id.* at § 3602(k). It is likewise unlawful to discriminate in the terms or conditions offered, to advertise that the sale or rental of property will be restricted on the basis of the protected traits, and to represent on the basis of the protected traits that an apartment is not available when in fact it is. *Id.* at § 3604(b)–(d). Finally, the statute contains protections for people with disabilities. *Id.* at § 3604(f). The FHA applies to all dwellings, except for single-family homes that are being sold and rented by the owner, as long as that owner does not own more than three such homes and does not use a mortgage broker, rental agency, or other agent to rent or sell the property. *Id.* at § 3603.

There are administrative law and civil litigation mechanisms for enforcing the FHA. I will focus here on the civil litigation mechanisms. An individual may bring a private cause of action under the FHA within two years of the violation; filing an administrative complaint is not a prerequisite. *Id.* at § 3612(a)(1)–(2). The remedies available for a violation of the FHA are actual and punitive damages, injunctive relief, and attorneys' fees (unless the prevailing party is the United States government). *Id.* at § 3613(c). The Attorney General may also bring a complaint under the FHA in cases where there is a pattern or practice of housing discrimination. *Id.* at § 3614(a).

Nothing in the FHA limits or invalidates any state or other laws that protect the right to fair housing, although state laws permitting discriminatory acts will be held invalid. *Id.* at § 3615.

CHAPTER 1 SKILLS EXERCISE

COMPLAINT

This exercise requires you to add factual allegations to Paula Patt's complaint describing her efforts to rent the apartment and her experience with Will Walters. Your portion of the complaint should be written on the Exercise 1 form where it reads *"Describe Paula Patt's claim against Dan Donner. This may require several paragraphs. Add numbered paragraphs as necessary."* Accordingly, the entire exercise should be drafted on that form prior to paragraph nine.

The critical portion that has been left for you to draft is the portion in which you will apply the facts you have learned from the materials in the casefile thus far. These materials include:

- The interview with Paula Patt

- The student notes after the interview with Paula Patt

- The internet ad for the apartment

- The email regarding 1357 Telegraph Avenue

- The rental application

- The legal memo on the Federal Fair Housing Act

Take that information and use it to add persuasive factual allegations to the complaint. A successful complaint will meet the pleading standard set out in *Swierkiewicz*, *Twombly*, and *Iqbal*. This exercise should be completed after you have studied these cases in your Civil Procedure course.

Some tips for drafting the complaint:

- Include all facts that are relevant and favorable to your lawsuit so that the reader understands what happened and why those incidents were a violation of the law.

- Anticipate what a motion to dismiss under *Twombly* and *Iqbal* might look like, and ensure you have enough facts and a strong enough narrative to overcome it.

- Do not argue; make objective statements of fact. But draft the facts in a logical and persuasive way.

- Although you do not need to cite sources for your allegations in a complaint, be sure that you have some basis for the facts that you allege. In this case, that means all of your allegations should be based on the materials listed above—do not add additional facts that you cannot support.

- Do not include any case law here.

- Note that Rule 5.2 of the Federal Rules of Civil Procedure provides that a minor may be identified only by initials in a public court filing. If you refer to Sally Patt, you should use "S.P." rather than her name.

- Remember how crucial the complaint is to your case going forward! The complaint is how you commence the litigation and will be your first opportunity to tell your client's story. If it is not well written, it could also be your last. In addition, this will be your first impression in front of the judge, so make sure there are no typos or grammatical mistakes.

1 | SAM PELLEGRINO (State Bar # 11235813)
spellegrino@berkeleylegalclinic.org
2 | BERKELEY LEGAL CLINIC
2013 Center Street, Suite 310
3 | Berkeley, CA 94704
Telephone: (510) 555-5151
4 | Facsimile: (510) 555-5155

Attorney for Plaintiff

5

UNITED STATES DISTRICT COURT
6 | NORTHERN DISTRICT OF CALIFORNIA

7 | PAULA PATT,   Case No. C 1357 DBO

8 | Plaintiff,
                                                  **COMPLAINT FOR VIOLATION OF THE
      v.   FAIR HOUSING ACT**
9 | DAN DONNER,
                                                  DEMAND FOR JURY TRIAL
10 | Defendant.
                                        /
11 | _____

Plaintiff Paula Patt alleges as follows:

PARTIES

1.   Plaintiff Paula Patt is an individual currently residing in Oakland, California, within the

Northern District of California. She is unmarried and is the mother of S.P., who is a five year old

girl.

2.   Upon information and belief, Defendant Dan Donner is an individual, resides in Brooklyn,

New York, and is the owner of the apartment building located at 1357 Telegraph Avenue, Berkeley,

California. This building is located within the Northern District of California.

NATURE OF ACTION

3.   This is a civil rights action for declaratory and injunctive relief and damages to remedy an

act of discrimination in the provision of housing committed by Defendant Dan Donner, the owner of

the apartment building located at 1357 Telegraph Avenue, Berkeley, California. Plaintiff Paula Patt

1 brings this action under the Fair Housing Act of 1968, as amended, 42 U.S.C. § 3601 *et seq.*, to

2 establish that she was rejected as a tenant on the basis of her familial status.

3   **JURISDICTION AND VENUE**

4   4.   This action is brought by Plaintiff Paula Patt, on her own behalf, pursuant to the Fair

5 Housing Act, 42 U.S.C. §§ 3604, 3613.

6   5.   This Court has subject matter jurisdiction over this action under 42 U.S.C. § 3613 and 28

7 U.S.C. § 1331.

8   6.   Venue is proper in that the claims alleged herein arose in the Northern District of

9 California.

10   **INTRADISTRICT ASSIGNMENT**

11   7.   The events giving rise to Plaintiff Paula Patt's claim occurred in substantial part in

12 Alameda County.

13   **STATEMENT OF CLAIM**

14   *8.   Describe Paula Patt's claim against Dan Donner. This may require several paragraphs. Add*

15 *numbered paragraphs as necessary.*

16   9.   Will Walters's refusal to rent the apartment to Plaintiff Paula Patt constitutes

17 discrimination against families with children in violation of the Fair Housing Act, 42 U.S.C. § 3604,

18 for which Defendant Dan Donner, Will Walters's employer and the owner of the apartment building

19 located at 1357 Telegraph Avenue, is liable.

20   10. Because she was unable to rent from Defendant Dan Donner, Plaintiff Paula Patt must

21 continue to search for an apartment and must currently stay in a motel.

22   11. Plaintiff Paula Patt has not yet found any other suitable and available apartment.

23

24

12. Plaintiff Paula Patt is currently living at a motel in Oakland, California, and paying $700 per week (approximately $3,000 per month).

13. The motel room where Plaintiff Paula Patt is currently living is smaller and more expensive than the apartment that Will Walters refused to rent to her. It is also located farther from the University of California-Berkeley campus where Plaintiff Paula Patt works.

14. Plaintiff Paula Patt has suffered emotional distress and humiliation caused by Will Walters's discriminatory conduct.

PRAYER FOR RELIEF

WHEREFORE, the Plaintiff Paula Patt prays that the Court enter judgment that:

15. Declares that Defendant Dan Donner has committed discriminatory housing practices, as set forth above, in violation of the Fair Housing Act, 42 U.S.C. § 3604;

16. Enjoins Defendant Dan Donner from discriminating on the basis of familial status against any person in any aspect of the rental of a dwelling pursuant to 42 U.S.C. § 3613(c)(1);

17. Orders Defendant Dan Donner to rent the apartment in question or the next available comparable apartment to Plaintiff Paula Patt pursuant to 42 U.S.C. § 3613(c)(1);

18. Awards monetary damages to Plaintiff Paula Patt pursuant to 42 U.S.C. § 3613(c)(1);

19. Awards punitive damages to Plaintiff Paula Patt pursuant to 42 U.S.C. § 3613(c)(1); and

20. Awards attorneys' fees and costs to Plaintiff Paula Patt pursuant to 42 U.S.C. § 3613(c)(2).

21. Plaintiff Paula Patt further prays for such additional relief as the interests of justice may require.

DEMAND FOR JURY TRIAL

Plaintiff Paula Patt demands a jury trial for all issues so triable.

Dated: August 28

1

2

3

4

5

6

7

8

9

10

11

12

13

14

15

16

17

18

19

20

21

22

23

24

Respectfully submitted,

/S/ _____

Sam Pellegrino
Attorney for Plaintiff

CHAPTER 2

TESTING THE SUFFICIENCY OF THE COMPLAINT

CHAPTER 2 MATERIALS

PROOF OF SERVICE

Proof of Service Form

Directions: A copy of this form shall be appropriately filled out and attached when proof of service or statement of delivery or mailing is required. Use Part 1 and Part 3 for delivery by mail. Use Part 2 and Part 3 for personal delivery.

Part 1: Delivery by U.S. Mail: Proof of Service by Mail

I declare that I am over 18 years and not a party to this action.

My address is _____2013 Center Street, Berkeley, CA____. On _____August 28_____, I
                                                                  (date)
served the attached _____Complaint_____ by placing a true copy enclosed in a
                      (name of document)
sealed envelope with postage fully prepaid and return receipt requested in the U.S. mail, addressed as follows:

Dan Donner, 1509 E 11th Street, Brooklyn, New York 11230 _____

_____

Part 2: Personal Delivery:

I declare that on _____, I personally delivered the attached _____ to
                (date)   (name of document)
_____ at _____.
   (name of recipient)   (location)

Part 3: I declare under penalty of perjury that the foregoing is true and correct and that this declaration was executed on ___August 28___ at ___Berkeley, California_____.
                                        (date)   (city)

_____Matt Madison_____   _____
     (type or print name)   (signature)

CHAPTER 2 MATERIALS

DAN DONNER INTAKE FORM

New Client Intake Form

Client Information

Name	Date	Client No.
Dan Donner	August 30	01234

Occupation
Accountant (full time); rental property owner (1357 Telegraph Avenue, Berkeley, CA)

Address		Apartment
1509 E 11th St.		N/A

City	State	Zip Code
Brooklyn	New York	11230

Telephone	Fax	Email
(718) 121-1234	(718) 555-5678	DonnerCPA@gmail.com

History

Prior Civil Case Experience
☐ Plaintiff   ☐ Defendant   ☒ No Prior Experience

Explanation
N/A

Matter Details

Mr. Donner has been served with a complaint by one Ms. (Mrs?) Paula Patt. Will Walters, Mr. Donner's property manager, showed her an available apartment at 1357 Telegraph Avenue recently and then decided to rent it to another applicant. She has alleged that his decision was discriminatory, based on her status as a single mother of a young child. She is requesting damages and injunctive relief. Mr. Donner would like to end this case with as little expense as possible.

Mr. Donner is the nephew of our late client Agnes Donner (Client No. 00876) and inherited this property upon her death.

CHAPTER 2 MATERIALS
INSURANCE CORRESPONDENCE

JOHNSON & SHERMEN LLP

10000 SHATTUCK AVE, SUITE 3500, BERKELEY, CA 94704 | 510.555.3500 | JOHNSONSHERMEN.COM

September 2

Yerba Buena Casualty Company
2100 Front Street, Floor 14
San Francisco, California 94111

RE: Tender Letter for Discrimination Claim

Dear Sir or Madam:

My client, Mr. Dan Donner, received a complaint for housing discrimination filed against him on August 28 alleging a violation of the Fair Housing Act. Mr. Donner is the holder of policy number 1710131923 issued by your company (the "Policy"), and hereby tenders the defense of this action.

I have enclosed copies of the complaint and the Policy. Relevant provisions of Policy are highlighted, including, *inter alia*, paragraphs II.5 ("Tenant Discrimination Coverage"), IV.1.xii (defining "Tenant Discrimination"), and IV.2.iv (defining "Litigation Expenses"), and Schedule III, listing 1357 Telegraph Avenue, Berkeley, California as the "Covered Property."

Yerba Buena Casualty Company has a duty to defend this action under paragraph II.5.iii of the Policy and basic principles of California insurance law. *E.g.*, *Scottsdale Ins. Co. v. MV Transp.*, 36 Cal.4th 643, 654 (2005) ("An insurer must defend its insured against claims that create a *potential* for indemnity under the policy.").

We recognize that you have discretion to appoint defense counsel for this case. Mr. Donner requests that you appoint Johnson & Shermen LLP to defend him. I am a member in good standing of the State Bar of California and have experience litigating housing discrimination cases in federal court. The same is true of my partner, Sheila Shermen. Our firm bills $375 per hour of attorney time and does not bill for non-attorney support staff.

Please confirm your acceptance of this defense and advise as to whether you agree to appoint Johnson & Shermen LLP as defense counsel.

Sincerely,

Jane Johnson, Attorney at Law
State Bar No. 31415927

Enclosures

Yerba Buena Casualty Company
2100 Front St., Floor 14, San Francisco, CA 94111
www.YerbaBuenaCasualty.com • (415) 413 0703

September 5

Jane Johnson
Johnson & Shermen LLP
10000 Shattuck Ave., Suite 3500
Berkeley, CA 94705

Dear Ms. Johnson,

I have reviewed your September 2 letter and the enclosed complaint. Yerba Buena Casualty Company (YBCC) has determined that the complaint filed against your client Dan Donner in Patt v. Donner (C 1357 DBO) alleges a claim that creates a potential for liability under the insurance policy held by Mr. Donner (Policy No. 1710131923) (the "Policy").

YBCC therefore accepts the tendered defense subject to the exclusion stated at section III.1 of the Policy regarding punitive or exemplary damages. This exclusion is based on California Civil Code section 533, which does not permit an insurer to indemnify such damages.

Your firm comes highly recommended from other attorneys we have worked with in the past. YBCC therefore agrees to appoint Johnson & Shermen LLP in this matter subject to the following conditions: YBCC will pay $300 per hour for attorney work, for a reasonable number of hours necessary to reach a favorable resolution of the matter. Any fee disputes will be arbitrated by the Alternative Dispute Resolution program of the San Francisco Bar Association. Neither Johnson & Shermen LLP nor Mr. Donner has the authority to enter a settlement agreement binding YBCC without our express approval. Johnson & Shermen LLP will apprise YBCC of the status of litigation and/or negotiations, and will immediately alert YBCC if a conflict of interest arises between Mr. Donner and YBCC. If these terms are agreeable, please send a complete retainer agreement for our review.

YBCC will reimburse any reasonable costs and expenses accrued for the defense of this matter starting September 2. YBCC will not consider any costs or expenses predating the tender of the defense or accrued seeking coverage. YBCC reserves the right to deny coverage and withdraw from the defense if at any time it becomes clear that the matter is not within the scope of the Policy.

I look forward to working with you.

Yours sincerely,

Ivan Inglewood
Senior Claims Specialist

CHAPTER 2 MATERIALS

CASE MANAGEMENT STATEMENT

UNITED STATES DISTRICT COURT
NORTHERN DISTRICT OF CALIFORNIA

Paula Patt,	)	Case Number C 1357 DBO
Plaintiff,	)	
vs.	)	JOINT CASE MANAGEMENT
Dan Donner,	)	STATEMENT
Defendant.	)	
	)	
_____	)	

The parties to the above-entitled action jointly submit this JOINT CASE MANAGEMENT STATEMENT & PROPOSED ORDER pursuant to Judge Osaka's Standing Order 19, which modifies the Standing Order for All Judges of the Northern District of California dated July 1, 2011 and Civil Local Rule 16–9. Standing Order 19 controls in this matter because the parties hereby consent to Judge Osaka's Rapid Order Calendar for Court Efficiency Trial Program (the "ROCCET Program"). The parties agree to abide by the special scheduling rules, page limits, and other procedural requirements of the ROCCET Program. Both parties understand that they will not have the opportunity to file reply briefs without special dispensation of the Court.

1 | **1.   Jurisdiction & Service**

2 | *The basis for the court's subject matter jurisdiction over plaintiff's claims and defendant's*

3 | *counterclaims, whether any issues exist regarding personal jurisdiction or venue, whether any parties*

4 | *remain to be served, and, if any parties remain to be served, a proposed deadline for service.*

5 | This Court has federal question subject matter jurisdiction pursuant to 28 U.S.C. § 1331,

6 | because Plaintiff is bringing a claim under a federal statute, specifically the Fair Housing Act, 42

7 | U.S.C. §§ 3604, 3613.

8 | The parties disagree as to this Court's personal jurisdiction over Defendant. Plaintiff contends

9 | that Defendant is subject to personal jurisdiction in California due to his ownership of 1357

10 | Telegraph Avenue and business activities leasing apartments. Defendant contends that, having

11 | never visited California, he is not subject to this Court's jurisdiction.

12 | **2.   Facts**

13 | *A brief chronology of the facts and a statement of the principal factual issues in dispute.*

14 | The parties agree to the following facts: Defendant owns an apartment building at 1357

15 | Telegraph Avenue in Berkeley, California, and employs Will Walters as his property manager. On

16 | or about August 15, Plaintiff viewed an internet advertisement for an available apartment at 1357

17 | Telegraph. She arranged with Mr. Walters to view the apartment the same day, and arrived to see

18 | it accompanied by a young girl. Plaintiff submitted an application to rent the apartment. On or

19 | about August 21, Plaintiff telephoned Mr. Walters, who informed her that he had rented the

20 | apartment to a different tenant.

21 | The parties dispute the following issues of fact: what reaction, if any, Mr. Walters had upon

22 | seeing Plaintiff and the minor child who came to see the apartment; whether Plaintiff's rental

23 |

24 |

1   application established that she was a qualified tenant; and what motivation Mr. Walters had for

2   selecting a different tenant.

3   At this time, Defendant does not yet have sufficient information to determine whether to

4   stipulate to or contest Plaintiff's assertion that she is a single mother.

5   **3.   Legal Issues**

6   *A brief statement, without extended legal argument, of the disputed points of law, including reference*

7   *to specific statutes and decisions.*

8   At this time, the disputed issues of law in this case are confined to preliminary issues: 1)

9   whether Plaintiff's complaint states sufficient facts to satisfy the pleading standard set forth in

10 *Ashcroft v. Iqbal* and related cases; and 2) whether this Court has personal jurisdiction over

11 Defendant. Should the case go forward, the parties expect it to turn on issues of fact.

12 **4.   Motions**

13 *All prior and pending motions, their current status, and any anticipated motions.*

14   Defendant intends to move to dismiss the Complaint under Rule 12(b)(6) for failure to state a

15 claim and under Rule 12(b)(2) for lack of personal jurisdiction over Mr. Donner. Defendant will

16 submit both motions simultaneously to prevent waiver of either motion. However, Defendant

17 requests the Court's permission to brief and argue each motion separately, because Defendant

18 strongly believes that the 12(b)(6) motion will dispose of the case without need to consider the issue

19 of personal jurisdiction.

20   Plaintiff consents to this unorthodox procedure. Plaintiff would not be prejudiced by

21 Defendant's proposal, and Plaintiff's counsel includes law students working under supervision,

22 whose education could benefit from the opportunity to approach the two issues separately. Plaintiff

23 emphatically disputes Defendant's view of the merits of the 12(b)(6) motion.

24

JOINT CASE MANAGEMENT STATEMENT

5. Amendment of Pleadings

The extent to which parties, claims, or defenses are expected to be added or dismissed.

Plaintiff is currently researching California state housing discrimination law, and may amend to add a state law claim.

6. Discovery

Discovery taken to date, if any, the scope of anticipated discovery, any proposed limitations or modifications of the discovery rules.

The parties consent to the limited discovery available under Judge Osaka's ROCCET Program. The parties expect that the bulk of discovery will consist of one deposition by each party. Plaintiff intends to depose Will Walters, Defendant's property manager. Defendant intends to depose Plaintiff Paula Patt.

7. Settlement and ADR

Prospects for settlement, ADR efforts to date, and a specific ADR plan for the case.

The parties have discussed settlement and have determined that the case cannot be settled at this time. The parties remain in contact and will continue to consider settlement throughout the proceedings. At this time, counsel for both parties have maintained an effective professional relationship and do not believe third-party ADR procedures would increase the likelihood of settlement.

8. Trial

Whether the case will be tried to a jury or to the court, the expected length of the trial, and the proposed trial date.

1   Plaintiff has demanded a jury trial. The parties anticipate that a trial of no more than two days

2   will be sufficient. In accordance with the ROCCET Program, the parties propose a trial beginning

3   December 2 of this year.

4   **9.   Disclosure of Non-party Interested Entities or Persons**

5   *Whether each party has filed the "Certification of Interested Entities or Persons" required by Civil*

6   *Local Rule 3–16. In addition, each party must restate in the case management statement the contents*

7   *of its certification by identifying any persons, firms, partnerships, corporations (including parent*

8   *corporations) or other entities known by the party to have either: (i) a financial interest in the subject*

9   *matter in controversy or in a party to the proceeding; or (ii) any other kind of interest that could be*

10 *substantially affected by the outcome of the proceeding.*

11   The parties have filed Certifications of Interested Entities or Persons under separate cover.

12 Plaintiff identifies her daughter, S.P., as a person with an interest in the proceeding. Defendant

13 identifies his insurer, Yerba Buena Casualty Company, as an interested entity.

14   The parties are not aware of any persons seeking to intervene or otherwise participate in the

15 proceedings. In the interest of speedy and efficient litigation, the parties would oppose any

16 intervention.

17
    Dated: September 2   /s/ Sam Pellegrino, Berkeley Legal Clinic
18   _____
                                Counsel for plaintiff
19 Dated: September 2   /s/ Jane Johnson, Johnson & Shermen LLP
20   _____
                                Counsel for defendant

21

22

23

24

CHAPTER 2 MATERIALS

SCHEDULING ORDER

UNITED STATES DISTRICT COURT

NORTHERN DISTRICT OF CALIFORNIA

Paula Patt,	)	Case Number C 1357 DBO
Plaintiff,	)	
vs.	)	ORDER SETTING INITIAL CASE MANAGEMENT CONFERENCE AND ADR DEADLINES
Dan Donner,	)	
Defendant.	)	
_____	)	

Following the case management conference held on September 3, IT IS HEREBY ORDERED that this action is assigned to the Honorable Judge Osaka. This matter shall be controlled by Judge Osaka's Standing Order 19, which modifies the Standing Order for All Judges of the Northern District of California dated July 1, 2011 and Civil Local Rule 16–9. Standing Order 19 controls in this matter because the parties have consented to Judge Osaka's Rapid Order Calendar for Court Efficiency Trial Program (the "ROCCET Program"). The parties hereby agree to follow the special scheduling rules, page limits and other procedural requirements of the ROCCET Program. Neither party will have the opportunity to file reply briefs without special dispensation of the Court.

Based on the consent of the parties, as well as the ROCCET Program's purpose of experimenting with adjustments to procedure, Defendant's request to separately brief his motions to dismiss under Rules 12(b)(2) and 12(b)(6) is GRANTED. The motions, as well as Defendant's briefing of the 12(b)(6) issue, should be filed at Defendant's earliest convenience and no later than September 6. Plaintiff's opposition and the hearing on this matter will take place in accordance with the schedule set forth in the ROCCET Program (Standing Order 19).

IT IS FURTHER ORDERED that this action is not assigned to Alternative Dispute Resolution (ADR) Multi-Option Program governed by ADR Local Rule 3 (see https://www.cand.uscourts.gov/

1 adr). At this time, the counsel for both parties have maintained an effective professional relationship

2 and do not believe third party ADR procedures would increase the likelihood of settlement.

3   **CASE SCHEDULE**

Date	Event
8/28	Complaint Filed
9/2	Case Management Statement Filed
9/6	Last day to submit Motions to Dismiss (except 12(b)(2))
9/10	Last day to submit Opposition to Motions to Dismiss
9/22	Last day to submit 12(b)(2) Motion to Dismiss
9/26	Last day to submit Opposition to 12(b)(2) Motion to Dismiss
10/11	Last day to submit Answer to Complaint
11/1	Last day to complete discovery
11/2	Last day to submit Motion for Summary Judgment
11/8	Last day to submit Opposition to the Motion for Summary Judgment
11/15	Settlement Conference

CHAPTER 2 MATERIALS

WILL WALTERS INTERVIEW TRANSCRIPT

To view the video-recording of the interview, go to: http://www.kaltura.com/tiny/blgsb

Subject: Re: Will Walters Interview
From: Andrew Adderland <andrew.adderland@johnsonshermen.com>
To: Sheila Shermen <sheila.shermen@johnsonshermen.com>
Date: September 4 1:17 PM

Sheila, here's the transcript you asked for. I hope the trip went well.

Andrew

Andrew Adderland
Assistant to Sheila Shermen
Johnson & Shermen LLP | www.johnsonshermen.com

<walters-transcript.pdf>

On September 4 at 11:36 AM, sheila.shermen@johnsonshermen.com wrote:

Hi Andrew, do you think you could write up a transcript of this for me? Jane recorded a witness interview but I don't think I'll have a chance to look it over until I'm on the plane, and I won't be able to access our video server. Should be fairly short. Thanks!

Sheila Shermen
Johnson & Shermen LLP | www.johnsonshermen.com
sheila.shermen@johnsonshermen.com | (510) 555-3500

On September 4 at 11:13 AM, jane.johnson@johnsonshermen.com wrote:
Sheila,

I interviewed Will Walters this morning, the property manager who will probably be the key witness in the Patt v. Donner case. His views on single parenthood aren't exactly ideal—and he apparently didn't realize that familial status discrimination is illegal—but the good news is that it seems the plaintiff canceled her check for an application fee before she was rejected, essentially withdrawing her application. I recorded the interview for you, here's a link to the video on our server. http://www.kaltura.com/tiny/blgsb

Let's discuss when you're back in town. Hope you're enjoying Seattle!

Jane

Jane Johnson
Johnson & Shermen LLP | www.johnsonshermen.com
jane.johnson@johnsonshermen.com | (510) 555-3500

Interview with Will Walters by Jane Johnson
Transcript by Andrew Adderland, assistant to Sheila Shermen

MR. WALTERS: Hi

MS. JOHNSON: Hi

MR. WALTERS: Jane?

MS. JOHNSON: Good morning Will. Yes, my name is Jane Johnson.

MR. WALTERS: Nice to meet you.

MS. JOHNSON: Nice to meet you.

MS. JOHNSON: Thank you very much for coming in today, and the reason why we asked you to come in is because there's been a complaint filed against your employer, Dan Donner, whom I represent. And it is alleging discrimination, and because you work for him as manager of the apartment, you're a very important witness because we need to figure out how to file Dan's response.

MR. WALTERS: Ok, I understand.

MS. JOHNSON: So again, thank you for coming in today.

MR. WALTERS: Of course. Um. . .

MS. JOHNSON: Yes?

MR. WALTERS: So is this confidential? How does this work?

MS. JOHNSON: Yes, it is confidential, but if you say something to me I may need to disclose it to Mr. Donner, as well as his insurance company.

MR. WALTERS: Sure. Ok, I understand.

MS. JOHNSON: But other than that, yes, it is confidential.

MR. WALTERS: Now you said it's a discrimination claim.

MS. JOHNSON: It is.

MR. WALTERS: This woman. . . this is about that Paula Patt woman, right?

MS. JOHNSON: Yes, Paula Patt.

MR. WALTERS: And, she's white—I think she's white—and I rented the apartment to another woman, I have other women in the. . . So I, you know, I'm not racist, I'm not sexist, I don't really understand what's going on.

MS. JOHNSON: Nobody's saying that you're racist or sexist. So the claim is, what Paula Patt is alleging here is that you discriminated against her because she has a child and that was why you didn't rent the apartment to her. So then, that's the claim.

MR. WALTERS: Ok, is there a law about that?

MS. JOHNSON: Yes, there are laws against that. The housing laws protect against any sort of discrimination against families and children.

MR. WALTERS: Oh. Ok.

MS. JOHNSON: But, you know, if you like, we can arrange a session or opportunity for you to have some training on what sort of things are prohibited for apartment managers, some online courses. I'm sure that will probably be very helpful.

MR. WALTERS: Ok, yeah, yeah, I could probably find time for that.

MS. JOHNSON: Great. So I guess first I just wanted to ask you some questions. Tell me a little bit about yourself and what it is you do for Mr. Donner.

MR. WALTERS: Ok, well I've been the um. . .

MS. JOHNSON: Oh, sorry, before we go ahead I just wanted to make sure—we are recording this conversation for my partner Sheila Shermen because she unfortunately could not be here today. And I just wanted to make sure that, she may find some things in our conversation that are significant that I didn't think about.

MR. WALTERS: Ok, sure.

MS. JOHNSON: Is that alright?

MR. WALTERS: That's no problem. Yeah, so for me, I'm the apartment manager, I've done this for a couple years now and I'm a business student at Haas. . .

MS. JOHNSON: At UC Berkeley?

MR. WALTERS: Yeah, that's right. And, yeah, Dan. . . I saw an ad online for this job, it came with free rent which is a great deal for me, and mostly I just fill vacancies when they arise. Sometimes I do some minor repairs and things like that.

MS. JOHNSON: Ok.

MR. WALTERS: A lot of it is just bringing people into the building.

MS. JOHNSON: Right. And what is the procedure that you usually go through? Is it whenever a place becomes empty you put up an ad or something?

MR. WALTERS: Yeah, when I know someone's planning to move out, or every now and then somebody does unexpectedly, but if there's a vacancy I'll put an ad up on gregslist.

MS. JOHNSON: Ok.

MR. WALTERS: And uh, usually I'll take the first qualified applicant. That's my policy.

MS. JOHNSON: The first qualified applicant.

MR. WALTERS: Yeah, absolutely.

MS. JOHNSON: Ok, do you happen to have a copy of the ad that you put on gregslist?

MR. WALTERS: Yeah, here you go.

MS. JOHNSON: Oh. Brilliant. Wonderful. So I notice it says here that you kind of don't specify any requirement or any sort of type of people that you rent to. Is there any other policy against who you prefer to rent to? Other than the first qualified candidate?

MR. WALTERS: Well, I like to rent to grad students. Because in Berkeley there are a lot of students in general and I think the grad students are quieter and a little more responsible than the undergrads. And so I'm a grad student, like I said, and most of the other tenants are too. So that's something that I look for, is people who are gonna kinda keep their head down, and focus on their work, and live a responsible life.

MS. JOHNSON: So are all people who are living in the apartment units, are they all grad students?

MR. WALTERS: Not all of them. Umm, there are a few other grad students. The woman who I most recently rented to—the same apartment—she's a barista, she works at a coffee shop, but she seems to kinda have her life together.

MS. JOHNSON: Ok. So let's talk about the facts of the case. Do you remember this person Paula Patt? Can you tell me a bit more about your first contact with her?

MR. WALTERS: Yeah, um, she sent me an email after I posted that ad.

MS. JOHNSON: Ok.

MR. WALTERS: And then we talked on the phone. And set up a chance for her to come in and see the apartment. She said she was interested, she was a student, and so we set that up for her to come in the same day.

MS. JOHNSON: Ok.

MR. WALTERS: And I gave her the application, which she brought with her.

MS. JOHNSON: Ok. Can you describe to me, in chronological order, what happened when she came to look at the apartment?

MR. WALTERS: Sure, so she showed up at the door, and she brought her kid with her. I didn't realize she had a kid.

MS. JOHNSON: She didn't mention this on the phone?

MR. WALTERS: No, no, that hadn't come up. But she had this daughter who was just out of control. Just loud, whiny, and seemed like she'd be really disruptive in the apartment building. And it kind of made me think that maybe Paula wasn't so responsible because she didn't have—didn't really have her kid under control. And the fact that she has a—single woman with a kid, maybe she made some bad choices there, I don't know.

MS. JOHNSON: Ok, so you kind of have a problem with her, kind of, lifestyle. Is that—

MR. WALTERS: Well, you know, me personally? Yeah I don't think that's the best way to raise a kid.

MS. JOHNSON: Ok.

MR. WALTERS: But that's you know, that's not why—I'm not discriminating against people who are, you know, single parents, it's just that that made me think twice about her. And also, mostly, you know if it had been a different kid, if her kid had been quiet and well behaved, that would have been a different story. But this kid was just all over the place.

MS. JOHNSON: Right. Did you mention of this to her? Or did you tell her that you didn't like, that you didn't think she would be a good fit for the apartment?

MR. WALTERS: No, not at the time. I just didn't want to start any conflict there. We chatted a little bit. I asked her about where she came from, things like that—just conversation.

MS. JOHNSON: Just conversation. OK.

MR. WALTERS: Right. But she looked around, and I said I'd be in touch, and she gave me the application and gave me a check for the application fee, and then she. . .

MS. JOHNSON: Can you tell me any more about this check for the application fee?

MR. WALTERS: Well yeah, it's for a background check. You know, I just want to make sure I'm getting responsible people in the building. So she gave me the check. . .

MS. JOHNSON: Right. How much is it, the check?

MR. WALTERS: It's thirty-five dollars.

MS. JOHNSON: Thirty five dollars. Ok.

MR. WALTERS: Yeah, and then she went on her way, and then later on I had also gotten an email from this other woman who's now in the apartment, and she came in the same day.

MS. JOHNSON: Same day, ok.

MR. WALTERS: She looked at it, she seemed great. And you know, I just didn't think Paula was the right fit for the apartment because she had this loud little kid.

MS. JOHNSON: Right.

MR. WALTERS: And so I ended up renting it to the barista, and she worked out great.

MS. JOHNSON: Ok. Wonderful. So can you tell me, is there anything other—because Paula, she seemed to say that she called you back a few days later, so what was. . .

MR. WALTERS: Yeah, I was surprised by that. Yeah she called and asked and I told her it was rented, but I was surprised she even called because, uh. . .

MS. JOHNSON: Why?

MR. WALTERS: When I went to deposit her check, it was canceled.

MS. JOHNSON: The check that she gave you—the thirty-five dollars.

MR. WALTERS: Yeah, yeah.

MS. JOHNSON: So she canceled the check.

MR. WALTERS: Yeah, that's what the bank told me.

MS. JOHNSON: I see.

MR. WALTERS: It wasn't that it bounced, it wasn't that she didn't have the money. That would have been a problem too, because, you know, she's gotta be able to pay the rent.

MS. JOHNSON: Right.

MR. WALTERS: But it wasn't that, it was that she had canceled it. So I didn't think she was still interested, and then she called me out of the blue about a week later.

MS. JOHNSON: So in your mind, when you went to the bank and you realized that the check had been canceled, in your mind you kind of assumed that she had canceled her application.

MR. WALTERS: Of course.

MS. JOHNSON: Paula. . . right?

MR. WALTERS: Yeah, of course. Why would she do that if she still wanted the apartment?

MS. JOHNSON: Right. Great. And so your reason for not moving forward with her application was because she didn't satisfy the requirements in the application, namely the background check?

MR. WALTERS: Well, that's why I thought she didn't want it anymore. Yeah, exactly. *didn't say that*

MS. JOHNSON: Ok. And then subsequently you rented to the barista, who was qualified, gave you the check, and everything went through fine.

MR. WALTERS: Everything went fine with her. She's been great since she moved in, so I think I made the right choice. Because she's been a good tenant, and you know now this Paula's causing trouble with this lawsuit. And I feel like I'm sorry that I'm putting Dan—that Dan's going through this now, but I think we made the right decision.

MS. JOHNSON: Yes. Well, you know, I think things—lawsuits like these, they generally don't last very long, so I wouldn't be too worried about it if I were you. You're not one of the named defendants.

MR. WALTERS: Ok. I'm not being sued here, just to be clear?

MS. JOHNSON: No, no, you're not being sued, so you don't have to worry, at least for now.

MR. WALTERS: Ok.

MS. JOHNSON: So, thank you very much. I think that's all the information I need to gather today. So thank you again for coming in.

MR. WALTERS: Ok, thank you.

MS. JOHNSON: We'll be in touch.

MR. WALTERS: Absolutely.

MS. JOHNSON: Thank you.

CHAPTER 2 SKILLS EXERCISE

12(b)(6) MOTION TO DISMISS

This exercise requires you to complete a Rule 12(b)(6) motion to dismiss for failure to state a claim upon which relief can be granted. The motion has been largely drafted for you, but you must complete the section where it reads, *"Apply the rule announced in* Bell Atlantic Corporation v. Twombly *and* Ashcroft v. Iqbal *to Ms. Patt's complaint."*

In the critical portion that has been left for you to draft, you will apply the rule of *Twombly* and *Iqbal* to the facts set forth in Ms. Patt's complaint. Your goal is to convince the judge that the facts alleged in Ms. Patt's complaint are insufficient to meet the relevant pleading standard. This exercise should be completed after you have studied the cases on pleading standards in your Civil Procedure course.

Some tips for drafting the motion:

- Address all relevant facts in the complaint. Do not simply ignore facts that may seem more favorable to the plaintiff; instead, try to frame those facts in a way that supports your argument.

- Support your arguments with analysis. For example, it is not enough to simply state that an allegation in the complaint is an unsupported legal conclusion. You must argue *why* it is only a legal conclusion, preferably by comparing it to the complaints discussed in case law. (Otherwise *your* argument is just a conclusion!)

- Be creative! Propose alternative explanations for the facts that do not support an inference of discrimination.

- This is not the time introduce new facts that the plaintiff has not alleged, or to dispute the accuracy of purely factual allegations in the complaint. Your goal is to demonstrate that the facts of the complaint, as alleged, are insufficient under *Twombly* and *Iqbal*.

- Include citations to cases and to the relevant sections of the complaint.

- Before starting, read the portions of the motion that have already been drafted. Avoid unnecessary repetition of points that were made earlier in the motion.

- Remember that a successful Rule 12(b)(6) motion to dismiss can prevent years of litigation! It is also often a defendant's first opportunity to make a good impression to the court. Be sure to carefully proofread your work before submission.

1 | JANE JOHNSON (State Bar No. 31415927)
Jane.Johnson@johnsonshermen.com
2 | JOHNSON & SHERMEN, LLP
10000 Shattuck Ave., Suite 3500
3 | Berkeley, California 94704
Telephone: (510) 555-3500
4 | Facsimile: (510) 555-3501

Attorney for Defendant

5

UNITED STATES DISTRICT COURT

6   NORTHERN DISTRICT OF CALIFORNIA

7 | PAULA PATT,   Case No. C 1357 DBO

Plaintiff,
8 | **NOTICE OF MOTION AND MOTION TO**
v.   **DISMISS**
9 | DAN DONNER,
                                         MEMORANDUM OF POINTS AND
10 | Defendant.   **AUTHORITIES**
                                      /
11 | _____   Date: September 13
                                         Time: 12:00 p.m.
12 | Judge: Hon. Dianne B. Osaka

13   TO PLAINTIFF AND HER ATTORNEY OF RECORD:

14   NOTICE IS HEREBY GIVEN that on September 6, at time 12:00 p.m., or as soon thereafter as

15   the matter may be heard in Courtroom 3 of the above-titled Court, located at 1301 Clay Street,

16   Oakland, California, Defendant Dan Donner will and hereby does move the Court, pursuant to Rule

17   12(b)(6) of the Federal Rules of Civil Procedure, to dismiss Plaintiff's Complaint. This Motion is

18   brought on the grounds that Plaintiff has failed to state a claim for relief under § 3604(a) of the Fair

19   Housing Act.

20   Defendant also moves to dismiss Plaintiff's Complaint for lack of personal jurisdiction pursuant

21   to Rule 12(b)(2) of the Federal Rules of Civil Procedure. However, the parties have stipulated and

22   the Court has ordered that Defendant shall withhold briefing on the Rule 12(b)(2) Motion until after

23   the determination of this Rule 12(b)(6) Motion, if the case is not dismissed.

24

NOTICE OF MOTION AND MOTION TO DISMISS

1   This Motion is based on the Supporting Memorandum of Points and Authorities, and on such

2   further written and oral argument as may be presented at or before the time the Court takes this

3   motion under submission.

4   Dated: September 6

5   Respectfully submitted,

6   /s/ _____.

7   JANE JOHNSON
                                                                     Attorney for Defendant

8

9

10

11

12

13

14

15

16

17

18

19

20

21

22

23

24

NOTICE OF MOTION AND MOTION TO DISMISS

MEMORANDUM OF POINTS AND AUTHORITIES

TABLE OF CONTENTS

TABLE OF AUTHORITIES

Ashcroft v. Iqbal, 556 U.S. 662 (2009)

Bell Atlantic Corp. v. Twombly, 550 U.S. 544 (2007)

Leatherman v. Tarrant County Narcotics Intelligence and Coordination Unit, 507 U.S. 163 (1993)

42 U.S.C. §§ 3604 *et seq.*

Rule 12(b)(6) of the Federal Rules of Civil Procedure

I.   INTRODUCTION

Plaintiff Paula Patt filed a claim against Defendant Dan Donner for violating the Fair Housing Act, which prohibits discrimination in the rental and sale of housing. 42 U.S.C. §§ 3604 *et seq.* Specifically, Ms. Patt claims that Will Walters, Mr. Donner's property manager, intentionally declined to rent her an apartment because she has a minor child, and that in doing so he violated 42 U.S.C. § 3604(a). Compl. ¶ 15. Ms. Patt alleges that Mr. Donner is liable on the sole grounds that he owns the apartment building in which Ms. Patt sought an apartment.[1] Mr. Donner moves to dismiss because Ms. Patt's claim fails as a matter of law, since it lacks sufficient factual allegations to render a finding of intentional discrimination plausible.

II.   STATEMENT OF FACTS

Ms. Patt has alleged the following facts, which the Court takes as true in the context of this Motion to Dismiss. *See Leatherman v. Tarrant Cty. Narcotics Intelligence & Coordination Unit*, 507 U.S. 163, 164 (1993). Mr. Donner is the owner of the apartment building located at 1357 Telegraph Avenue. Compl. ¶ 14. Mr. Walters is Mr. Donner's property manager for the building. Compl. ¶ 6. Ms. Patt is the mother of S.P., age five. Compl. ¶ 7. Ms. Patt further alleges that on or about August 15, Mr. Walters showed Ms. Patt an apartment at 1357 Telegraph Avenue. Compl. ¶¶ 9–11. Ms. Patt alleges that she submitted an application to rent the apartment but was subsequently declined. Compl. ¶¶ 12–13.

---

[1]   Mr. Donner does not currently move to dismiss on the basis that he is not responsible for any alleged action by Mr. Walters. Should the case go forward, Mr. Donner intends to preserve his argument that he is not vicariously liable for Mr. Walters's alleged conduct for a later stage of the proceedings.

III. ARGUMENT

A. A Motion to Dismiss Should Be Granted Where the Plaintiff Fails to State a Claim Upon Which Relief Can Be Granted.

Our federal system of notice pleading seeks to balance, on the one hand, the plaintiff's interest in bringing a dispute before the attention of a court with, on the other hand, the defendant's right to fair notice of the claims against her and a societal interest in conserving our limited judicial resources. Though more liberal than the fact-pleading regime that it succeeded, notice pleading nonetheless requires that complaints meet a certain threshold in order to survive a motion to dismiss. Ms. Patt's Complaint does not reach this threshold, and should therefore be dismissed for failure to state a claim upon which relief can be granted. Fed. R. Civ. P. 12(b)(6).

Recent cases have clarified the standard by which courts must assess complaints in determining whether or not they fail to state a claim. In *Bell Atlantic v. Twombly*, the Court explained that "labels and conclusions" or a "formulaic recitation of the elements of a cause of action" are not sufficient. 550 U.S. 544, 555 (2007). In *Ashcroft v. Iqbal*, the Court picked up this thread of reasoning to state that a complaint must state sufficient factual matter that, if accepted as true, would render the claim plausible on its face. 556 U.S. 662, 677 (2009). While the Federal Rules of Civil Procedure state only that a complaint must contain "a short and plain statement of the claim showing that the pleader is entitled to relief," a plaintiff's statement does not show entitlement to relief unless it meets the plausibility standard established by *Twombly* and *Iqbal*. Fed. R. Civ. P. 8(a). "Plausibility" requires something more than "sheer possibility that a defendant has acted unlawfully." *Iqbal*, 556 U.S. at 677. "[W]here the well-pleaded facts do not permit the court to infer more than the mere possibility of misconduct," the complaint must be dismissed. *Id.* at 679. The ultimate inquiry is thus

1   whether the complaint contains "factual matter that, if taken as true, states a claim" on which relief

2   can be granted. *Id.* at 666.

3   **B. Ms. Patt's Complaint Fails to Include Sufficient Factual Allegations to Render a**

4   **Claim of Intentional Discrimination Plausible.**

5   Ms. Patt's Complaint states conclusions of law without providing sufficient factual basis to

6   support those conclusions.

7   In the leading case on the issue, *Ashcroft v. Iqbal*, the U.S. Supreme Court dismissed plaintiff

8   Javaid Iqbal's complaint alleging that high-ranking government officials—including the Attorney

9   General of the United States and the Director of the Federal Bureau of Information—orchestrated

10   a harsh detention program that discriminated against individuals based on their race, religion, and

11   national origin. 556 U.S. at 662. Although Mr. Iqbal's complaint described the conditions of his

12   detention and alleged that the defendants knew about the program, condoned its existence, and

13   even brought it into being, the Court nonetheless held that it did not contain sufficient factual

14   matter concerning the defendants' actions and states of mind to render his claim plausible. *Id.* at

15   666. In other words, it stated only conclusions of law, which are insufficient on their own to meet

16   the plausibility standard. *Id.* at 681–83.

17   Ms. Patt's Complaint is similarly conclusory. *(Apply the rule announced in* Bell Atlantic

18   Corporation v. Twombly *and* Ashcroft v. Iqbal *to Ms. Patt's complaint.)*

19   **IV. CONCLUSION**

20   Notice pleading does not "unlock the doors of discovery" for a plaintiff who, like Ms. Patt, is

21   "armed with nothing more than conclusions." *Iqbal*, 556 U.S. at 679. The civil justice system is not

22   an appropriate forum for individuals to try every personal disappointment. Although Ms. Patt would

23   have preferred the apartment owned by Mr. Donner to her current living arrangements, Mr. Donner

24

1 | had no obligation to rent to her, and the facts she offers are simply not enough to state a plausible

2 | claim of intentional discrimination. Mr. Donner respectfully asks that the Court dismiss the

3 | Complaint, with prejudice.

4 | Dated: September 6

5

6 | Respectfully submitted,

                                       /s/ _____ .

7 | JANE JOHNSON
                                       Attorney for Defendant

8

9

10

11

12

13

14

15

16

17

18

19

20

21

22

23

24

NOTICE OF MOTION AND MOTION TO DISMISS

CHAPTER 2 MATERIALS

OPPOSITION TO 12(b)(6) MOTION TO DISMISS

1 | SAM PELLEGRINO (State Bar # 11235813)
spellegrino@berkeleylegalclinic.org
2 | BERKELEY LEGAL CLINIC
2013 Center Street, Suite 310
3 | Berkeley, CA 94704
Telephone: (510) 555-5151
4 | Facsimile: (510) 555-5155

Attorney for Plaintiff
5 |

6 | UNITED STATES DISTRICT COURT
                         NORTHERN DISTRICT OF CALIFORNIA

7 | PAULA PATT,   Case No. C 1357 DBO

8 | Plaintiff,   **PLAINTIFF'S OPPOSITION TO
                                       DEFENDANT'S MOTION TO DISMISS
9 | v.   FOR FAILURE TO STATE A CLAIM**
   DAN DONNER,
10 | Defendant.   Date: September 13
                                  /   Time: 12:00 p.m.
11 | _____   Judge: Hon. Dianne B. Osaka

12 |
13 |
14 |
15 |
16 |
17 |
18 |
19 |
20 |
21 |
22 |
23 |
24 |

1   MEMORANDUM OF POINTS AND AUTHORITIES

2   **TABLE OF CONTENTS**

13   **TABLE OF AUTHORITIES**

14   *Ashcroft v. Iqbal*, 556 U.S. 662 (2009)

15   *Bell Atlantic Corp. v. Twombly*, 550 U.S. 544 (2007)

16   *Swierkiewicz v. Sorema N. A.*, 534 U.S. 506 (2002)

17   *McDonnell Douglas Corp. v. Green*, 411 U.S. 792 (1973)

18   *Conley v. Gibson*, 355 U.S. 41 (1957)

19   *Johnson v. Riverside Healthcare System*, 534 F.3d 1116 (9th Cir. 2008)

20   *Ring v. First Interstate Mortgage, Inc.*, 984 F.2d 924 (9th Cir. 1993)

21   *Walker v. Crigler*, 976 F.2d 900 (4th Cir. 1992)

22   *Llanos v. Estate of Coehlo*, 24 F. Supp. 2d 1052 (E.D. Cal. 1998)

23

24

1 | 42 U.S.C. §§ 3602 *et seq.*

2 | Rule 12(b)(6) of the Federal Rules of Civil Procedure

3

4

5

6

7

8

9

10

11

12

13

14

15

16

17

18

19

20

21

22

23

24

1

I.   INTRODUCTION

2   Defendant Dan Donner has moved to dismiss Plaintiff Paula Patt's complaint for intentional

3 housing discrimination for failure to state a claim. However, Ms. Patt's complaint properly states a

4 claim for discrimination on the basis of familial status under the federal Fair Housing Act (FHA).

5 42 U.S.C. § 3604(a). Accordingly, Defendant's Motion to Dismiss should be denied and Ms. Patt's

6 case allowed to move forward.

7

II.   STATEMENT OF FACTS

8   The Complaint includes the following allegations of fact, which are taken as true in the context

9 of a motion to dismiss. *See Swierkiewicz v. Sorema*, 534 U.S. 506, 508 n.1 (2002). Plaintiff Paula

10 Patt is the mother of S.P., age five. Compl. ¶¶ 1, 10. Ms. Patt is not married. Compl. ¶¶ 1, 11. Will

11 Walters is the manager of the apartment building located at 1357 Telegraph Avenue. Compl. ¶ 9.

12 Defendant Dan Donner is the owner of said apartment building and employs Mr. Walters as

13 manager. Compl. ¶¶ 17–18. On or about August 15 Ms. Patt, accompanied by her daughter, viewed

14 an apartment that was being offered for rent by Mr. Walters and is located at 1357 Telegraph

15 Avenue. Compl. ¶¶ 8–9, 12. During the viewing, Mr. Walters asked Ms. Patt about her marital

16 status, acted uncomfortable, and gave S.P. unpleasant looks. Compl. ¶ 14. Ms. Patt submitted an

17 application to rent the apartment but Mr. Walters declined to rent to her. Compl. ¶¶ 15–16. Ms.

18 Patt has brought this action to establish that the reason Mr. Walters declined to rent to her is that

19 she is an unmarried mother. Compl. ¶ 19.

20

21

22

23

24

1

2

3

4

5

6

7

8

9

10

11

12

13

14

15

16

17

18

19

20

21

22

23

24

III. ARGUMENT

A. A Motion to Dismiss Should Be Denied Where the Plaintiff States a Claim Upon Which Relief Can Be Awarded.

The Federal Rules of Civil Procedure replaced the "hyper-technical" system of code pleading with a system notice pleading in order to increase access to the courts and prevent meritorious complaints from being dismissed on purely formalistic grounds. *Ashcroft v. Iqbal*, 556 U.S. 662, 678–79 (2009). Accordingly, the Rules require only that a complaint must contain "a short and plain statement of the claim showing that the pleader is entitled to relief." Fed. R. Civ. P. 8(a); *see Iqbal*, 556 U.S. at 677–78 (2009); *Conley v. Gibson*, 355 U.S. 41 (1957). A complaint need only "give the defendant fair notice of what the plaintiff's claim is and the grounds upon which it rests" *Conley*, 355 U.S. at 47. For the purposes of ruling on a Motion to Dismiss, a court must assume all facts pled in a complaint to be true and must view the complaint in the light most favorable to the plaintiff. *Swierkiewicz*, 534 U.S. at 508 n.1, *Johnson v. Riverside Healthcare Sys.*, 534 F.3d 1116, 1122 (9th Cir. 2008). This rule does not oblige a plaintiff to plead "detailed factual allegations." *Bell Atlantic v. Twombly*, 550 U.S. 544, 555 (2007).

Furthermore, there are other legal mechanisms in place to conserve the valuable resources of the judicial system, including most notably liberal discovery rules and the motion for summary judgment. Fed. R. Civ. P. 26–37, 56. These tools help resolve disputed issues and uncover the weaknesses of non-meritorious claims. *See Swierkiewicz*, 534 U.S. at 512. A motion to dismiss should only be granted where the plaintiff fails to state a claim upon which relief can be awarded. Fed. R. Civ. P. 12(b)(6).

B. Ms. Patt's Complaint States a Claim for Relief Under the Fair Housing Act.

Defendant's Motion to Dismiss goes to the merits of Ms. Patt's claim, arguing in essence that her complaint fails to prove her claim of discrimination. The evidentiary burden that Ms. Patt would carry at trial need not be met at the pleading stage. *Sweirkiewicz*, 534 U.S. at 510. The Supreme Court made clear in *Swierkiewicz* that it "has never indicated that the requirements for a establishing a *prima facie* case [of discrimination] also apply to the pleading standard that plaintiffs must satisfy in order to survive a motion to dismiss." *Id.*

The FHA makes it unlawful to "refuse to . . . rent, after the making of a bona fide offer, or to refuse to negotiate the . . . rental of, or otherwise make unavailable or deny, a dwelling to any person because of . . . familial status." 42 U.S.C. § 3604(a). A "dwelling" is defined as "any building, structure, or portion thereof which is occupied as, or designed or intended for occupancy as, a residence by one or more families" 42 U.S.C. § 3602(b). "Familial status" denotes "one or more individuals (who have not attained the age of 18 years) being domiciled with (1) a parent or another person having legal custody of such individual or individuals." 42 U.S.C. § 3602(k). Mr. Walters's refusal to rent an apartment to Ms. Patt because of her status as a single parent falls squarely within the conduct prohibited by this statute.

Ms. Patt states a claim for discrimination under the Fair Housing Act. Ms. Patt's complaint clearly lays out all the elements necessary to establish a *prima facie* case of housing discrimination under *McDonnell Douglas Corp. v. Green*, 411 U.S. 792, 802 (1973). However, while those elements are relevant to Ms. Patt's burden at trial, they are not at issue in considering the sufficiency of her complaint. "[T]he ordinary rules for assessing the sufficiency of a complaint apply" in discrimination cases. *Sweirkiewicz*, 534 U.S. at 510. The ordinary rule is to assess whether complaint contains sufficient factual allegations to render the claim plausible. *Iqbal*, 556 U.S at 678.

PLAINTIFF'S OPPOSITION TO DEFENDANT'S MOTION TO DISMISS FOR FAILURE TO STATE A CLAIM

1   A reasonable person would plausibly conclude that Mr. Walters, on behalf of Mr. Donner,

2   discriminated against Ms. Patt and her daughter. Prior to meeting Ms. Patt and her daughter, Mr.

3   Walters was friendly with Ms. Patt on the telephone. Compl. ¶ 9. When he first saw Ms. Patt he

4   was friendly and had a smile on his face. Compl. ¶ 13. Then something changed, immediately and

5   dramatically. Mr. Walters looked down, saw S.P., and his entire manner changed. Compl. ¶ 14.

6   Nothing happened between these two moments that could explain this change other than Mr.

7   Walters' realization that Ms. Patt had a young daughter. He then began examining Ms. Patt about

8   her marriage, her daughter, and her personal life. Compl. ¶ 14. Ultimately he refused to rent to Ms.

9   Patt. Compl. ¶ 16. A plausible explanation, indeed the most likely explanation based on facts now

10   known, is that Mr. Walters changed his mind about renting to Ms. Patt at the moment he saw her

11   daughter, and refused to rent to her because she has a daughter.

12   Defendant's Motion to Dismiss states that "there might be another" explanation for Mr.

13   Walters's decision. Mot. to Dismiss at 6. However, it does not go so far as to state what that reason

14   is. Suggesting that perhaps Ms. Patt did not meet one of the criteria for rental is itself an empty

15   and conclusory statement that fails to meet Defendant's burden to provide a legitimate, non-

16   discriminatory reason for the denial of the apartment to Ms. Patt. *See McDonnell Douglas*, 411 U.S.

17   at 802. If he indeed has such a reason then he must present it.

18   **C.   The Owner of an Apartment Building is Liable for the Discrimination on the Part of**

19   **its Landlord.**

20   Mr. Donner, as the owner of the apartment building located at 1357 Telegraph Avenue, is liable

21   for the discriminatory act or acts of Mr. Walters, even if Mr. Donner did not directly participate in

22   them. In an action for housing discrimination against both the owners and the manager of a housing

23   complex for discrimination on the basis of familial status in violation of state and federal law, owners

24

PLAINTIFF'S OPPOSITION TO DEFENDANT'S MOTION TO DISMISS FOR FAILURE TO STATE A CLAIM

1   cannot delegate their duty not to discriminate and thus can be held liable for the intentional actions

2   of their managers or agents. *Llanos v. Estate of Coehlo*, 24 F. Supp. 2d 1052, 1061 (E.D. Cal. 1998).

3   The Llanos court noted that it was necessary to hold owners responsible in order for housing

4   antidiscrimination law to have the intended effect of preventing discrimination. *Id.* It further noted

5   that *respondeat superior* provides an alternate theory underpinning an owner's liability for a

6   manager or agent's conduct. *Id.*; see also *Walker v. Crigler*, 976 F.2d 900, 904 & n.5 (4th Cir. 1992).

7   Thus, Ms. Patt's complaint states a valid claim for discrimination against Mr. Donner.

8   **D.   The Fair Housing Act Affords the Remedies Ms. Patt Seeks.**

9   A private plaintiff may bring an action under the Fair Housing Act. 42 U.S.C. § 3613(a)(1)(A).

10 In such an action, the court may award actual and punitive damages. *Id.* at § 3613(c)(1). The court

11 may also grant any injunctive relief it deems appropriate. *Id.* The court may likewise award

12 attorneys' fees to any party other than the United States government. *Id.* at § 3613(c)(2). Ms. Patt

13 prays for actual damages to compensate her for the additional expenses she incurred in her

14 continued search for an apartment and the increased rent and transportation costs she must pay in

15 her current residence. She also prays for injunctive relief so that she can obtain the apartment for

16 which she is qualified and that she prefers, and to prevent Defendant or his agents from committing

17 discriminatory acts in the future. All of these remedies are properly available to her under the law.

18   **IV.   CONCLUSION**

19 Defendant's Motion to Dismiss must not be used to decide Ms. Patt's case on the merits.

20 *Sweirkiewicz*, 534 U.S. at 510; *see also Ring v. First Interstate Mortg., Inc.*, 984 F.2d 924, 926–27

21 (9th Cir. 1993). Under our liberal system of notice pleading, it is more than sufficient that Ms. Patt

22 has alleged all the elements of a *prima facie* case of discrimination. *See Sweirkiewicz*, 534 U.S. at

23 510. The facts laid out render her claim plausible on its face. Even if Defendant's Motion to Dismiss

24

1   met the burden of stating a legitimate and non-discriminatory reason for the denial of the

2   apartment, an inquiry which is more appropriate for a motion for summary judgment than a motion

3   to dismiss, Ms. Patt would still have an opportunity to show that reason was a pretext. *See*

4   *Sweirkiewicz*, 534 U.S. at 510; *McDonnell Douglas*, 411 U.S. at 803. Ms. Patt's Complaint properly

5   states a claim for discrimination under the Fair Housing Act. Ms. Patt therefore respectfully

6   requests that the Court deny Defendant's Motion to Dismiss.

7   Dated: September 10

8

                                                Respectfully submitted,

9   /s/ _____ .

                                               Sam Pellegrino

10   Attorney for Plaintiff

11

12

13

14

15

16

17

18

19

20

21

22

23

24

ORDER DENYING 12(b)(6) MOTION TO DISMISS

IN THE UNITED STATES DISTRICT COURT
FOR THE NORTHERN DISTRICT OF CALIFORNIA
OAKLAND DIVISION

PAULA PATT,   No. C 1357 DBO

                    Plaintiff,

        v.   **ORDER DENYING MOTION TO DISMISS**

DAN DONNER,

                    Defendant.

                                        /

This matter comes before the Court on Defendant Dan Donner's Motion to Dismiss for failure to state a claim. Fed. R. Civ. P. 12(b)(6). Plaintiff Paula Patt has made the following allegations, which for the limited purpose of this Motion the Court assumes to be true. *Ashcroft v. Iqbal*, 556 U.S. 662, 678 (2009); *Leatherman v. Tarrant Cnty. Narcotics Intelligence & Coordination Unit*, 507 U.S. 163, 164 (1993). On August 15, Mr. Donner's manager Will Walters showed an apartment for rent located at 1357 Telegraph Avenue to Plaintiff Paula Patt, who was accompanied by her five-year-old daughter, S. Compl. ¶¶ 8–9, 12. Mr. Walters is the manager of the building, which is owned by Mr. Donner. Compl. ¶¶ 9, 17–18. During the appointment, Ms. Patt noted that Mr. Walters displayed apparent discomfort, that he asked her about her marital status, and that he gave "unpleasant" looks to her daughter. Compl. ¶ 14. Ms. Patt nonetheless submitted an application for the apartment, but when she called Mr. Walters on August 21, he brusquely informed her that he would not rent it to her. Compl. ¶ 16. Ms. Patt alleges intentional housing discrimination on the basis of familial status. Compl. ¶ 19. Mr. Donner moves to dismiss, arguing that the claim fails to state sufficient factual matter to be plausible. Mot. to Dismiss at 5–6.

The Federal Rules of Civil Procedure require that a complaint contain "a short and plain statement of the claim showing that the pleader is entitled to relief." Fed. R. Civ. P. 8(a); *see Iqbal*, 556 U.S. at 677; *Swierkiewicz v. Sorema N. A.*, 534 U.S. 506, 508, 512 (2002); *Conley v. Gibson*, 355

1   U.S. 41, 47 (1957). A motion to dismiss should be granted where the plaintiff fails to state a claim

2   upon which relief can be granted. Fed. R. Civ. P. 12(b)(6). A complaint must state sufficient factual

3   matter that, if accepted as true, would render the claim plausible on its face. *Iqbal*, 556 U.S. at 678.

4   A *prima facie* case for violation of the Fair Housing Act requires that the plaintiff show either

5   intentional discrimination or disparate impact. *Harris v. Itzhaki*, 183 F.3d 1043, 1051 (9th Cir.

6   1999); *Gamble v. City of Escondido*, 104 F.3d 300, 304–05 (9th Cir. 1999). Here, Ms. Patt appears to

7   allege intentional discrimination. Compl. ¶¶ 8–19. Intentional discrimination may be supported by

8   either direct or indirect evidence; however, if the plaintiff presents only indirect evidence, the Court

9   must apply the burden-shifting framework set forth for Title VII discrimination claims in *McDonnell*

10 *Douglas Corp. v. Green. Harris*, 183 F.3d at 1051; *see McDonnell Douglas Corp. v. Green*, 411 U.S.

11 792, 802 (1973). Since Ms. Patt's Complaint does not state direct evidence of discrimination, we

12 must determine whether her claim will plausibly meet the requirements that apply when a plaintiff

13 relies on indirect evidence alone.

14   A plaintiff relying on indirect evidence of discrimination must show the following in order to

15 raise a rebuttable presumption of intentional discrimination: 1) she is a member of a protected class;

16 2) she applied for the apartment and was qualified to rent it; 3) she was not accepted as a tenant;

17 4) the apartment remained vacant or was rented to another tenant who was not a member of a

18 protected class. *See McDonnell Douglas*, 411 U.S. at 802 (applying a version of these factors in the

19 context of employment discrimination); *Gamble*, 104 F.3d at 305 (applying a version of these factors

20 under the FHA to a claim challenging a city's decision to deny a building permit). Once the plaintiff

21 has shown these four elements, the burden shifts to the defendant to present a legitimate reason

22 (one that is not discriminatory) for having denied the applicant. *Id.*

23

24

1   It is important to note that the plaintiff must fully prove these elements at trial but does not

2   per force need to include them in her complaint. *Sweirkiewicz*, 534 U.S. at 510. However, "the

3   elements of [an] alleged cause of action help to determine whether Plaintiff has set forth a plausible

4   claim." *Khalik v. United Air Lines*, 671 F.3d 1188, 1192 (10th Cir. 2012). Based on Ms. Patt's

5   allegations as to three of the four elements, and regarding Mr. Walters's demeanor, it is plausible

6   that she would be able to prevail at trial, and therefore the motion to dismiss should be denied.

7   The first question is whether Ms. Patt is a member of a protected class. The Fair Housing Act

8   prohibits all housing discrimination on the basis of familial status. 42 U.S.C. § 3604(a). Ms. Patt's

9   status as a single mother in a society that privileges two-parent families exposes her to criticism

10   and mistreatment—exactly the kind of mistreatment that the Fair Housing Act was intended to

11   prevent. Thus, Ms. Patt's right to rent an apartment for which she is qualified is protected by the

12   Fair Housing Act, and the first prong of *McDonnell Douglas* is established. *See McDonnell Douglas*,

13   411 U.S. at 802; *Gamble*, 104 F.3d at 305.

14   Further, Ms. Patt's complaint states that she applied for the apartment and was qualified to

15   rent it. Compl. ¶ 15; *see McDonnell Douglas*, 411 U.S. at 802; *Gamble*, 104 F.3d at 305. Although

16   she does not provide further factual detail on her qualifications, such detail is not necessary in order

17   to survive a motion to dismiss. It is sufficient that she allege as much in the pleading stage for the

18   court to permit her case to go forward. The burden will be on her to prove this at trial.

19   Third, Ms. Patt alleges that Mr. Donner, through his manager Mr. Walters, rejected Ms. Patt's

20   application for the apartment. Compl. ¶ 16. This satisfies the third element of *McDonnell Douglas*.

21   *See McDonnell Douglas*, 411 U.S. at 802; *Gamble*, 104 F.3d at 305.

22   Ms. Patt does not address the fourth and final element: the Complaint does not state that the

23   apartment remained vacant after her application, *see McDonnell Douglas*, 411 U.S. at 802, or that

24

ORDER DENYING MOTION TO DISMISS

1　Mr. Donner rented to the apartment to someone without a child, *see Gamble*, 104 F.3d at 305.

2　However, a complaint need not establish a *prima facie* case of discrimination, only facts sufficient

3　to render its claim plausible. *Sweirkiewicz*, 534 U.S. at 510. Reading the complaint as a whole, the

4　Court determines that Ms. Patt has made such a showing. Ms. Patt of course retains the burden of

5　proving a *prima facie* case at summary judgment or trial, but need not do so in her Complaint.

6　　　Furthermore, although the motion to dismiss suggests an alternate explanation for the denial

7　of the apartment, this alternate explanation does not diminish the plausibility of Ms. Patt's claim.

8　Mot. to Dismiss at 6. The standard to survive a motion to dismiss does not require that a plaintiff's

9　complaint provide the most likely explanation available, but only that it be plausible. *See Iqbal*, 556

10　U.S. at 678 ("The plausibility standard is not akin to a 'probability requirement' . . . .").

11　　　In sum, Ms. Patt's Complaint "contain[s] sufficient factual matter, accepted as true, to state a

12　claim to relief that is plausible on its face," including three of the four factors to state a *prima facie*

13　case of housing discrimination on the basis of familial status and to raise a rebuttable presumption

14　of discrimination at trial. *See id.* (citation and internal quotation marks omitted). Her claim is

15　therefore facially plausible and Defendant's Motion to Dismiss is denied.

16　**IT IS SO ORDERED.**

17　Dated: September 13

18
19　　　　　　　　　　　　　　　　　　DIANNE B. OSAKA
　　　　　　　　　　　　　　　　　　UNITED STATES DISTRICT JUDGE

20

21

22

23

24

CHAPTER 3
PROVISIONAL REMEDIES

CHAPTER 3 MATERIALS

EMAIL RE: TEMPORARY RESTRAINING ORDER

Subject:	Patt Case: TRO/Preliminary Injunction
From:	Matt Madison <mmadison@berkeleylegalclinic.org>
To:	Sam Pellegrino <spellegrino@berkeleylegalclinic.org>
Date:	September 13 11:49 AM

Hi Sam,

As you suggested, I called Ms. Johnson, the defense attorney, to inform her of our intent to seek a Temporary Restraining Order preventing Mr. Donner from renting the newly vacant apartment pending the decision about the preliminary injunction.

She seemed surprised and said that she would call me back. She called back about half an hour later, confirmed that there was an available apartment, and said that there was no need for us to go to court for a TRO because her client would agree not to rent the apartment until the court rules on the preliminary injunction. She explained that this is a normal professional courtesy in this community.

I've forwarded an email she sent me following our conversation.

I will set aside the TRO motion and work on the preliminary injunction motion today unless I hear otherwise from you.

Best,
Matt

Matt Madison
J.D. Candidate
U.C. Berkeley School of Law

On September 13 at 11:23 AM, jane.johnson@johnsonshermen.com wrote:

Dear Mr. Madison,

Per our telephone conversation, this email confirms that my client Mr. Dan Donner agrees not to rent the available apartment at 1357 Telegraph Avenue until the court has ruled on Ms. Patt's forthcoming Motion for Preliminary Injunction, so long as Ms. Patt files her motion without delay and arranges for a prompt hearing.

Again, thank you for your call this morning. The legal community in this area places a premium on professional courtesy, and I have no doubt that you will fit in well as you begin to practice law.

Sincerely,
Jane Johnson
Johnson & Shermen LLP | www.johnsonshermen.com
jane.johnson@johnsonshermen.com | (510) 555-3500

CHAPTER 3 SKILLS EXERCISE

MOTION FOR PRELIMINARY INJUNCTION

This exercise requires you to complete a motion for a preliminary injunction. Portions of the brief in support of the motion (also referred to as the "Memorandum of Points and Authorities") have been drafted for you, but you must complete Section B, specifically where it reads, *"apply the facts from the declarations, below, to argue that Plaintiff Paula Patt is likely to succeed on the merits."*

As you have learned in your Civil Procedure course, preliminary injunctive relief may be issued, at the discretion of the district court, to protect a plaintiff from an irreparable injury. *Herb Reed Enters., LLC v. Fla. Entm't Mgmt.*, 736 F.3d 1239, 1247 (9th Cir. 2013). A plaintiff seeking preliminary injunctive relief must establish the following four criteria: (1) a strong likelihood of success on the merits; (2) the threat of irreparable injury if injunctive relief is denied; (3) a balance of hardships favoring the plaintiff; and (4) that injunctive relief will advance the public interest. *Winter v. Nat. Res. Def. Council, Inc.*, 555 U.S. 7, 20 (2008).

In the critical portion of the exercise that has been left for you to draft, you will complete the section of the motion regarding Paula Patt's likelihood of success on the merits of her claim. To do so, you will apply the facts provided in the declarations of Paula Patt and Tara Tenenbaum, as well as any allegations set forth in the case record thus far. Your goal is to use the facts provided to convince the judge that Paula Patt is likely to prevail on her Fair Housing Act claim. This exercise should be completed after you have studied the topic of preliminary injunctive relief in your Civil Procedure course.

Some tips for drafting the brief:

- Before starting, read the portions of the motion that have already been drafted! Avoid unnecessary repetition of points that were made earlier in the motion.

- Avoid unsupported conclusory statements. You must explain *why* the facts you are using make it likely that Paula Patt will succeed on the merits of her Fair Housing Act claim.

- Do not simply ignore facts that may seem more favorable to the Defendant; instead, try to frame those facts in a way that supports your argument.

- Do not introduce any facts that are not included in the declarations attached to the motion or set forth in the case record thus far.

- There is no need to add additional case law in the section you are completing. Instead, focus on the facts, with citations to the record.

1 | SAM PELLEGRINO (State Bar # 11235813)
spellegrino@berkeleylegalclinic.org
2 | BERKELEY LEGAL CLINIC
2013 Center Street, Suite 310
3 | Berkeley, CA 94704
Telephone: (510) 555-5151
4 | Facsimile: (510) 555-5155

Attorney for Plaintiff
5

UNITED STATES DISTRICT COURT
6 | NORTHERN DISTRICT OF CALIFORNIA

7 | PAULA PATT,   Case No. C 1357 DBO

8 | Plaintiff,   **NOTICE OF MOTION AND MOTION FOR**
    v.   **PRELIMINARY INJUNCTION**
9 | DAN DONNER,
                                               MEMORANDUM OF POINTS AND
10 | Defendant.   **AUTHORITIES**
                                          /
11 | ─────────────────────────────────────   Date: September 20
                                               Time: 12:00 p.m.
12 | Judge: Hon. Dianne B. Osaka

13 | TO DEFENDANT AND HIS ATTORNEY OF RECORD:

14 | NOTICE IS HEREBY GIVEN that on September 20, at 12:00 p.m. in Courtroom 3 of the above-

15 | titled Court, located at 1301 Clay Street, Oakland, California, Plaintiff Paula Patt ("Plaintiff") will

16 | and hereby does move the Court, pursuant to Rule 65 of the Federal Rules of Civil Procedure, to

17 | grant Plaintiff a preliminary injunction preventing Defendant Dan Donner ("Defendant") from

18 | renting Apartment 3B at 1357 Telegraph Avenue, which is currently available, to anyone besides

19 | Plaintiff, prior to resolution of the above-captioned action.

20 | This Motion is brought on the grounds that Plaintiff is likely to prevail on the claim that the

21 | Defendant has violated the Fair Housing Act, and injunctive relief is necessary because future

22 | financial damages will be insufficient to remedy the claim where Plaintiff seeks to rent the

23 | apartment at issue.

24 |

NOTICE OF MOTION AND MOTION FOR PRELIMINARY INJUNCTION
1

1   This Motion is based on the Supporting Memorandum of Points and Authorities, and on such

2   further written and oral argument as may be presented at or before the time the Court takes this

3   motion under submission.

4

5

6

Respectfully submitted,

/s/ _____.

Sam Pellegrino
Attorney for Plaintiff

7

8

9

10

11

12

13

14

15

16

17

18

19

20

21

22

23

24

1

MEMORANDUM OF POINTS AND AUTHORITIES

2

TABLE OF CONTENTS

3

18

TABLE OF AUTHORITIES

19

Cases

20

All. for the Wild Rockies v. Cottrell, 632 F.3d 1127 (9th Cir. 2011)

21

Am. Passage Media Corp. v. Cass Commc'ns Inc., 750 F.2d 1470 (9th Cir. 1985)

22

Ashcroft v. ACLU, 542 U.S. 656 (2004)

23

24

1 | *Benda v. Grand Lodge of the Int'l Ass'n of Machinists & Aerospace Workers*, 584 F.2d 308 (9th Cir.

2 | 1978)

3 | *Herb Reed Enters., LLC v. Fla. Entm't Mgmt.*, 736 F.3d 1239 (9th Cir. 2013)

4 | *Meyer v. Holley*, 537 U.S. 280 (2003)

5 | *Park Vill. Apartment Tenants Ass'n v. Mortimer Howard Trust*, 636 F.3d 1150 (9th Cir. 2011)

6 | *Price v. Pelka*, 690 F.2d 98 (6th Cir.1982)

7 | *Winter v. Nat. Res. Def. Council, Inc.*, 555 U.S. 7 (2008)

8 | Statutes and Rules

9 | 42 U.S.C. § 3613(c)(1) (2006)

10 | Rule 65(b) of the Federal Rules of Civil Procedure

I.   INTRODUCTION

Plaintiff Paula Patt moves for a preliminary injunction enjoining Defendant from renting Apartment 3B at 1357 Telegraph Avenue to anyone besides Plaintiff, in order to maintain the available apartment while the Court is given sufficient time to consider the merits of the Plaintiff's Fair Housing Act claim.[1] *See* Fed. R. Civ. P. 65(b); 42 U.S.C. § 3613(c)(1) (2006). Ms. Patt brings this motion to receive an Order from the court that Defendant cannot rent the available apartment to anyone besides Ms. Patt pending the resolution of Plaintiff's Fair Housing Act claim.

II.   STATEMENT OF FACTS

Plaintiff Paula Patt is the mother of S.P., age five. Patt Decl. (Ex. 2) ¶ 3. Ms. Patt is not married. Patt Decl. ¶ 4. Defendant Dan Donner is the owner of the apartment building located at 1357 Telegraph Avenue, Berkeley, CA. Compl. ¶ 12. On or about August 15, Ms. Patt, accompanied by her daughter, viewed an apartment that was being offered for rent by Mr. Donner. Patt Decl. ¶¶ 1–2, 5. At the beginning of the viewing, Defendant's Building Manager Will Walters was pleasant and welcoming toward Ms. Patt. Patt Decl. ¶ 6. However, as soon as he saw that she was accompanied by her daughter S.P., he asked Ms. Patt about her marital status, acted uncomfortable, and gave S.P. unpleasant looks. *Id.* Mr. Walters' demeanor and attitude towards Ms. Patt changed dramatically upon learning she had a child. *Id.* Ms. Patt submitted an application to rent the apartment but the Manager refused to rent the apartment to her. Patt Decl. ¶¶ 7–9. Ms. Patt asserts that his refusal was based on the fact that she has a minor child and is not married. Compl. ¶ 13. As of September 5, a second apartment in the same building, Apartment 3B, is now available. Gregslist Advertisement (Ex. 1); Patt Decl. ¶ 15; Tenenbaum Decl. (Ex. 3) ¶¶ 7–8. As of September 5, Ms. Patt continues to look for an apartment while living in temporary housing. Patt Decl. ¶ 10.

---

[1]   The parties have agreed that Defendant will not rent this apartment until the Court has ruled on this Motion for Preliminary Injunction. Based on this agreement, Plaintiff has agreed to forgo filing a motion for a temporary restraining order.

1   Ms. Patt seeks a preliminary injunction so that she can rent the open apartment at 1357 Telegraph

2   Avenue, either now or if and when the Fair Housing Act claim is resolved in her favor.

3   III. ARGUMENT

4   **A.   Ms. Patt Should Be Granted a Preliminary Injunction Because the Application of a**

5   **Judicial Remedy After a Hearing on the Merits Cannot Redress Ms. Patt's Injuries.**

6   A preliminary injunction may be issued to protect the Plaintiff from irreparable injury. *Herb*

7   *Reed Enters., LLC v. Fla. Entm't Mgmt.*, 736 F.3d 1239, 1247 (9th Cir. 2013). The grant of a

8   preliminary injunction rests in the discretion of the district court. *Ashcroft v. ACLU*, 542 U.S. 656,

9   664 (2004). This discretion should be exercised based on the existence of the four prerequisites for

10 injunctive relief: (1) a substantial likelihood that Plaintiff will prevail on the merits; (2) a substantial

11 threat that Plaintiff will suffer irreparable injury if the injunctive relief is not granted; (3) that the

12 threatened injury to Plaintiff outweighs the threatened harm the inunction may do to Defendant;

13 and (4) that granting the preliminary injunction will not disserve the public interest. *Winter v. Nat.*

14 *Res. Def. Council, Inc.*, 555 U.S. 7, 20 (2008).

15 **B.   Ms. Patt Should Be Granted a Preliminary Injunction Because Plaintiff Is Likely to**

16   **Prevail on the Merits of Her Claim.**

17   In deciding whether to grant a motion for a preliminary injunction, the Ninth Circuit considers

18 the moving party's probable success on the merits. *Benda v. Grand Lodge of the Int'l Ass'n of*

19 *Machinists & Aerospace Workers*, 584 F.2d 308, 314 (9th Cir. 1978).

20   In this case, Ms. Patt is likely to prevail on her Fair Housing Act claim. *(Apply the facts from*

21 *the declarations, below, to argue that Plaintiff Paula Patt is likely to succeed on the merits.)*

22

23

24

1 **C. Ms. Patt Should Be Granted a Preliminary Injunction Because There Is a Substantial**

2 **Threat of Irreparable Injury to Plaintiff Without Injunctive Relief.**

3 To obtain injunctive relief, the moving party must show that there is a significant threat of

4 irreparable injury. *See Am. Passage Media Corp. v. Cass Commc'ns Inc.*, 750 F.2d 1470, 1473 (9th

5 Cir. 1985).

6 In this case, there is a significant chance of irreparable injury to Ms. Patt if the preliminary

7 injunction is not granted. Ms. Patt seeks to rent the available apartment at 1357 Telegraph Avenue.

8 Patt Decl. ¶ 7. This apartment is ideal for Ms. Patt and her daughter in terms of location, space,

9 and price. Patt Decl. ¶¶ 7, 11. Ms. Patt is currently living in temporary housing, and has been unable

10 to locate permanent housing that is comparable to the apartment in question. Patt Decl. ¶ 10. Since

11 she seeks to rent the open apartment at 1357 Telegraph Avenue, later monetary damages, even

12 including punitive damages, will not redress the harm. In addition, there is now a similar apartment

13 in the building available. Ex. 1; Patt Decl. ¶ 15. However, if a new tenant rents the available

14 apartment, Ms. Patt will not be able to rent that apartment, regardless of the outcome of her claim.

15 *See Park Vill. Apartment Tenants Ass'n v. Mortimer Howard Trust*, 636 F.3d 1150, 1159 (9th Cir.

16 2011) (holding that the loss of an interest in real property constitutes an irreparable injury).

17 Therefore, unless Defendant Donner is enjoined from renting to another tenant, there is a

18 significant chance of irreparable injury to Ms. Patt.

19 **D. Ms. Patt Should Be Granted a Preliminary Injunction Because the Balance of**

20 **Hardships in this Case Favors Plaintiff Over Defendant.**

21 In order to grant preliminary injunctive relief, the court weighs the hardship of the Plaintiff

22 against that of the Defendant. *See Alliance for the Wild Rockies v. Cottrell*, 632 F.3d 1127, 1134–35

23 (9th Cir. 2011). Here, Ms. Patt's hardship outweighs that of Mr. Donner. Ms. Patt is currently losing

24

1   money by staying in temporary housing that is more expensive than the 1357 Telegraph Avenue

2   apartment. Patt Decl. ¶ 13. In addition to financial loss, she has to spend time continuing to search

3   for apartments. Patt Decl. ¶¶ 10, 12. Ms. Patt also has to spend extra time commuting to work and

4   taking her daughter to her school, both of which are closer to the apartment than to Ms. Patt's

5   current temporary housing. Patt Decl. ¶ 14. In contrast, Mr. Donner's potential hardship is less

6   significant. Currently, an apartment in the building is open. Ex. 1. Therefore, Mr. Donner would

7   not lose any money if enjoined from changing the status of the apartment. Even if the preliminary

8   injunction is issued, Mr. Donner would merely lose the rental amount of the apartment for the

9   duration of the injunction. However, even this loss could be fully mitigated if he simply rents the

10 apartment to Ms. Patt pending the resolution of the litigation. In weighing the relative hardships

11 of Ms. Patt and Mr. Donner, Ms. Patt's financial and time hardships outweigh the potential financial

12 loss for Defendant if enjoined from renting the apartment.

13 **E.   Ms. Patt Should Be Granted a Preliminary Injunction Because Doing So Is in the**

14 **Public Interest.**

15   The fourth factor to consider before granting injunctive relief is whether the preliminary

16 injunction is in the public interest. *Winter*, 555 U.S. at 24. Congress established a national policy

17 against housing discrimination by passing the Fair Housing Act, which the Supreme Court found

18 to serve an "overriding societal priority." *Meyer v. Holley,* 537 U.S. 280 (2003); *see also Price v. Pelka,*

19 690 F.2d 98, 102 (6th Cir.1982) (eradicating housing discrimination serves the public interest). Ms.

20 Patt's situation is consistent with these public interest concerns of eradicating housing

21 discrimination. If injunctive relief is not granted, there is a substantial chance the Defendant will

22 rent the open apartment to a third party, and the Plaintiff will not be able to obtain the relief that

23

24

1 she seeks, even if her claim is successful. Since that result would be against the public interest of

2 fully remedying discrimination, granting a preliminary injunction is in the public interest.

3 ## IV. CONCLUSION

4 The Court should grant the motion for a preliminary injunction enjoining Mr. Donner from

5 renting the apartment at 1367 Telegraph Avenue because there is a substantial likelihood that Ms.

6 Patt will prevail on the merits of her claim; a substantial threat that Ms. Patt will suffer irreparable

7 injury if injunctive relief is not granted; the threatened injury to Ms. Patt outweighs the threatened

8 harm the inunction may do to Mr. Donner; and granting the preliminary injunction will not disserve

9 the public interest.

10 Dated: September 16

11   Respectfully submitted,

12   /s/ _____

13   Matt Madison
                                                  Certified Law Student
                                                  Supervised by Sam Pellegrino
14   *Attorney for Plaintiff*

15

16

17

18

19

20

21

22

23

24

EXHIBIT 1

$1,800/1br-1 brm in cozy apt bldng close to campus (berkeley) (map)

Date: 09-01, 9:30AM PDT

Reply to: 456789@gregslist.org

Please call 510-123-4567

Nice 1brm apartment in quiet building. Located within walking distance to UC Berkeley, Downtown Berkeley.

Address: 1357 Telegraph Avenue, Apartment 3B

One bedroom

Rent: $1,800

Deposit: $1,000

Available: October 1

Remodeled Kitchen

Stove/Range: Gas

New carpet

Owner Pays: Water and Garbage

Lease Term: 10 months or 1 year

1357 Telegraph Avenue (google map) (yahoo map)

• it's NOT ok to contact this poster with services or other commercial interests

PostingID: 789

1   **EXHIBIT 1**

2

3

4

5

6

7

8

9

10

11

12

13

14

15

16

17

18

19

20

21

22

23

24

EXHIBIT 2

DECLARATION OF PAULA PATT IN SUPPORT OF

PLAINTIFF'S MOTION FOR A PRELIMINARY INJUNCTION

1. On or about August 15, I saw an advertisement on Gregslist indicating that a one-bedroom apartment was available for rent located at 1357 Telegraph Avenue in Berkeley California. The apartment was listed for $1,800 per month, exclusive of gas and electricity. The advertisement made no mention of the building's policy regarding children.

2. I placed a call to the number listed and reached Will Walters, who identified himself as the individual who had posted the listing for 1357 Telegraph Avenue, Berkeley, California. Will Walters' manner for the duration of the telephone call was pleasant and friendly. He assured me that the apartment was available for rent, at a monthly rental of $1,800. An appointment was set for me to view the apartment that afternoon.

3. I am the mother of a five-year-old girl, S.P.

4. I am not married.

5. My daughter accompanied me to see the apartment.

6. When my daughter S.P. and I arrived for the afternoon appointment, Will Walters initially acted friendly. As soon as he saw S.P., however, he looked and acted uncomfortable. Prior to that moment, Mr. Walters did not know I had a daughter. After seeing S.P., Will Walters asked me about my age, marital status, the identity and whereabouts of S.P.'s father, and on several instances gave S.P. unpleasant looks. His tone towards me was curt and no longer positive. His attitude and conduct towards me changed immediately and dramatically after he saw S.P.

7. The apartment was ideal so I submitted an application for the apartment establishing that I was fully qualified to rent the apartment.

1　EXHIBIT 2

2　8.　My application included a detailed rental history as well as a credit check fee. I have a very

3　　　good rental history from before I moved to California this summer.

4　9.　About a week after I submitted the application, I telephoned Will Walters to inquire about the

5　　　status of the apartment. He briefly informed me that he would not rent the apartment to me.

6　　　Mr. Walters did not tell me why, and he did not explain his change of demeanor when I visited

7　　　the apartment.

8　10.　Because I was unable to rent the available apartment at 1357 Telegraph Avenue, I am still

9　　　visiting a number of additional apartments. S.P. and I are temporarily staying at a motel until

10　　　we find something permanent that is reasonable in terms of price and location.

11　11.　The apartment in question is ideal in terms of space, price, and location.

12　12.　So far I have not been able to find a suitable replacement apartment, despite the significant

13　　　amount of time I have spent searching and visiting apartments.

14　13.　The motel S.P. and I are staying in now is more expensive than a permanent apartment.

15　14.　It takes me extra time each day to commute to school and to reach S.P.'s school for drop off and

16　　　pick up from the motel than if we were living the 1357 Telegraph Avenue Apartment.

17　15.　On or about September 4, I viewed a second Gregslist posting for an apartment in the same

18　　　building at 1357 Telegraph Avenue that will be available to rent next month.

19　16.　Based on the Gregslist post and the apartment number, it appears that the newly available

20　　　apartment is located directly above the apartment that Mr. Walters refused to rent to me, and

21　　　has a substantially similar layout.

22

23

24

DECLARATION OF PAULA PATT IN SUPPORT OF PLAINTIFF'S MOTION FOR A PRELIMINARY INJUNCTION

2

EXHIBIT 2

17. Through my attorneys at the Berkeley Legal Clinic, I contacted Dan Donner, the owner of the building, about the newly available apartment. Mr. Donner informed my attorneys that he will not consider renting this apartment to me and my daughter.

Dated: September 16

/s/ _____

Paula Patt

EXHIBIT 3

DECLARATION OF TARA TENENBAUM IN SUPPORT OF

PLAINTIFF'S MOTION FOR A PRELIMINARY INJUNCTION

1. I live in apartment 3A at 1357 Telegraph Avenue in Berkeley California.

2. I am a twenty-six year old graduate student at UC Berkeley, and have lived in Berkeley for a year, since August of last year.

3. When I first moved to Berkeley, I responded to an ad posted about what is now my apartment at 1357 Telegraph Avenue. I met with Will Walters, the building manager, to see the apartment and then he approved my application later the same day. I have lived in the apartment since then.

4. During the year I have lived in the building, there have been no tenants with children in any of the apartments.

5. In August of this year, apartment 2B became available in the building. It is now occupied by tenant who moved in after Mr. Walters showed the apartment to at least two potential tenants. To the best of my knowledge, this tenant works as a barista, lives alone, and does not have children.

6. I recently spoke with Matt Madison, who told me he was a law student working at the Berkeley Legal Clinic. He asked me several questions about my experience living in the building, the rental policies, and if I knew of any additional availability in the building. At the time I did not know of any availability.

7. I have since learned that the tenant in apartment 3B intends to move out at the end of this month, and that Mr. Walters is currently advertising that apartment.

DECLARATION OF TARA TENENBAUM IN SUPPORT OF PLAINTIFF'S MOTION FOR A PRELIMINARY INJUNCTION

1

1 **EXHIBIT 3**

2 8.   To my knowledge, as of today apartment 3B has the same floor plan and is otherwise similar to

3   apartment 2B, and is available to rent starting next month.

4   Dated: September 16

5   /s/ _____

6   Tara Tenenbaum

7

8

9

10

11

12

13

14

15

16

17

18

19

20

21

22

23

24

DECLARATION OF TARA TENENBAUM IN SUPPORT OF PLAINTIFF'S MOTION FOR A PRELIMINARY INJUNCTION
2

OPPOSITION TO MOTION FOR PRELIMINARY INJUNCTION

1

JANE JOHNSON (State Bar No. 31415927)
Jane.Johnson@johnsonshermen.com

2

JOHNSON & SHERMEN, LLP
10000 Shattuck Ave., Suite 3500

3

Berkeley, California 94704
Telephone: (510) 555-3500

4

Facsimile: (510) 555-3501

5

Attorney for Defendant

6

UNITED STATES DISTRICT COURT
NORTHERN DISTRICT OF CALIFORNIA

7

PAULA PATT,   Case No. C 1357 DBO

8

       Plaintiff,   **OPPOSITION TO MOTION FOR**
    v.   **PRELIMINARY INJUNCTION**

9

DAN DONNER,

10

       Defendant.   **MEMORANDUM OF POINTS AND**
                                /   **AUTHORITIES**

11

                                         Date: September 20

12

                                         Time: 12:00 p.m.
                                         Judge: Hon. Dianne B. Osaka

13

TO PLAINTIFF AND HER ATTORNEY OF RECORD:

14

    Defendant Dan Donner submits the attached Memorandum of Points and Authorities in

15

opposition to Plaintiff's Motion for Preliminary Injunction.

16

Dated: September 19

17

18

                                    Respectfully submitted,
                                    /s/ _____.

19

                                    JANE JOHNSON
                                    Attorney for Defendant

20

21

22

23

24

1 ## MEMORANDUM OF POINTS AND AUTHORITIES

2 ### TABLE OF CONTENTS

14 ### TABLE OF AUTHORITIES

15 *All. for the Wild Rockies v. Cottrell*, 632 F.3d 1127 (9th Cir. 2011)

16 *Action Apartment Ass'n, Inc. v. Santa Monica Rent Control Bd.*, 509 F.3d 1020 (9th Cir. 2007)

17 *Bivens v. Six Unknown Fed. Narcotics Agents*, 403 U.S. 388 (1971)

18 *Chevron USA, Inc. v. Cayetano*, 224 F.3d 1030 (9th Cir. 2000)

19 *Cnty. of Santa Barbara v. Hickel*, 426 F.2d 164 (9th Cir. 1970)

20 *Dollar Rent A Car of Wash., Inc. v. Travelers Indem. Co.*, 774 F.2d 1371 (9th Cir. 1985)

21 *Franklin v. Gwinnett Cnty. Pub. Schs.*, 503 U.S. 60 (1992)

22 *Houtan Petroleum, Inc. v. ConocoPhillips Co.*, No. 07–5627, 2007 WL 4107984 (N.D. Cal. Nov. 16,

23 2007)

24

1 | *Jarrow Formulas, Inc. v. Nutrition Now, Inc.*, 304 F.3d 829 (9th Cir. 2002)

2 | *Meyer v. Holley*, 537 U.S. 280 (2003)

3 | *Monsanto Co. v. Geertson Seed Farms*, 561 U.S. 139 (2010)

4 | *Sossamon v. Texas*, 563 U.S. 277 (2011)

5 | *Winter v. Nat. Res. Def. Council, Inc.*, 555 U.S. 7 (2008)

6

7

8

9

10

11

12

13

14

15

16

17

18

19

20

21

22

23

24

1

MEMORANDUM OF POINTS AND AUTHORITIES

2

I.   INTRODUCTION

3   Plaintiff Paula Patt has moved for a preliminary injunction enjoining Defendant Dan Donner

4   from renting Apartment 3B at 1357 Telegraph Avenue to anyone besides Ms. Patt.[1] Mot. for

5   Preliminary Injunction at 5. This is not a case where such an "extraordinary remedy" is warranted.

6   Mr. Donner opposes preliminary injunctive relief.

7

II. STATEMENT OF FACTS

8   Plaintiff alleges that she sought to rent an apartment owned by Mr. Donner. Patt Decl. ¶ 9.

9   Plaintiff fails to disclose that, soon after submitting an application, she stopped payment on her

10 check required to pay for the background check that Defendant's rental manager performs for each

11 prospective tenant. Walters Decl. ¶ 8. Plaintiff now claims, based on an alleged change in the

12 building manager's demeanor when she visited, that she did not receive the apartment because she

13 has a child. Compl. at 2. Defendant denies these allegations. Now, a different apartment than the

14 one Ms. Patt originally sought to rent is available in the same building. Patt Decl. ¶ 15. Ms. Patt

15 asks the Court to enjoin Mr. Donner from renting this other apartment to anyone except Ms. Patt

16 for the duration of this lawsuit, even before "the Court [has been] given sufficient time to consider

17 the merits of the Plaintiff's Fair Housing Act claim" Mot. for Prelim. Inj. at 5.

18

III. ARGUMENT

19 "An injunction is a drastic and extraordinary remedy, which should not be granted as a matter

20 of course." *Monsanto Co. v. Geertson Seed Farms*, 561 U.S. 139, 165 (2010); *see also Winter v. Nat.*

21 *Res. Def. Council, Inc.*, 555 U.S. 7, 24 (2008) ("A preliminary injunction is an extraordinary remedy

22 never awarded as of right."). The decision to grant a preliminary injunction falls within the

23

OPPOSITION TO MOTION FOR PRELIMINARY INJUNCTION
4

24

---

[1]   Mr. Donner has agreed not to rent this apartment to anyone else until the Court has ruled on the Motion for a Preliminary Injunction.

1   discretion of the district court, which must be mindful of the burden an injunction would impose on

2   a defendant. *See Winter*, 555 U.S. at 24. The Court should consider four factors before granting a

3   preliminary injunction: (1) whether there is a substantial likelihood that Plaintiff will prevail on

4   the merits; (2) whether there is a substantial threat that Plaintiff will suffer irreparable injury if

5   the injunctive relief is not granted; (3) whether the threatened injury to Plaintiff outweighs the

6   threatened harm the injunction may do to Defendant; and (4) whether granting the preliminary

7   injunction will disserve the public interest. *Id.* at 20. These factors weigh against Plaintiff's

8   application for injunctive relief.

9   **A.   The Court Should Not Impose a Preliminary Injunction Because Ms. Patt's Claim is**

10   **Unlikely to Succeed on the Merits**

11   The first factor to consider is whether Ms. Patt has "a ***strong*** likelihood of success on the

12   merits." *Dollar Rent A Car of Wash., Inc. v. Travelers Indem. Co.*, 774 F.2d 1371, 1374 (9th Cir.

13   1985) (emphasis added). Ms. Patt has submitted only the most circumstantial evidence of

14   discrimination: that she has a child, that the six current tenants—most of whom are students—do

15   not have children, and that, based on her own self-serving declaration, Mr. Walters' demeanor

16   changed when Ms. Patt visited the apartment. Patt Decl. ¶¶ 3, 6; Tenenbaum Decl. ¶ 4. At most,

17   Ms. Patt has presented the bare accusation of discrimination—certainly not a "strong likelihood of

18   success." *See Dollar Rent A Car*, 774 F.2d at 1374.

19   Further, Ms. Patt fails to disclose in her Motion for a Preliminary Injunction that she

20   voluntarily chose to stop payment on her check for the building manager's background check, a

21   required element of her application. Walters Decl. ¶ 8. Without a background check, Mr. Donner's

22   building manager was unable to select her as a tenant in the building. *See id.* Ms. Patt's unilateral

23   actions invoke the equitable principle of unclean hands, as Ms. Patt has participated in causing the

24

OPPOSITION TO MOTION FOR PRELIMINARY INJUNCTION
5

1   harm that she now objects to. *Jarrow Formulas, Inc. v. Nutrition Now, Inc.*, 304 F.3d 829, 841 (9th

2   Cir. 2002) ("The unclean hands doctrine closes the doors of a court of equity to one tainted with

3   inequitableness or bad faith relative to the matter in which he seeks relief.") Thus, Ms. Patt is

4   unlikely to succeed on the merits of her claim.

5   **B. The Court Should Not Impose a Preliminary Injunction Because There Is No**

6   **Possibility of Irreparable Injury**

7   "An essential prerequisite to the granting of a preliminary injunction is a showing of

8   irreparable injury to the moving party in its absence." *Id.* at 1375 (citing *Cnty. of Santa Barbara v.*

9   *Hickel*, 426 F.2d 164, 168 (9th Cir. 1970)); *see also Houtan Petroleum, Inc. v. ConocoPhillips Co.*, No.

10 07–5627, 2007 WL 4107984, at *9 (N.D. Cal. Nov. 16, 2007). The very fact that Ms. Patt has

11 requested this injunction shows that there is no risk of irreparable harm: she is willing to accept a

12 different apartment than the one for which she originally applied. The apartment she now asks the

13 court to reserve for her is not the same apartment she originally sought to rent. *See* Patt Decl. ¶ 16.

14 While this exact apartment may not be available at the conclusion of litigation, other apartments

15 in the Berkeley area certainly will be.

16   "[D]amages have been regarded as the ordinary remedy for an invasion of personal interests in

17 liberty." *Sossamon v. Texas*, 563 U.S. 277, 296 (2011) (quoting *Bivens v. Six Unknown Fed. Narcotics*

18 *Agents*, 403 U.S. 388, 396 (1971)). It is therefore "axiomatic that a court should determine the

19 adequacy of a remedy in law before resorting to equitable relief." *Id.* (quoting *Franklin v. Gwinnett*

20 *Cnty. Pub. Schs.*, 503 U.S. 60, 75–76 (1992)). In the unlikely event that Ms. Patt prevails in this

21 lawsuit, she can use any damages she recovers to obtain a comparable apartment. Ms. Patt's claim

22 to irreparable harm—that she may not be able to rent a specific apartment, distinct from the one

23 she originally sought to rent—is simply not comparable to cases where courts have found this

24

1 condition to be satisfied. *Cf., e.g., All. for the Wild Rockies v. Cottrell*, 632 F.3d 1127, 1135 (9th Cir.

2 2011) (holding that the environmental harm stemming from imminent deforestation and logging of

3 wilderness area satisfied the irreparable injury requirement).

4   Because Ms. Patt has conceded that she would accept a different apartment than the one she

5 originally sought, she cannot show that the lack of a preliminary injunction will cause irreparable

6 harm. Because she cannot show irreparable harm, she is not entitled to a preliminary injunction.

7 *See Dollar Rent A Car*, 774 F.2d at 1375.

8 **C. A Preliminary Injunction Would Impose a Significant Burden on Mr. Donner**

9   A preliminary injunction would impose significant hardship on Mr. Donner, while the absence

10 of a preliminary injunction would impose no significant hardship on Ms. Patt. Ms. Patt's argument

11 to the contrary assumes that Mr. Donner would rent the available apartment to her, and would

12 therefore continue to receive rent payments. Mot. for Prelim. Inj. at 7. This is not the case. Mr.

13 Donner and Mr. Walters did not consider Ms. Patt to be a well-qualified applicant for the first

14 apartment, and Ms. Patt has done nothing in the interim that would change that determination. If

15 the preliminary injunction is granted, the apartment will remain vacant and Mr. Donner will suffer

16 a significant loss of income. Ms. Patt, on the other hand, would be in exactly the same position she

17 is in now, and the same position she would be in if the injunction is denied, because Mr. Donner

18 does not intend to rent her this apartment unless compelled to do so by a final order of injunctive

19 relief.

20 **D. A Preliminary Injunction in This Case Is Not in the Public Interest**

21   "In exercising their sound discretion, courts of equity should pay particular regard for the public

22 consequences in employing the extraordinary remedy of injunction." *Winter*, 555 U.S. at 24 (citation

23 omitted); *see also Dollar Rent A Car*, 774 F.2d at 1374. Mr. Donner certainly does not dispute that

24

1   fighting discrimination is a "societal priority," *see Meyer v. Holley,* 537 U.S. 280 (2003), but

2   punishing landlords who have not discriminated, simply because an unsuccessful applicant brings

3   a lawsuit, does not serve that legitimate purpose. Ms. Patt's purported public interest justification

4   is simply a thinly-veiled reiteration of her own baseless claims. *See* Mot. for Prelim. Inj. at 7.

5   The actual effect of this injunction would be that an apartment would remain vacant for the

6   indefinite duration of Ms. Patt's lawsuit against Mr. Donner. A reduced supply of housing is

7   certainly not in the public interest. *See Action Apartment Ass'n, Inc. v. Santa Monica Rent Control*

8   *Bd.,* 509 F.3d 1020, 1023 (9th Cir. 2007) ("[R]emedy[ing] housing shortages constitutes a legitimate

9   public purpose."); *Chevron USA, Inc. v. Cayetano,* 224 F.3d 1030, 1048 (9th Cir. 2000) (Fletcher, J.,

10   concurring) (listing "reduced supplies of housing" as a negative policy consideration). Nor is the

11   public interest served by incentivizing baseless claims of discrimination by providing injunctive

12   relief without proof of wrongdoing. Fighting discrimination is an important public interest, but

13   would not be served by this injunction.

14   **IV. CONCLUSION**

15   This case meets none of the criteria for a preliminary injunction. Mr. Donner therefore

16   respectfully requests that the Court decline to impose this "drastic and extraordinary remedy." *See*

17   *Monsanto,* 561 U.S. at 142.

18   Dated: September 16

19

20   Respectfully submitted,

                                     /s/ _____ .

21   JANE JOHNSON
                                 Attorney for Defendant

22

23

24

1 | **EXHIBIT A**

2 | **DECLARATION OF WILL WALTERS IN SUPPORT OF DEFENDANT'S**

3 | **OPPOSITION TO MOTION FOR PRELIMINARY INJUNCTION**

4 | I, the undersigned, do hereby swear, certify, and affirm that:

5 | 1.   I am over the age of 18 and a resident of the State of California. I have personal knowledge

6 | of the facts herein, and, if called as a witness, could testify competently thereto.

7 | 2.   My name is Will Walters. I am currently a business student at the Haas School of Business

8 | at the University of California, Berkeley. I also work as an apartment manager for the apartment

9 | building located at 1357 Telegraph Avenue in Berkeley, California.

10 | 3.   My job duties as apartment manager include filling vacancies when they arise and

11 | completing minor repairs in the building.

12 | 4.   On August 15 of this year, I posted an advertisement on Gregslist regarding an available

13 | apartment unit, apartment 2B, in the building located at 1357 Telegraph Avenue.

14 | 5.   After posting the advertisement, I received an email from a prospective tenant, the Plaintiff

15 | in this case, Paula Patt, requesting to view the apartment.

16 | 6.   After receiving Ms. Patt's email, we spoke on the phone and scheduled a time for her to see

17 | the apartment that same day.

18 | 7.   Ms. Patt arrived at the apartment on August 15 with her daughter. Ms. Patt also brought

19 | with her a completed rental application and a thirty-five dollar check for her application fee, which

20 | covers a required background check.

21 | 8.   When I attempted to deposit Ms. Patt's application fee, I received notice from the bank that

22 | Ms. Patt had stopped payment on the check. As the application fee was a required element of her

23 | rental application, I concluded at that time that Ms. Patt had withdrawn her application.

24 | DECLARATION OF WILL WALTERS IN SUPPORT OF DEFENDANT'S OPPOSITION TO
MOTION FOR PRELIMINARY INJUNCTION

1

1 **EXHIBIT A**

2   9.   I ultimately rented the apartment to another prospective tenant.

3 Dated: September 19

4

5 /s/

      Will Walters

6

7

8

9

10

11

12

13

14

15

16

17

18

19

20

21

22

23

24
     DECLARATION OF WILL WALTERS IN SUPPORT OF DEFENDANT'S OPPOSITION TO MOTION FOR PRELIMINARY INJUNCTION

CHAPTER 3 MATERIALS

ORDER DENYING PRELIMINARY INJUNCTION

1
2
3
4
5
6
7
8
9
10
11
12
13
14
15
16
17
18
19
20
21
22
23
24

IN THE UNITED STATES DISTRICT COURT
FOR THE NORTHERN DISTRICT OF CALIFORNIA
OAKLAND DIVISION

PAULA PATT,   No. C 1357 DBO
                    Plaintiff,
          v.   **ORDER DENYING MOTION FOR**
                                      PRELIMINARY INJUNCTION
DAN DONNER,
                    Defendant.

_____/

Plaintiff has moved for a preliminary injunction preventing Defendant, the owner of an apartment building, from renting a newly-vacant apartment to anyone except for Plaintiff for the duration of this civil action. Plaintiff claims that Defendant violated the Fair Housing Act by discriminating against her based on familial status, because she is the mother of a child. Because the original apartment is already rented, the proposed injunction would apply to a *different* apartment that has recently become available.

"A preliminary injunction is an extraordinary remedy never awarded as of right." *Winter v. Natural Res. Def. Council, Inc.*, 555 U.S. 7, 24 (2008). "The traditional equitable criteria for granting preliminary injunctive relief are (1) a strong likelihood of success on the merits, (2) the possibility of irreparable injury to plaintiff if the preliminary relief is not granted, (3) a balance of hardships favoring the plaintiff, and (4) advancement of the public interest . . . ." *Dollar Rent A Car of Wash., Inc. v. Travelers Indem. Co.*, 774 F.2d 1371 (9th Cir. 1985).

"An essential prerequisite to the granting of a preliminary injunction is a showing of irreparable injury to the moving party in its absence." *Id.* at 1375 (citation omitted). Here, the required showing of irreparable injury has not been established. If the injunction is denied and the plaintiff subsequently prevails on the merits, she will be able to recover legal damages to fully compensate her for her injuries. If Plaintiff rents an apartment that differs in price or quality, and if she

1   ultimately prevails on her claim, those differences may be considered in evaluating her claim for

2   damages. *See Sossamon v. Texas*, 131 S. Ct. 1651, 1665 (2011) (noting that "it is axiomatic that a

3   court should determine the adequacy of a remedy in law before resorting to equitable relief," and

4   that "damages have been regarded as the ordinary remedy for an invasion of personal interests in

5   liberty" (citations omitted)).

6   Because irreparable injury is an "essential prerequisite," the Court declines to grant a

7   preliminary injunction in this case. *See Dollar Rent A Car*, 774 F.2d at 1375. The Court need not

8   reach the remaining three criteria, including Plaintiff's likelihood of success on the merits. *See Allen*

9   *v. Rowland*, No. 91–15853, 1992 WL 37371 (9th Cir. Feb. 27, 1992) (unpublished disposition)

10 (affirming denial of a preliminary injunction based solely on the lack of irreparable injury).

11   For the foregoing reasons, Plaintiff's Motion for Preliminary Injunction is DENIED.

12 **IT IS SO ORDERED.**

13 Dated: September 20

14   DIANNE B. OSAKA

15   UNITED STATES DISTRICT JUDGE

16

17

18

19

20

21

22

23

24

CHAPTER 4
OBJECTING TO PERSONAL JURISDICTION

CHAPTER 4 SKILLS EXERCISE

MOTION TO DISMISS FOR LACK OF PERSONAL JURISDICTION

This exercise requires you to argue a 12(b)(2) motion to dismiss for lack of personal jurisdiction. Recall that the applicable standard is whether the Defendant has such minimum contacts with the forum state that the exercise of jurisdiction does not offend traditional notions of fair play and substantial justice. *Int'l Shoe Co. v. Washington*, 326 U.S. 310, 316 (1945). Recall further that the test has been refined in *Burger King Corp. v. Rudzewicz*, 471 U.S. 462, 471–79 (1985).

Your assignment is to complete Parts III C and III D of the motion to dismiss, which argue that the Defendant Dan Donner is not subject to personal jurisdiction in California. First, complete the section that reads *"Apply the purposeful or intentional contacts portion of the minimum contacts test and analogize Mr. Donner's circumstances to relevant case law."* Second, complete the section that reads *"Apply the fair and reasonable standard of the minimum contacts test and analogize Mr. Donner's circumstances to relevant case law."*

In the critical portions that have been left for you to draft, you will apply the rule of *International Shoe* as refined in *Burger King* and its progeny to the facts of this case. Your goal is to convince the judge that Mr. Donner's ties to California do not meet the intentional and purposeful contacts portion of the minimum contacts test and that California's exercise of personal jurisdiction over Mr. Donner would violate the fair and reasonable standard of the minimum contacts test. This exercise should be completed after you have studied the cases on personal jurisdiction in your Civil Procedure course.

Some tips for drafting the Motion:

- There are many personal jurisdiction cases in your tool chest with widely varying fact patterns. Be strategic in analogizing and distinguishing from these cases to our set of facts.

- Make sure you are clear as to which grounds for personal jurisdiction you are attacking, be it specific jurisdiction or general jurisdiction.

- Remember that in actual practice a failure to bring your motion to dismiss for lack of personal jurisdiction at the same time as any other pretrial motions and prior to an answer will result in a waiver of this defense. Recall that in this case the Defendant moved to dismiss under both 12(b)(2) and 12(b)(6), and the judge granted leave to withhold briefing on the 12(b)(2) motion until after determination of the 12(b)(6) motion.

- Also remember that in actual practice, just because you might be able to win a motion to dismiss for lack of personal jurisdiction does not mean that you should always bring it. You should carefully assess whether the current forum presents any competitive advantage to your client or whether another potential forum creates any disadvantage.

1 JANE JOHNSON (State Bar No. 31415927)
   Jane.Johnson@johnsonshermen.com
2 JOHNSON & SHERMEN, LLP
   10000 Shattuck Ave., Suite 3500
3 Berkeley, California 94704
   Telephone: (510) 555-3500
4 Facsimile: (510) 555-3501

5 Attorney for Defendant

6   IN THE UNITED STATES DISTRICT COURT
        FOR THE NORTHERN DISTRICT OF CALIFORNIA

7 PAULA PATT,   No. C 1357 DBO

8   Plaintiff,
                                            DEFENDANT DAN DONNER'S NOTICE
       v.   **OF MOTION AND MOTION TO DISMISS**
9 DAN DONNER,
                                            MEMORANDUM OF POINTS AND
10   Defendant.   **AUTHORITIES IN SUPPORT OF**
                                         / **MOTION TO DISMISS**
11 _____

                                            Date: September 27
12   Time: 12:00 p.m.
                                            Judge: Hon. Dianne B. Osaka
13

14   On September 6, Defendant Dan Donner moved to dismiss Plaintiff Paula Patt's Complaint on

15 multiple grounds, including this Court's lack of personal jurisdiction over Mr. Donner. The Court

16 had previously granted leave for Mr. Donner to brief and argue his personal jurisdiction motion

17 following the Court's decision on the portion of the Motion to Dismiss seeking dismissal for failure

18 to state a claim upon which relief could be granted under Fed. R. Civ. P. 12(b)(6). That motion was

19 denied on September 13. Mr. Donner now submits the following Memorandum of Points and

20 Authorities, and renews his request that the Court dismiss this case pursuant to Fed. R. Civ. P.

21 12(b)(2), based on the following memorandum and on such further written and oral argument as

22 may be presented at or before the time the Court takes this motion under submission.

23

24

DEFENDANT DAN DONNER'S NOTICE OF MOTION AND MOTION TO DISMISS
1

1

TABLE OF CONTENTS

14

TABLE OF AUTHORITIES

Cases

16   *Asahi Metal Industry Co. v. Superior Court of California*, 480 U.S. 102 (1987) west law

17   *Bristol-Myers Squibb Co. v. Superior Court*, 137 S. Ct. 1773 (2017) p40

18   *Burger King Corp. v. Rudzewicz*, 471 U.S. 462 (1985) west law

19   *International Shoe Co. v. Washington*, 326 U.S. 310 (1945) p79

20   *J. McIntyre Mach., Ltd. v. Nicastro*, 564 U.S. 873 (2011) p111

21   *Pennoyer v. Neff*, 95 U.S. 714 (1878) p63

22   *Shaffer v. Heitner*, 433 U.S. 186 (1977) p90

23   *World-Wide Volkswagen Corp. v. Woodson*, 444 U.S. 286 (1980) p106

24

1 | <u>Statutes, Rules, and Other Sources</u>

2 | 42 U.S.C. § 3604(a)

3 | Rule 12(b)(2) of the Federal Rules of Civil Procedure

4 | United States, Constitution Amendment XIV, § 1

5

6

7

8

9

10

11

12

13

14

15

16

17

18

19

20

21

22

23

24

1

2

3

4

5

6

7

8

9

10

11

12

13

14

15

16

17

18

19

20

21

22

23

24

MEMORANDUM OF POINTS AND AUTHORITIES

I. INTRODUCTION

Plaintiff Paula Patt filed a claim against Defendant Dan Donner for violating the Fair Housing Act, which prohibits discrimination in the rental and sale of housing. 42 U.S.C. §§ 3604 *et seq.* Specifically, Ms. Patt claims that Will Walters, Defendant's property manager, intentionally declined to rent an apartment to her because she has a minor child and is not married, and that in doing so he violated the Fair Housing Act. Compl. ¶ 19. Ms. Patt alleges that Mr. Donner, the owner of the apartment building, is liable for Mr. Walters's alleged discrimination. Mr. Donner moves to dismiss the Complaint because the U.S. District Court for the Northern District of California lacks personal jurisdiction over him, and defending a suit in California would thus be a violation of his right to due process of law under the Fourteenth Amendment to the United States Constitution.

II. STATEMENT OF FACTS

Mr. Donner is a lifelong resident of the State of New York. Affidavit of Dan Donner ¶¶ 1, 3. He inherited the apartment building located at 1357 Telegraph Avenue in October 2007. *Id.* ¶ 5. In January of last year, he hired Mr. Walters, via telephone, to manage the apartment building. *Id.* ¶¶ 6–7 Mr. Walters's responsibilities include: maintaining the facilities, collecting rent, and interviewing and selecting prospective tenants. *Id.* ¶¶ 8–9. Mr. Walters continues in this position today, handling all day-to-day operations. *Id.* ¶ 8. Mr. Donner's only involvement with the apartment building is to deposit the monthly checks that Mr. Walters sends; he has never set foot in the State of California. *Id.* at ¶¶ 4, 9–10.

Plaintiff Paula Patt is the mother of S.P., age five. Compl. ¶ 10. On or about August 15, Mr. Walters showed Ms. Patt an apartment that was then available at 1357 Telegraph Avenue. Compl. ¶¶ 8–9, 12. Ms. Patt allegedly submitted an application to rent the apartment, which was instead

1　rented to a different, well-qualified, applicant. Compl. ¶¶ 15–16. Mr. Donner had no knowledge of

2　Ms. Patt's alleged application until this suit was filed. Donner Aff. ¶ 11.

3　## III. ARGUMENT

4　**A.　A Motion to Dismiss Should be Granted Where the Court Lacks Personal Jurisdiction**

5　**　　Over the Defendant.**

6　A court deprives a party of its right to due process of law under the Constitution if it imposes

7　obligations or restricts the rights of that party over whom it does not have personal jurisdiction. *See*

8　*Pennoyer v. Neff*, 95 U.S. 714, 733 (1878); *International Shoe Co. v. Washington*, 326 U.S. 310, 316

9　(1945); *Shaffer v. Heitner*, 433 U.S. 186, 212 (1977); U.S. Const. amend. XIV, § 1. A party may assert

10　that the Court lacks personal jurisdiction in a pre-Answer motion to dismiss. Fed. R. Civ. P. 12(b)(2).

11　**B.　A Finding of Personal Jurisdiction Requires that the Defendant Have Minimum**

12　**　　Contacts with the Forum State and that Jurisdiction is Reasonable.**

13　A determination of personal jurisdiction is comprised of two parts. First, a defendant must have

14　intentional purposeful contact with the forum state. *Burger King Corp. v. Rudzewicz*, 471 U.S. 462,

15　476–78 (1985); *International Shoe*, 326 U.S. at 316. Second, a defendant's contacts with the forum

16　state must be sufficiently strong that the exercise of personal jurisdiction does not "offend

17　traditional notions of fair play and substantial justice." *Id*. These two requirements must be satisfied

18　in order for a court to have personal jurisdiction over a defendant, even if the defendant owns

19　property in the forum state. *Shaffer*, 433 U.S. at 212.

20　A court may only find that a defendant has sufficient contact with the forum state where the

21　defendant has purposefully availed himself or herself of the protection of the forum state's laws or

22　intentionally directed his or her activities toward the forum state. *World-Wide Volkswagen Corp. v.*

23　*Woodson*, 444 U.S. 286, 297 (1980).

24

1   In assessing whether personal jurisdiction offends fair play and substantial justice, a court

2   must consider several factors, including: (1) the burden on the defendant of defending a suit in the

3   forum state; (2) the forum state's interest in the case; (3) the plaintiff's interest in being heard in

4   the forum state; and (4) other interests (such as the efficiency of the interstate judicial system) that

5   favor the case being heard in a different state. *Burger King Corp.*, 471 U.S. at 477. While each factor

6   should be considered, the "primary concern" is the burden on the defendant. *See Bristol-Myers*

7   *Squibb Co. v. Superior Court*, 137 S. Ct. 1773, 1780 (2017).

8   **C.   Mr. Donner Does Not Have Minimum Contacts with California Because Mere**

9   **Ownership of Property is Not Sufficient to Establish Minimum Contacts.**

10   *(Apply the purposeful or intentional contacts portion of the minimum contacts test and analogize*

11   *Mr. Donner's circumstances to relevant case law.)*

12   **D.   California's Exercise of Personal Jurisdiction Over Mr. Donner Would Be Contrary**

13   **to Fair Play and Substantial Justice.**

14   *(Apply the fair and reasonable standard of the minimum contacts test and analogize Mr.*

15   *Donner's circumstances to relevant case law.)*

16   **IV.   CONCLUSION**

17   Since Mr. Donner does not have sufficient minimum contacts with California, such that

18   personal jurisdiction in this case would offend traditional notions of fair play and substantial justice,

19   the Court does not have personal jurisdiction over Mr. Donner and should grant this motion to

20   dismiss pursuant to Fed. R. Civ. P. 12(b)(2).

21   Respectfully submitted,

22   _____

23   Jane Johnson
       On behalf of Dan Donner

24   Date: September 22

DAN DONNER SUPPORTING AFFIDAVIT

AFFIDAVIT OF DAN DONNER IN SUPPORT
OF MOTION TO DISMISS

I, the undersigned, do hereby swear, certify, and affirm that:

1. I am over the age of 18 and a resident of the State of New York. I have personal knowledge of the facts herein, and, if called as a witness could testify competently thereto.

2. My name is Dan Donner. I am 42 years old and employed as an accountant.

3. I was born in Brooklyn, New York, and have resided there for 42 years.

4. I have never been to the state of California.

5. In October 2007, I inherited the apartment building located at 1357 Telegraph Avenue ("the apartment building").

6. In January of last year, I posted an Internet advertisement to run in the Bay Area seeking a manager for the apartment building. In the ad, I offered a rent-free apartment in the building in exchange for basic maintenance and repairs, collecting rent, and screening and selecting tenants.

7. Will Walters telephoned me in response to the ad, and after a fifteen-minute conversation, I hired him. Our correspondence has consisted entirely of emails since then.

8. Mr. Walters is still the manager of the apartment building. He is solely responsible for making sure the building is in good repair, collecting rent, interviewing prospective tenants, and ultimately selecting new tenants.

9. Every month, Mr. Walters collects the rent checks for the five other apartments in the building and mails them to me. I have provided him with a credit card that he may use for building-related expenses. That is my only contact with the apartment building.

10. Prior to my hiring Mr. Walters, his predecessor, whom I hired through a similar process, had the same responsibilities, and my contact with the apartment building was the same as now.

11. I have never met Ms. Patt and I did not know anything about her interview or Mr. Walters's decision until the filing of the action against me.

I declare under penalty of perjury that the foregoing is true and correct.

Executed this September 16, in Brooklyn, New York.

_____

Dan Donner

CHAPTER 4 SKILLS EXERCISE

OPPOSITION TO MOTION TO DISMISS FOR LACK OF PERSONAL JURISDICTION

This exercise requires you to oppose the Defendant's 12(b)(2) motion to dismiss for lack of personal jurisdiction. Recall again that the applicable standard is whether the Defendant has such minimum contacts with the forum state that the exercise of jurisdiction does not offend traditional notions of fair play and substantial justice. *Int'l Shoe Co. v. Washington*, 326 U.S. 310, 316 (1945). Recall further that the test has been refined in *Burger King Corp. v. Rudzewicz*, 471 U.S. 462, 471–79 (1985).

Your assignment is to complete Parts III B and III C of the opposition to the motion to dismiss, which argue that the Defendant Dan Donner is subject to personal jurisdiction in California. First, complete the section that reads *"Apply the purposeful or intentional contacts portion of the minimum contacts test and analogize Mr. Donner's circumstances to relevant case law."* Second, complete the section that reads *"Apply the fair and reasonable standard of the minimum contacts test and analogize Mr. Donner's circumstances to relevant case law."*

In the critical portions that have been left for you to draft, you will apply the facts of this case to the rule of *International Shoe* as refined in *Burger King* and its progeny. Your goal is to convince the judge that Mr. Donner's ties to California meet the intentional and purposeful contacts portion of the minimum contacts test and that California's exercise of personal jurisdiction over Mr. Donner would not violate the fair and reasonable standard of the minimum contacts test. This exercise should be completed after you have studied the cases on personal jurisdiction in your Civil Procedure course.

Some tips for drafting the Motion:

- There are many personal jurisdiction cases in your tool chest with widely varying fact patterns. Be strategic in analogizing and distinguishing from these cases to our set of facts.

- Make sure you are clear as to which grounds for personal jurisdiction applies, be it specific jurisdiction or general jurisdiction.

1 | SAM PELLEGRINO (State Bar # 11235812)
sampellegrino@berkeleylegalclinic.org
2 | MATT MADISON (Certified Law Student)
BERKELEY LEGAL CLINIC
3 | 2013 Center Street, Suite 310
Berkeley, CA 94704
4 | Telephone: (510) 584-1515
Facsimile: (510) 555-5155

5 | Attorney for Plaintiff

6 | IN THE UNITED STATES DISTRICT COURT
FOR THE NORTHERN DISTRICT OF CALIFORNIA
7 |

8 | PAULA PATT,   No. C 1357 DBO
          Plaintiff,

9 | v.   **PLAINTIFF PAULA PATT'S
                                                  OPPOSITION TO MOTION TO DISMISS**
  | DAN DONNER,
10 | Defendant.
                                                  Date: September 27
11 | Time: 12:00 p.m.
                                      /   Judge: Hon. Dianne B. Osaka

12 |

13 |

14 |

15 |

16 |

17 |

18 |

19 |

20 |

21 |

22 |

23 |

24 |

1

TABLE OF CONTENTS

12

TABLE OF AUTHORITIES

13

<u>Cases</u>

14   *Asahi Metal Industry Co. v. Superior Court of California*, 480 U.S. 102 (1987)

15   *Bristol-Myers Squibb Co. v. Superior Court*, 137 S. Ct. 1773 (2017)

16   *Burger King Corp. v. Rudzewicz*, 471 U.S. 462 (1985)

17   *Hanson v. Denckla*, 357 U.S. 235 (1958)

18   *International Shoe Co. v. Washington*, 326 U.S. 310 (1945)

19   *J. McIntyre Mach., Ltd. v. Nicastro*, 564 U.S. 873 (2011)

20   *Pennoyer v. Neff*, 95 U.S. 714 (1878)

21   *Shaffer v. Heitner*, 433 U.S. 186 (1977)

22   *World-Wide Volkswagen Corp. v. Woodson*, 444 U.S. 286 (1980)

23

24

1 | <u>Statutes, Rules, and Other Sources</u>

2 | 42 U.S.C. § 3604(a)

3 | Rules 12(b)(2), (g)(2), and (h)(1) of the Federal Rules of Civil Procedure

4 | United States, Constitution Amendment XIV, § 1

5 |

6 |

7 |

8 |

9 |

10 |

11 |

12 |

13 |

14 |

15 |

16 |

17 |

18 |

19 |

20 |

21 |

22 |

23 |

24 |

1

2

3

4

5

6

7

8

9

10

11

12

13

14

15

16

17

18

19

20

21

22

23

24

MEMORANDUM OF POINTS AND AUTHORITIES

I.   INTRODUCTION

Defendant Dan Donner has moved to dismiss Plaintiff Paula Patt's complaint for housing discrimination for lack of personal jurisdiction. However, as set forth herein, this court has jurisdiction over Mr. Donner under the minimum contacts test based on his ongoing ownership of rental property located in the state of California, from which he derives monthly rental income and over which he retains full decision-making responsibility and financial control. Furthermore, it would not be unfair or unjust to subject Mr. Donner to personal jurisdiction in California since he should have been on notice of this possibility.

II.   STATEMENT OF FACTS

Mr. Donner, an accountant, inherited the apartment building located at 1357 Telegraph Avenue in October 2007. Donner Aff. ¶ 5. In January of last year, he hired Will Walters, via telephone, to manage the apartment building; Mr. Walters responsibilities include maintaining the facilities, collecting rent, and interviewing and selecting prospective tenants. *Id.* at ¶¶ 6–9. Mr. Donner receives rent checks each month from Mr. Walters, which are deposited in his personal account for his personal benefit. *Id.* at ¶ 9. Mr. Donner pays all bills and expenses for the property. *Id.* at ¶ 9.

Plaintiff Paula Patt is the mother of S.P., age five. Compl. ¶ 7. On or about August 15, Mr. Walters showed Ms. Patt an apartment that was then available at 1357 Telegraph Avenue. *Id.* at ¶¶ 6, 7, 10–12. Ms. Patt submitted an application to rent the apartment but Mr. Walters declined to rent to her. *Id.* at ¶¶ 13–14. Ms. Patt has brought this action to establish that the reason Mr. Walters declined to rent to her is that she is an unmarried mother. *Id.* at ¶¶ 16–17.

III. ARGUMENT

A. This Case Does Not Turn on *Pennoyer v. Neff,* but Rather on the Minimum Contacts Test of *International Shoe Co. v. Washington*

Defendant relies on the cases of *Pennoyer v. Neff* and *Shaffer v. Heitner* in support of his motion to dismiss. However, the rule articulated by the Supreme Court in *Pennoyer v. Neff* was displaced in the nineteen-forties because jurisdiction was easily evaded by corporations exploiting technicalities in an overly rigid framework. *International Shoe Co. v. Washington,* 326 U.S. 310, 318–19 (1945). The old rule was replaced by a more flexible standard, intended to better reflect the actual effects of interstate transactions. *Id.* The current standard is neither "mechanical [n]or quantitative" but instead looks to the "quality and nature of the activity in relation to the fair and orderly administration of the laws." *Id.* at 319.

The present inquiry into whether a court has personal jurisdiction over a defendant comprises two parts. First, as a threshold matter, a defendant must have engaged in a sufficient level of intentional purposeful contact with the forum state. *Burger King Corp. v. Rudzewicz,* 471 U.S. 462, 476–78 (1985); *International Shoe,* 326 U.S. at 316. Second, the exercise of personal jurisdiction must not "offend traditional notions of fair play and substantial justice." *Burger King,* 471 U.S. at 476–78; *International Shoe,* 326 U.S. at 316. These two requirements must be satisfied in order for a court to exercise personal jurisdiction over a defendant, even if the defendant owns property in the forum state. *Shaffer v. Heitner,* 433 U.S. 186, 212 (1977).

B. Defendant's Motion Should Be Denied Because Defendant's Continuing Ownership of Rent-Generating Property Constitutes Contact with the State of California

(Apply the purposeful or intentional contacts portion of the minimum contacts test and analogize Mr. Donner's circumstances to relevant case law.)

C. Defendant's Motion to Dismiss Should Be Denied Because It Would Not Be Unfair or Unjust for Defendant to Face Trial in California

(Apply the fair and reasonable standard of the minimum contacts test and analogize Mr. Donner's circumstances to relevant case law.)

IV. CONCLUSION

Mr. Donner's Motion to Dismiss for lack of personal jurisdiction should be denied because Mr. Donner's continuing ownership and rental of units in an apartment building in California constitutes contact with the state sufficient to support a finding of personal jurisdiction. Furthermore, it is entirely fair and just for the party with greater means to travel to the state where the injury occurred, especially since that state has a strong interest in seeing an effective resolution of the case to ensure the protection of its residents from unlawful discrimination.

Respectfully submitted,

_____

Sam Pellegrino
On behalf of Ms. Paula Patt
Date: September 26

CHAPTER 4 MATERIALS

ORDER DENYING MOTION TO DISMISS FOR LACK OF PERSONAL JURISDICTION

IN THE UNITED STATES DISTRICT COURT
FOR THE NORTHERN DISTRICT OF CALIFORNIA
OAKLAND DIVISION

PAULA PATT, and individual, Plaintiff, v. DAN DONNER, Defendant.	No. C 1357 DBO **ORDER DENYING MOTION TO DISMISS FOR LACK OF PERSONAL JURISDICTION**

/

This matter comes before the court on Defendant Dan Donner's motion to dismiss for lack of personal jurisdiction under FRCP Rule 12(b)(2). Plaintiff Paula Patt has made the following allegations, which for the limited purpose of this motion the court assumes to be true. *Ashcroft v. Iqbal*, 556 U.S. 662, 678 (2009). On August 15, Will Walters showed an apartment for rent located at 1357 Telegraph Avenue to Plaintiff Paula Patt, who was accompanied by her five-year-old daughter, S.P. Compl. ¶¶ 6, 7, 10–12. Mr. Walters is the manager of the building, which is owned by Mr. Donner. Compl. ¶ 15. During the appointment, Ms. Patt noted that Mr. Walters displayed apparent discomfort, that he asked her about her marital status, and that he gave "unpleasant" looks to her daughter. Compl. ¶ 12. Ms. Patt nonetheless submitted an application for the apartment, but when she called Mr. Walters on August 21, he brusquely informed her that he would not rent it to her. Compl. ¶ 14. Ms. Patt, who is unmarried, alleges intentional housing discrimination on the basis of familial status and marital status. Compl. ¶¶ 9, 16–17.

Mr. Donner first responded by filing a Motion to Dismiss for failure to state a claim, and lack of personal jurisdiction. The parties agreed to argue the 12(b)(6) issues first, reserving the 12(b)(2) motion for later argument should the need arise. Now Mr. Donner submits that since he has never physically entered the state of California and that his ownership of the apartment building, acquired

1   through inheritance, constitutes his sole contact with the state, the complaint should be dismissed

2   against him for lack of personal jurisdiction.

3   The Federal Rules of Civil Procedure dictate that the personal jurisdiction of federal courts is

4   in most circumstances identical to that of general jurisdiction courts of the state in which the court

5   is located. Fed. R. Civ. P. 4(k)(1)(A). California authorizes its courts to exercise jurisdiction "on any

6   basis not inconsistent with the Constitution of this state or of the United States." Cal. Civ. Proc.

7   Code § 410.10. The issue is therefore a matter of constitutional due process of law, the right to which

8   is guaranteed by both the Fifth and the Fourteenth Amendments to the United States Constitution.

9   *See* U.S. Const. amend. V, XIV, § 1. A court may not impose obligations or restrict the rights of a

10   party over whom it does not have personal jurisdiction without depriving that party of its

11   constitutional right to due process of law. *Pennoyer v. Neff*, 95 U.S. 714, 733 (1878); *International*

12   *Shoe Co. v. Washington*, 326 U.S. 310, 316 (1945); *Shaffer v. Heitner*, 433 U.S. 186, 212 (1977); U.S.

13   Const. amend. XIV, § 1.

14   The governing rule on personal jurisdiction is a flexible standard, intended to reflect the actual

15   state of interstate transactions. *International Shoe*, 326 U.S. at 318–19. The standard is neither

16   "mechanical [n]or quantitative" but instead looks to the "quality and nature of the activity in

17   relation to the fair and orderly administration of the laws." *Id.* at 319. This standard is composed of

18   two parts. First, a defendant must have engaged in intentional purposeful contact with the forum

19   state. *Burger King Corp. v. Rudzewicz*, 471 U.S. 462, 476–78 (1985); *International Shoe*, 326 U.S. at

20   316. Second, the contact must be sufficiently strong that the exercise of personal jurisdiction does

21   not "offend traditional notions of fair play and substantial justice." *Id.*

22   First, we consider whether Mr. Donner has sufficient intentional contact with the State of

23   California. When a defendant "purposefully avails itself of the privilege of conducting activities

24

1   within the forum State, thus invoking the benefits and protections of its laws," it engages in contact

2   sufficient to subject itself to the jurisdiction of that state. *Hanson v. Denckla*, 357 U.S. 235, 253

3   (1958). Although Mr. Donner did not intentionally bring about his initial contact with the State,

4   which arose with his inheritance of the apartment building, he has intentionally maintained and

5   pursued that contact. Had he sold his building after acquiring it, we would be facing a very different

6   factual landscape. However, Mr. Donner retained the building, engaged a manager, and has

7   continued for these several years to profit from its rental. If profiting from the sale of shoes in

8   Washington State was sufficient contact with Washington, then this court fails to see how profiting

9   from the rental of apartments is not. *International Shoe*, 326 U.S. at 321. The lack of Mr. Donner's

10   physical presence in the State is immaterial given that he benefits directly from the State's laws of

11   contract and real property. Thus we find that Mr. Donner has sufficient contact with California to

12   be subject to its personal jurisdiction.

13   Before we may conclude, we must consider whether our finding of personal jurisdiction would

14   offend traditional notions of fair play and substantial justice. *Burger King Corp.*, 471 U.S. at 464.

15   In doing so we may take into account, as appropriate, the burden on the defendant, the interest of

16   the forum state in adjudicating the dispute, the plaintiff's interest in a convenient and effective

17   resolution of the case, the interstate judicial system's interest in an effective resolution, and the

18   interest of the several states in furthering their social policies. *Id.* at 476–77.

19   Here, the interest of California in preventing housing discrimination within its borders is of

20   paramount importance and strongly favors a finding of personal jurisdiction. This finding is further

21   supported by the fact that the events in issue took place in California, and most of the relevant

22   evidence and witnesses are located there. Furthermore, subjecting the defendant to personal

23   jurisdiction would not intrude on any particular policies advanced by the state of New York of which

24

1 we are aware. Although defending against a lawsuit in California will inconvenience the defendant

2 to a certain extent, there is no indication that this inconvenience will offend our Constitutional

3 principles, especially given his ongoing relationship with the state. In sum, there are no fairness

4 concerns that would deprive California of personal jurisdiction over Mr. Donner in this case. The

5 Motion to Dismiss for lack of personal jurisdiction should therefore be denied.

6 IT IS SO ORDERED.

7 Dated: September 27

8 _____

   DIANNE B. OSAKA
9 UNITED STATES DISTRICT JUDGE

10

11

12

13

14

15

16

17

18

19

20

21

22

23

24

CHAPTER 5
AMENDING THE PLEADINGS

CHAPTER 5 SKILLS EXERCISE

MOTION TO AMEND COMPLAINT

This exercise requires you to complete Plaintiff Paula Patt's motion to amend her complaint. The motion has largely been drafted for you, but you must complete Section C, specifically where it reads, *Explain the rule codified in Title 28 U.S.C. § 1367(a) and apply it to Ms. Patt's motion, comparing the facts in her case to those in the Gibbs case.*

As you have learned in your Civil Procedure course, when a federal court has original jurisdiction over a given claim, it may also have supplemental jurisdiction over other claims within the civil action. 28 U.S.C. § 1367(a); *see also United Mine Workers of America v. Gibbs*, 383 U.S. 715 (1966). In the critical portion of the exercise, which has been left for you to draft, you will apply the law of 28 U.S.C. § 1367(a). To do so, you will apply the facts set forth in the case record thus far. This exercise should be completed after you have studied the topics of supplemental jurisdiction and amendment of pleadings in your Civil Procedure course.

Some tips for drafting the Motion:

- Before starting, read the portions of the motion that have already been drafted. Avoid unnecessary repetition of points made earlier in the motion.

- Avoid unsupported conclusory statements. You must explain *why* the facts you are using support the court's exercise of supplemental jurisdiction over Paula Patt's state claim.

- Do not introduce any facts that are not included in the declarations attached to the motion or set forth in the case record thus far.

1 | SAM PELLEGRINO (State Bar # 11235813)
spellegrino@berkeleylegalclinic.org
2 | BERKELEY LEGAL CLINIC
2013 Center Street, Suite 310
3 | Berkeley, CA 94704
Telephone: (510) 555-5151
4 | Facsimile: (510) 555-5155

Attorney for Plaintiff

5

IN THE UNITED STATES DISTRICT COURT
6
FOR THE NORTHERN DISTRICT OF CALIFORNIA
7
OAKLAND DIVISION

8 | PAULA PATT, an individual,   No. C 1357 DBO
                    Plaintiff,
9 | v.   **PLAINTIFF PAULA PATT'S NOTICE OF
                                                  MOTION AND MOTION TO AMEND
10 | DAN DONNER,   COMPLAINT**
                    Defendant.
11 | **MEMORANDUM OF POINTS AND
                                            /   AUTHORITIES**

12
                                                  Date: October 4
13   Time: 12:00 p.m.
                                                  Judge: Hon. Dianne B. Osaka
14

TO DEFENDANT AND HIS ATTORNEY OF RECORD:
15

16 | NOTICE IS HEREBY GIVEN that on October 4, at 12:00 p.m. or as soon thereafter as the

matter may be heard in Courtroom 3 of the above-entitled Court, located at 1301 Clay Street,
17

18 | Oakland, California, Plaintiff Paula Patt will and hereby does move the Court, pursuant to Rule

15(a)(1)(B) of the Federal Rules of Civil Procedure, to grant Plaintiff leave to amend her Complaint.
19

This Motion is brought on the grounds that Plaintiff has a proper and related state law claim that
20

21 | Defendant has violated the California Fair Housing and Employment Act and that the court has

jurisdiction over this state supplemental claim pursuant to 28 U.S.C. § 1367.
22

23

24

1   This Motion is based on this Notice of Motion and Motion and Supporting Memorandum of

2   Points and Authorities, and on such further written and oral argument as may be presented at or

3   before the time the Court takes this motion under submission.

4

5

6

7

8

9

10

11

12

13

14

15

16

17

18

19

20

21

22

23

24

MEMORANDUM OF POINTS AND AUTHORITIES

TABLE OF CONTENTS

TABLE OF AUTHORITIES

Cases

1   <u>Statutes, Rules, and Other Sources</u>

2   28 U.S.C. § 1367(a), (c)

3   Cal. Gov't Code § 12955(d)

4   42 U.S.C. § 3604(a)

5   Rule 15(a)(1)(B) of the Federal Rules of Civil Procedure

6

7

8

9

10

11

12

13

14

15

16

17

18

19

20

21

22

23

24

I. INTRODUCTION

Plaintiff Paula Patt moves to amend her complaint against Defendant Dan Donner for violation of the Federal Fair Housing Act to add a supplemental claim that Defendant violated the California Fair Housing and Employment Act ("FEHA") when Will Walters, Defendant Donner's property manager, declined to rent an apartment to Ms. Patt. Cal. Gov't Code § 12955(d). Ms. Patt brings this complaint to establish that Mr. Walters declined to rent to her because she is unmarried and has a minor child.

II. STATEMENT OF FACTS

Plaintiff Paula Patt is the mother of S.P., age five. Compl. ¶¶ 1, 10. Ms. Patt is not married. Compl. ¶¶ 1, 11. Will Walters is the manager of the apartment building located at 1357 Telegraph Avenue. Compl. ¶ 9. Defendant Dan Donner is the owner of said apartment building and personally retained Mr. Walters to serve as manager. Donner Decl., ¶¶ 5–8. On or about August 15, Ms. Patt, accompanied by her daughter, viewed an apartment that was being offered for rent by Mr. Donner and is located at 1357 Telegraph Avenue. Compl. ¶¶ 9–12. During the viewing, Mr. Walters asked Ms. Patt about her marital status, asked the identity and whereabouts of S.P.'s father, acted uncomfortable, and gave S.P. unpleasant looks. Compl. ¶ 14. Mr. Walters' entire demeanor changed upon seeing S.P., and learning Ms. Patt had a child. *Id.* Mr. Walters went from being friendly and interested in Ms. Patt to being dismissive and curt. Compl. ¶¶ 13–14. Ms. Patt submitted an application to rent the apartment but Mr. Walters refused to rent the apartment to her. Compl. ¶¶ 15–16. Ms. Patt intends to establish that his refusal was based on the fact that she has a minor child and is not married. *See* Compl. ¶ 19.

1

III. ARGUMENT

2   **A.   Plaintiff Paula Patt Should Be Granted Leave to Amend Her Complaint Because**

3   **Justice So Requires.**

4   A court should grant a motion to amend freely when justice requires. Fed. R. Civ. P. 15(a)(1)(B).

5   This rule is intended to ensure that cases are decided on their merits and not on the technical

6   requirements of pleading and should be applied with "extreme liberality." *United States v. Webb*,

7   655 F.2d 977, 979 (9th Cir. 1981). Justice requires the motion be granted in this case because Ms.

8   Patt has a valid claim against the Defendant for a violation of state law that she would be unable

9   to bring in a later suit because it would be merged into or barred by the judgment in this case. *See*

10 *Davis v. Dallas Area Rapid Transit*, 383 F.3d 309 at 313 (5th Cir. 2004).

11 **B.   Plaintiff Paula Patt Should Be Granted Leave to Amend Her Complaint Because It Will**

12 **Not Cause Undue Prejudice or Delay, Is Not Sought in Bad Faith, and Is Not Futile.**

13   In deciding whether to grant a Motion to Amend, the Ninth Circuit considers four factors, three

14 of which are independently sufficient grounds for denying the motion. *DCD Programs v. Leighton*,

15 833 F.2d 183, 186 (9th Cir. 1987). If the motion will cause undue prejudice to the other party, was

16 filed in bad faith, or would be futile even if granted, the motion should be denied. *Id.* In addition,

17 the court will consider whether granting the motion would cause undue delay, although a finding of

18 delay on its own is not sufficient for denial of a motion. *Id.* Granting Ms. Patt's Motion to Amend

19 would not trigger any of these factors because the motion was filed early on in the case, properly

20 states a claim upon which relief can be granted, and was filed in a good faith effort to obtain

21 compensation for harm done. Therefore, her Motion to Amend should be granted.

22   Granting Ms. Patt's Motion to Amend would not cause undue prejudice to the Defendant

23 because it was filed early on in the course of the case (neither party has yet begun discovery) leaving

24

1   Mr. Donner ample time in which to respond. Prejudice is a concern when a motion to amend is

2   perceived as being "tactical" or "strategic," that is, where such motions are made in order to delay

3   the proceedings or avoid an adverse ruling that cannot be defeated on the merits. *Acri v. Int'l Ass'n*

4   *of Machinists & Aerospace Workers*, 781 F.2d 1393, 1398–99 (9th Cir. 1986) (affirming denial of

5   motion to amend because it was made to "avoid the possibility of an adverse summary judgment

6   ruling, and . . . would prejudice the Union because of the need for further discovery"); *United States*

7   *v. Twin Falls, Idaho*, 806 F.2d 862, 876 (9th Cir. 1986) (affirming denial of motion to amend to add

8   claim for punitive damages because bringing it two years after filing of original complaint and two

9   months after start of jury trial was too late in the proceedings). Ms. Patt's motion does not raise any

10   of these concerns. Ms. Patt is not seeking to add an additional Defendant nor dissimilar claims from

11   those she brought initially. Crucially, she is bringing this motion early on in the proceedings, before

12   discovery has even begun. *See DCD Programs*, 833 F.2d at 187–88 ("Given that this case is still at

13   the discovery stage with no trial date pending . . . there is no evidence that [Defendant] would be

14   prejudiced by the timing of the proposed amendment."). Therefore, Mr. Donner will have ample time

15   to review the supplemental claim, obtain discovery on the matter, and prepare his defense.

16   Ms. Patt's motion is not futile because it properly states a claim for which relief can be granted.

17   The FEHA prohibits discrimination against a prospective renter on the basis of marital and familial

18   status. Cal. Gov't Code § 12955(d). It is therefore broader than the federal Fair Housing Act, which

19   prohibits discrimination based on familial status but does not address marital status. Plaintiff seeks

20   to prove that Mr. Walters declined to rent an apartment to Ms. Patt because she is not married and

21   has a minor child, in direct contravention of the FEHA. *See* Compl. ¶ 19. By seeking to add a claim

22   under state law, Ms. Patt is not merely restating the facts in her original complaint nor seeking to

23

24

1   add a claim that is already covered by her existing causes of action. *See DCD Programs*, 833 F.2d at

2   188.

3   Finally, there are no facts evidencing bad faith on the part of Ms. Patt. This motion is not made

4   to add a defendant who would destroy diversity and the jurisdiction of the court. *See DCD Programs*,

5   833 F.2d at 186. It has not been made to cause delay or hinder the proceedings, which have only

6   just begun.

7   As there is no evidence of prejudice, delay, futility, or bad faith, the court should grant Ms.

8   Patt's Motion to Amend.

9   **C.   The Court Has Jurisdiction Over Plaintiff Paula Patt's State Law Claim Because It**

10   **Is Part of the Same Constitutional Case as the Federal Law Claim.**

11   When a federal court has original jurisdiction over a federal claim, it also has supplemental

12   jurisdiction over all other claims that are part of the same constitutional case. 28 U.S.C. § 1367(a);

13   *see also United Mine Workers of America v. Gibbs*, 383 U.S. 715 (1966). In order to be part of the

14   "same constitutional case," a federal and state law claim must share a "common nucleus of operative

15   fact." *Gibbs*, 383 U.S. at 725. Supplemental jurisdiction is subject to only a few limitations—a federal

16   court may only decline to exercise supplemental jurisdiction over claims that raise novel issues of

17   state law, where state claims predominate over federal law claims, in cases where the federal claim

18   or claims have been dismissed, or if there are other similarly exceptional circumstances in play. 28

19   U.S.C. § 1367(c). Ms. Patt's state law claim emerges from the same nucleus of operative fact as her

20   federal law claim, and does not predominate over the federal claim or raise novel issues of law.

21   Therefore, the court has supplemental jurisdiction over her state law claim.

22   Section 1367 codifies the rule introduced in *Gibbs* and thus the facts of that case provide a key

23   illustration of what is meant by the phrase "common nucleus of operative fact." *See* 28 U.S.C.

24

1   § 1367(a). Mr. Gibbs was hired by a coal company to oversee the opening of a mine and was awarded

2   a contract to haul coal, but members of UMW forcibly blocked the mine opening, costing Mr. Gibbs

3   both his job and his contract. *Gibbs*, 383 U.S. at 717–20. He subsequently found himself unable to

4   obtain additional trucking contracts or mine leases. *Id.* at 720. Mr. Gibbs brought a federal claim

5   against UMW under the Labor Management Relations Act (LMRA) for a secondary boycott. *Id.*; *see*

6   29 U.S.C. §§ 141 *et seq.* He also brought a state law claim against UMW for an unlawful conspiracy

7   and boycott intended to interfere with his employment contract. *Gibbs*, 383 U.S. at 720. At the

8   District Court level, the jury awarded damages pursuant to Mr. Gibbs' state law cause of action, but

9   the court held that he had no cognizable claim under the LMRA. *Id.* at 720–21. On appeal, the

10 Supreme Court considered the "threshold question" of subject matter jurisdiction and held that the

11 court had pendant (now "supplemental") jurisdiction over the state law claim because the two claims

12 were part of the same constitutional case. *Id.* at 725. The Court defined a "constitutional case" as

13 comprising claims that "derive from a common nucleus of operative fact." *Id.* Since Mr. Gibbs' two

14 claims derived from a single set of operative facts, they were part of the same "case" and could be

15 heard in federal court. *Id.* Furthermore, the Court held that even though the District Court

16 ultimately found Mr. Gibbs had no claim under the LMRA, it was still within the District Court's

17 discretion to rule on the state law claim. *Id.* at 728.

18 *(Compare the facts in Ms. Patt's case with those in Gibbs to argue why the motion should be*

19 *granted.)*

20   **IV. CONCLUSION**

21   Since Ms. Patt has a valid claim for violation of California state law over which the court has

22 supplemental jurisdiction, since her amended complaint would not cause undue prejudice or delay,

23

24

1 | and since there is no evidence of bad faith, justice requires that the court grant Ms. Patt leave to

2 | amend her complaint.

3 | Dated: September 27

4 | Respectfully submitted,

5 | /s/ _____

6 | Matt Madison
   | Certified Law Student

7 | Sam Pellegrino
   | *Attorney for Plaintiff*

8

9

10

11

12

13

14

15

16

17

18

19

20

21

22

23

24

ORDER GRANTING MOTION TO AMEND COMPLAINT

IN THE UNITED STATES DISTRICT COURT
FOR THE NORTHERN DISTRICT OF CALIFORNIA
OAKLAND DIVISION

PAULA PATT,

       Plaintiff,

     v.

DAN DONNER,

       Defendant.

/

No. C 1357 DBO

ORDER GRANTING MOTION TO AMEND COMPLAINT

Plaintiff Paula Patt has moved to amend her complaint against Defendant Dan Donner for violation of the Federal Fair Housing Act to add a supplemental claim that Defendant violated the California Fair Housing and Employment Act ("FEHA") when Will Walters, Defendant Donner's property manager, declined to rent an apartment to Ms. Patt.

Plaintiff's Motion to Amend the Complaint is GRANTED.

IT IS SO ORDERED.

Dated: October 4

DIANNE B. OSAKA
UNITED STATES DISTRICT JUDGE

CHAPTER 5 MATERIALS
AMENDED COMPLAINT

1 SAM PELLEGRINO (State Bar # 11235813)
   spellegrino@berkeleylegalclinic.org
2 BERKELEY LEGAL CLINIC
   2013 Center Street, Suite 310
3 Berkeley, CA 94704
   Telephone: (510) 555-5151
4 Facsimile: (510) 555-5155

   Attorney for Plaintiff
5
                          UNITED STATES DISTRICT COURT
6   NORTHERN DISTRICT OF CALIFORNIA

7 PAULA PATT,   Case No. C 1357 DBO

8   Plaintiff,   **FIRST AMENDED COMPLAINT FOR**
       v.   **VIOLATION OF THE FAIR HOUSING**
9 DAN DONNER,   **ACT AND THE CALIFORNIA FAIR**
                                            HOUSING AND EMPLOYMENT ACT
             Defendant.
10
                                            DEMAND FOR JURY TRIAL
11 _____

12
   Plaintiff Paula Patt alleges as follows:
13
                                      PARTIES
14
       1.   Plaintiff Paula Patt is an individual currently residing in Oakland, California, within the
15
   Northern District of California. She is unmarried and is the mother of S.P., who is a five-year-old
16
   girl.
17
       2.   Upon information and belief, Defendant Dan Donner is an individual, resides in Brooklyn,
18
   New York, and is the owner of the apartment building located at 1357 Telegraph Avenue, Berkeley,
19
   California. This building is located within the Northern District of California.
20
                                   NATURE OF ACTION
21
       3.   This is a civil rights action for declaratory and injunctive relief and damages to remedy an
22
   act of discrimination in the provision of housing committed by Defendant Dan Donner, the owner of
23

24
                    FIRST AMENDED COMPLAINT FOR VIOLATION OF THE FAIR HOUSING ACT AND THE
                              CALIFORNIA FAIR HOUSING AND EMPLOYMENT ACT

1 || the apartment building located at 1357 Telegraph Avenue, Berkeley, California. Plaintiff Paula Patt

2 || brings this action under the Fair Housing Act of 1968, as amended, 42 U.S.C. § 3601 *et seq.*, and

3 || under the California Fair Employment and Housing Act. Cal. Gov't Code § 12955(d), to establish

4 || that she was rejected as a tenant on the basis of her familial status.

JURISDICTION AND VENUE

6 || 4.   This action is brought by Paula Patt, on her own behalf, pursuant to the Fair Housing Act,

7 || 42 U.S.C. §§ 3604, 3613, and the California Fair Employment and Housing Act, Cal. Gov't Code

8 || § 12955(d).

9 || 5.   This Court has subject matter jurisdiction over this action under 42 U.S.C. § 3613 and 28

10 || U.S.C. § 1331.

11 || 6.   The Court has supplemental subject matter jurisdiction over the related California state

12 || law claim, Cal. Gov't Code § 12955(d), under 28 U.S.C. § 1367.

13 || 7.   Venue is proper in that the claims alleged herein arose in the Northern District of

14 || California.

INTRADISTRICT ASSIGNMENT

16 || 8.   The events giving rise to Plaintiff Paula Patt's claim occurred in substantial part in

17 || Alameda County.

STATEMENT OF CLAIM

19 || 9.   On or about August 15, Plaintiff Paula Patt saw an advertisement on Gregslist indicating

20 || that a one-bedroom apartment was available for rent located at 1357 Telegraph Avenue in Berkeley

21 || California. The apartment was listed for $1,800 per month, exclusive of gas and electricity. The

22 || advertisement made no mention of the building's policy regarding children.

23

24 ||

FIRST AMENDED COMPLAINT FOR VIOLATION OF THE FAIR HOUSING ACT AND THE
CALIFORNIA FAIR HOUSING AND EMPLOYMENT ACT

1   10. Plaintiff Paula Patt placed a call to the number listed and reached Will Walters, who

2 identified himself as the manager of the apartment building and the individual who had posted the

3 listing for 1357 Telegraph Avenue, Berkeley, California. Will Walters's manner for the duration of

4 the telephone call was pleasant and friendly. He assured her that the apartment was available for

5 rent, and confirmed that he was asking for $1,800 per month in rent. An appointment was set for

6 Plaintiff Paula Patt to view the apartment that afternoon.

7   11. Plaintiff Paula Patt is the mother of a five-year-old girl, S.P.

8   12. Plaintiff Paula Patt is not married.

9   13. Plaintiff Paula Patt's daughter S.P. accompanied her to see the apartment.

10   14. When Will Walters answered the door for Plaintiff Paula Patt, he was initially friendly and

11 smiling.

12   15. When Will Walters saw S.P., he immediately looked and acted uncomfortable. Will Walters

13 asked Plaintiff Paula Patt about her age, her marital status and sexual history, the identity and

14 whereabouts of S.P.'s father, and on several instances gave S.P. unpleasant looks. After learning

15 about S.P., Mr. Walters was curt and dismissive of Ms. Patt, and tried to finish the viewing as

16 quickly as possible.

17   16. Plaintiff Paula Patt submitted an application for the apartment establishing that she was

18 fully qualified to rent the apartment.

19   17. On or about August 21, Plaintiff Paula Patt telephoned Will Walters to inquire about the

20 status of the apartment. He briefly informed Plaintiff Paula Patt that he would not rent the

21 apartment to her.

22   18. Defendant Dan Donner has owned the apartment building located at 1357 Telegraph

23 Avenue, Berkeley, California since 2007.

24

19. At all times relevant, Will Walters was acting as an agent of Defendant Dan Donner.

20. Because she was unable to rent from Defendant Dan Donner, Plaintiff Paula Patt must continue to search for an apartment and must currently stay in a hotel.

21. Plaintiff Paula Patt has not yet found any other suitable and available apartment.

22. Plaintiff Paula Patt is currently living at the Road Inn at 1423 University Avenue, Oakland, California, and paying $700 per week (approximately $3000 per month).

23. The hotel where Plaintiff Paula Patt is currently living is more expensive than the apartment that Will Walters refused to rent to her. It is also located farther from the University of California-Berkeley campus where Plaintiff Paula Patt works.

24. Plaintiff Paula Patt has suffered emotional distress and humiliation caused by Will Walters's discriminatory conduct.

FIRST CAUSE OF ACTION

Violation of Fair Housing Act

25. Will Walters's refusal to rent the apartment to Plaintiff Paula Patt constitutes discrimination against families with children in violation of the Fair Housing Act, for which Defendant Dan Donner, the owner of the apartment building located at 1357 Telegraph Avenue, is liable. 42 U.S.C. § 3604.

SECOND CAUSE OF ACTION

Violation of California Fair Employment and Housing Act

26. Will Walters's refusal to rent the apartment to Plaintiff Paula Patt constitutes discrimination on the basis of familial status and marital status in violation of the Fair Employment and Housing Act, for which Defendant Dan Donner, the owner of the apartment building located at 1357 Telegraph Avenue, is liable. Cal. Gov't Code § 12955(d).

FIRST AMENDED COMPLAINT FOR VIOLATION OF THE FAIR HOUSING ACT AND THE
CALIFORNIA FAIR HOUSING AND EMPLOYMENT ACT

<u>PRAYER FOR RELIEF</u>

WHEREFORE, the Plaintiff prays that the Court enter an ORDER that:

27. Declares that Defendant Dan Donner has committed discriminatory housing practices, as set forth above, in violation of the Fair Housing Act, 42 U.S.C. § 3604;

28. Enjoins Defendant Dan Donner from discriminating on the basis of familial status against any person in any aspect of the rental of a dwelling pursuant to 42 U.S.C. § 3613(c)(1);

29. Declares that Defendant Dan Donner has committed discriminatory housing practices, as set forth above, in violation of California's Fair Employment and Housing Act, Cal. Gov't Code § 12955(d);

30. Orders Defendant Dan Donner to rent the next available comparable apartment to Plaintiff Paula Patt pursuant to 42 U.S.C. § 3613(c)(1);

31. Awards monetary damages to Plaintiff Paula Patt pursuant to 42 U.S.C. § 3613(c)(1) and Cal. Gov't Code § 12955;

32. Awards punitive damages to Plaintiff Paula Patt pursuant to 42 U.S.C. § 3613(c)(1) and Cal. Gov't Code § 12955; and

33. Awards attorneys' fees to Plaintiff Paula Patt pursuant to 42 U.S.C. § 3613(c)(2) and Cal. Gov't Code § 12955.

34. The Plaintiff further prays for such additional relief as the interests of justice may require.

<u>DEMAND FOR JURY TRIAL</u>

35. Plaintiff Paula Patt demands a jury trial for all issues so triable.

Dated: September 27

1

2

3

4

5

6

7

8

9

10

11

12

13

14

15

16

17

18

19

20

21

22

23

24

Respectfully submitted,

/S/ _____ .

Matt Madison
Certified Law Student

Sam Pellegrino
Attorney for Plaintiff

FIRST AMENDED COMPLAINT FOR VIOLATION OF THE FAIR HOUSING ACT AND THE
CALIFORNIA FAIR HOUSING AND EMPLOYMENT ACT

CHAPTER 5 MATERIALS

ANSWER TO COMPLAINT

1 | JANE JOHNSON (State Bar # 31415927)
  | *Jane.Johnson@johnsonshermen.org*
2 | JOHNSON & SHERMEN, LLP
  | 1000 Shattuck Ave., Suite 3500
3 | Berkeley, CA 94704
  | Telephone: (510) 555-3500
4 | Facsimile: (510) 555-3501
  | Attorney for Defendant
5 |

UNITED STATES DISTRICT COURT

NORTHERN DISTRICT OF CALIFORNIA

7 | PAULA PATT,   Case No. C 1357 DBO

             Plaintiff,

8 | **ANSWER TO PLAINTIFF'S FIRST
      v.   AMENDED COMPLAINT**

9 | DAN DONNER,

             Defendant.

10 |

                                        /

_____

Defendant Dan Donner hereby respectfully submits the following Answer to Plaintiff Paula Patt's

Amended Complaint filed September 27. Defendant denies any allegations in the Amended

Complaint to which he does not specifically respond below.

PARTIES

1.   As to paragraph 1, Defendant lacks sufficient knowledge or information to admit or deny

the allegations therein, and on that basis DENIES them.

2.   Defendant ADMITS the allegations of paragraph 2.

NATURE OF ACTION

3.   Paragraph 3 is a characterization of Plaintiff's claim to which no response is required. To

the extent a response is required, Defendant ADMITS that Plaintiff has alleged discrimination and

purports to bring a claim on that basis, and DENIES any other allegations therein.

JURISDICTION AND VENUE

4.   Paragraph 4 is a characterization of Plaintiff's claim to which no response is required. To the extent a response is required, Defendant ADMITS the allegations of paragraph 4.

5.   Paragraph 5 is a legal conclusion to which no answer is required. To the extent an answer is required, Defendant ADMITS the allegations of paragraph 5.

6.   Paragraph 6 is a legal conclusion to which no answer is required. To the extent an answer is required, Defendant ADMITS the allegations of paragraph 6.

7.   Paragraph 7 is a legal conclusion to which no answer is required. To the extent an answer is required, Defendant ADMITS the allegations of paragraph 7.

INTRADISTRICT ASSIGNMENT

8.   Defendant ADMITS the allegations of paragraph 8.

STATEMENT OF CLAIM

9.   Paragraph 9 describes an internet advertisement that speaks for itself and no response is required to such description. Defendant ADMITS the remaining allegations of paragraph 9.

10. As to paragraph 10, Defendant lacks sufficient knowledge or information to admit or deny the allegations therein, and on that basis DENIES them.

11. As to paragraph 11, Defendant lacks sufficient knowledge or information to admit or deny the allegations therein, and on that basis DENIES them.

12. As to paragraph 12, Defendant lacks sufficient knowledge or information to admit or deny the allegations therein, and on that basis DENIES them.

13. Defendant ADMITS that Plaintiff was accompanied by a young girl to view the apartment. Defendant lacks sufficient knowledge or information to admit or deny any remaining allegations in paragraph 13, and on that basis DENIES them.

1   14. As to paragraph 14, Defendant lacks sufficient knowledge or information to admit or deny

2   the allegations therein, and on that basis DENIES them.

3   15. As to paragraph 15, Defendant ADMITS that Mr. Walters had a conversation with Plaintiff

4   when Plaintiff viewed the apartment. Defendant DENIES the remaining allegations therein.

5   16. As to paragraph 16, Defendant ADMITS that Plaintiff submitted a partial application to

6   rent the apartment. Defendant DENIES that Plaintiff submitted a complete application, that

7   Plaintiff's application established qualification to rent the apartment, and any remaining

8   allegations in paragraph 16.

9   17. Defendant ADMITS the allegations of paragraph 17.

10   18. Defendant ADMITS the allegations of paragraph 18.

11   19. Paragraph 19 is a legal conclusion to which no answer is required. To the extent an answer

12   is required, Defendant DENIES the allegations of paragraph 19.

13   20. As to paragraph 20, Defendant lacks sufficient knowledge or information to admit or deny

14   the allegations therein, and on that basis DENIES them.

15   21. As to paragraph 21, Defendant lacks sufficient knowledge or information to admit or deny

16   the allegations therein, and on that basis DENIES them.

17   22. As to paragraph 22, Defendant lacks sufficient knowledge or information to admit or deny

18   the allegations therein, and on that basis DENIES them.

19   23. As to paragraph 23, Defendant lacks sufficient knowledge or information to admit or deny

20   the allegations therein, and on that basis DENIES them.

21   24. Defendant DENIES the allegations of paragraph 24.

22

23

24

ANSWER TO PLAINTIFF'S FIRST AMENDED COMPLAINT

1

FIRST CAUSE OF ACTION

2

Violation of Fair Housing Act

3   25. Paragraph 25 is a legal conclusion to which no answer is required. To the extent an answer

4   is required, Defendant DENIES the allegations of paragraph 25.

5

SECOND CAUSE OF ACTION

6

Violation of California Fair Employment and Housing Act

7   26. Paragraph 26 is a legal conclusion to which no answer is required. To the extent an answer

8   is required, Defendant DENIES the allegations of paragraph 26.

9

PRAYER FOR RELIEF

10   27. Plaintiff's Prayer for Relief is not an allegation, and therefore no response is required. To

11   the extent that a response is required, Defendant DENIES that Plaintiff is entitled to any relief

12   whatsoever, including but not limited to the relief requested in paragraph 27 through 34.

13

DEMAND FOR JURY TRIAL

14   35. Defendant does not object to Plaintiff's demand for a jury trial for issues so triable.

15   Dated: October 11

16   Respectfully submitted,

17   /S/ _____.

18   Jane Johnson
                                                     Attorney for Defendant

19

20

21

22

23

24

CHAPTER 6
INTERVENTION

MOTION TO INTERVENE

1

Andrea Anderson
2345 Derby Street,
2   Berkeley, CA 94705
510-555-9998

3   *Counsel for proposed intervenor Berkeley*
Association for Fair Rental Policy, Inc.

4
                    IN THE UNITED STATES DISTRICT COURT
5   FOR THE NORTHERN DISTRICT OF CALIFORNIA
6   OAKLAND DIVISION

7   PAULA PATT,   No. C 1357 DBO

              Plaintiff,
8   **NOTICE OF MOTION AND MOTION TO**
        v.   **INTERVENE**
9   DAN DONNER,
                                          MEMORANDUM OF POINTS AND
              Defendant.   **AUTHORITIES**
10   /

11   _____ Date: October 16
                                          Time: 12:00 p.m.
12   Judge: Hon. Dianne B. Osaka

13

14

15

16

17

18

19

20

21

22

23

24
                                    1

TABLE OF CONTENTS

TABLE OF AUTHORITIES

1   TO PLAINTIFFS AND DEFENDANTS AND THEIR ATTORNEYS OF RECORD:

2   NOTICE IS HEREBY GIVEN that on October 16, at time 12:00 p.m., or as soon thereafter as

3   the matter may be heard in Courtroom 3 of the above-entitled Court, located at 1301 Clay Street,

4   Oakland, California, Berkeley Association for Fair Rental Policy, Inc. ("Fair Rental") will and hereby

5   does move the Court, pursuant to Rule 24 of the Federal Rules of Civil Procedure, to grant its motion

6   to intervene as a Defendant in this matter. This Motion is brought on the grounds that Fair Rental

7   has an interest that will be impaired by the disposition of this litigation and no existing party

8   represents that interest.

9   This Motion is based on this Notice of Motion and Motion and Supporting Memorandum of

10   Points and Authorities, and on such further written and oral argument as may be presented at or

11   before the time the Court takes this motion under submission.

12   **MEMORANDUM OF POINTS AND AUTHORITIES**

13   **I.   INTRODUCTION**

14   Plaintiff Paula Patt filed a claim against Defendant Dan Donner for violating the Fair Housing

15   Act and the California Fair Employment and Housing Act, which prohibit discrimination in the

16   rental and sale of housing. 42 U.S.C. §§ 3604 *et seq.*; Cal. Gov't Code § 12955(d). Specifically, Ms.

17   Patt claims that Will Walters, the building manager, discriminated against her as a prospective

18   tenant when he rejected her application after she withheld the required application fee. Am. Compl.

19   ¶ 20. Fair Rental moves to intervene in the interest of ensuring that antidiscrimination law, with

20   respect to rental housing markets, is enforced in an efficient and reliable manner in California.

21   **II.   STATEMENT OF FACTS**

22   Fair Rental was founded in 1976 to promote the development of just and reliable rental housing

23   policies. Over the past forty years, its mission has expanded to ensuring that all affected parties

24

1 have a meaningful voice in Berkeley's rental housing market. The organization is fueled by the belief

2 that the availability and efficient distribution of affordable rental housing is of paramount

3 importance to the Berkeley community, and that policies should be designed to reduce unneeded

4 constraints and costs in this essential market. While acts of discrimination may harm individuals

5 and groups, frivolous claims of housing discrimination can inhibit the broader availability of

6 affordable rental housing by imposing substantial costs and delays on rental housing providers. Fair

7 Rental strives to ensure that antidiscrimination laws are enforced in an efficient and reliable

8 manner to ensure the continued availability of housing for the Berkeley community.

9   Mr. Donner owns the building located at 1357 Telegraph Avenue, which is managed by Mr.

10 Walters. Declaration of Dan Donner at ¶¶ 5, 7. Plaintiff Paula Patt is the mother of S.P., age five.

11 Am. Compl. ¶ 11. On or about August 15, Mr. Walters showed Ms. Patt an apartment that was then

12 available at 1357 Telegraph Avenue. *Id.* at ¶¶ 9–10, 13. Ms. Patt submitted an application to rent

13 the apartment, but subsequently withheld the required application fee, at which point Mr. Walters

14 rejected her application. *Id.* at ¶¶ 16–17. Ms. Patt then brought a claim alleging that Mr. Walters

15 denied her the apartment because she is unmarried and has a child and that in doing so he violated

16 federal and state law. *Id.* at ¶ 20.

17   **III. ARGUMENT**

18 **A.   Fair Rental Should Be Permitted to Intervene Because It Has an Interest in the**

19   **Efficient and Reliable Enforcement of Housing Discrimination Law.**

20   A court must permit a party to intervene when it has an interest that may be impaired by the

21 outcome of litigation, and no existing party adequately represents that interest. Fed. R. Civ. P.

22 24(a)(2); *Grutter v. Bollinger*, 188 F.3d 394, 397 (6th Cir. 1999). Fair Rental has an interest in the

23 efficient and reliable enforcement of antidiscrimination law, which is at stake in Ms. Patt's suit.

24

1   In *Grutter v. Bollinger*, a white student claimed that the University of Michigan's Law School

2 improperly used race as a factor in admissions. 188 F.3d at 396–97. A group of minority applicants

3 and current students, as well as a non-profit organization dedicated to preserving higher education

4 opportunities for minorities, sought to intervene. *Id.* The court held that the intervening parties had

5 a substantial interest in the action because of their mission to ensure that minorities had access to

6 institutions like Michigan's Law School, which might be jeopardized by a change in their admissions

7 policy. *Id.* at 399.

8   Like the non-profit organization in *Grutter* whose mission was ensuring access to higher

9 education, Fair Rental has an interest in protecting access to housing by ensuring that Berkeley's

10 rental housing market remains free of burdensome delays and costs arising from premature or

11 frivolous discrimination claims. *See id.* at 394.

12 **B. Fair Rental Should Be Permitted to Intervene Because Its Interest in the Efficient**

13 **and Reliable Enforcement of Housing Discrimination Law Would Otherwise Be**

14 **Impaired.**

15   Fair Rental's interest in the efficient and reliable enforcement of housing discrimination law

16 will be impaired if it is not allowed to intervene in Ms. Patt's suit.

17   In *Bustop v. Superior Court*, an organization representing white parents sought to intervene in

18 the court's determination of whether a school reassignment plan formulated by the community

19 complied with the California Supreme Court's desegregation mandate. 69 Cal. App. 3d 66 (1977).

20 The court held that the parents had an interest that could be impaired or impeded by the court's

21 determination, since reassigning students to schools would directly impact their education, which

22 in turn would impact their social environment, economic opportunities, and other aspects of their

23

24

1   lives. *Id.* at 71. The court permitted the parents to intervene in the lawsuit, even though the record

2   showed that "citizen as well as staff participation was involved" in formulating the plan. *Id.* at 68.

3   Fair Rental's interest in the efficient and reliable enforcement of housing discrimination law

4   could likewise be impaired or impeded by the court's determination in this case. By stopping

5   payment on her check, Ms. Patt failed to fully complete a rental application. If Ms. Patt's claim of

6   discrimination is permitted to proceed despite her failure to complete an application, the courts

7   would open to a slew of premature housing discrimination claims. The need to defend against such

8   frivolous claims would impose a substantial financial burden on property owners and other

9   participants in Berkeley's rental housing market. This potential burden is similar in both

10 magnitude and breadth to the economic and social interests found to justify intervention in *Bustop*.

11 *Id.* at 71. Furthermore, removal of the basic prerequisite that a plaintiff must actually apply for

12 housing before claiming discrimination in her rejection would introduce an alarming degree of

13 uncertainty into this area of law. Because the efficiency and reliability of antidiscrimination

14 enforcement in Berkeley's rental housing market would be undermined by an adverse finding in

15 this lawsuit, Fair Rental should be permitted to intervene.

16 **C. Fair Rental Should Be Permitted to Intervene Because Existing Parties Do Not**

17   **Adequately Represent Its Interests.**

18   Fair Rental's interest in Mr. Donner's case is unique since Fair Rental has a stake in ensuring

19 the efficient and reliable enforcement of the body of housing discrimination law as a whole, as

20 opposed to advocating against relief only in this isolated instance.

21   Mr. Donner is in a similar position to the University of Michigan in *Grutter*; the University

22 might have been satisfied with an outcome that minimized its liability and might not have been

23 willing to fight hard to protect an inclusive admissions policy. *See* 188 F.3d at 394. Likewise, Mr.

24

1 Donner as an absentee property owner is not necessarily motivated to safeguard the interests of

2 other participants in Berkeley's rental housing market. He would be entirely justified in pursuing

3 only the beneficial resolution of Ms. Patt's claim. Fair Rental, however, acts in the interest of all

4 potential targets of frivolous housing discrimination claims in Berkeley and thus would approach

5 the case from a different angle, seeking to improve and clarify the requirements for discrimination

6 claims to proceed into costly litigation.

7   IV. CONCLUSION

8 Since Fair Rental has a substantial legal interest in ensuring the efficient and reliable

9 enforcement of housing discrimination law, since its interest would be impeded if Ms. Patt's suit

10 were adversely decided, and since Mr. Donner does not share Fair Rental's interest and thus will

11 not adequately represent it, the court should grant this motion to intervene as of right.

12 Respectfully submitted,

13 _____

   Andrea Anderson
14 On behalf of Berkeley Association for Fair Rental Policy, Inc.
   Date: October 7
15

16

17

18

19

20

21

22

23

24

CHAPTER 6 SKILLS EXERCISE

OPPOSITION TO MOTION TO INTERVENE

Berkeley Association for Fair Rental Policy, Inc. ("Fair Rental") has moved to intervene on behalf of Defendant Dan Donner. This exercise requires you to complete Plaintiff Paula Patt's motion opposing the putative intervention. The motion has largely been drafted for you, but you must complete Section C, specifically where it reads, *Compare this case to the facts from Bustop and Grutter, above, to argue that the court order will have no effect on Fair Rental or its landlord members.*

As you have learned in your Civil Procedure course, Rule 24(a)(2) allows an outside party to intervene in a lawsuit if (1) the application is timely, (2) the applicant has a significantly protectable interest in the pending lawsuit, (3) disposition of the lawsuit may adversely affect applicant's interest absent intervention, and (4) the existing parties do not adequately represent the applicant's interests. Fed. R. Civ. P. 24(a)(2); *Arakaki v. Cayetano,* 324 F. 3d 1078, 1083 (9th Cir. 2003). In the critical portion of the exercise, which has been left for you to draft, you will apply Rule 24(a)(2) and the relevant case law to argue that the outcome of Ms. Patt's case will have no impact on Fair Rental or its members. This exercise should be completed after you have studied the topic of intervention in your civil procedure course.

Some tips for drafting the Motion:

- Before starting, read the motion to intervene and the portions of the opposition motion that have already been drafted. Avoid unnecessary repetition of points made earlier in the motion.

- Avoid unsupported conclusory statements. You must explain *why* the facts you are using make it likely that the court should deny Fair Rental's motion to intervene.

1   SAM PELLEGRINO (State Bar # 11235813)
spellegrino@berkeleylegalclinic.org

2   BERKELEY LEGAL CLINIC
2013 Center Street, Suite 310

3   Berkeley, CA 94704
Telephone: (510) 555-5151

4   Facsimile: (510) 555-5155

5   Attorney for Plaintiff

6   IN THE UNITED STATES DISTRICT COURT
FOR THE NORTHERN DISTRICT OF CALIFORNIA

7   PAULA PATT,   No. C 1357 DBO

8   Plaintiff,   **PLAINTIFF PAULA PATT'S**

9   v.   **OPPOSITION TO MOTION TO**
DAN DONNER,   **INTERVENE**

10   Defendant.

Date: October 16

11   _____ / Time: 12:00 p.m.
Judge: Hon. Dianne B. Osaka

12

13

14

15

16

17

18

19

20

21

22

23

24

1

TABLE OF CONTENTS

2

16

TABLE OF AUTHORITIES

17

Arakaki v. Cayetano, 324 F.3d 1078 (9th Cir. 2003)

18

Bustop v. Superior Court, 69 Cal. App. 3d 66 (1977)

19

California ex rel. Lockyer v. United States, 450 F.3d 436 (9th Cir. 2006)

20

Freedom from Religion Foundation., Inc. v. Geithner, 644 F.3d 836 (9th Cir. 2011)

21

Grutter v. Bollinger, 188 F.3d 394 (6th Cir. 1999)

22

In re Estate of Marcos, 536 F.3d 980 (9th Cir. 2008)

23

League of United Latin American Citizens v. Wilson, 131 F.3d 1297 (9th Cir. 1997)

24

1 | *Smith v. Pangilian*, 651 F.2d 1320, 1324 (9th Cir. 1981)

2 | Cal. Gov't. Code § 12955(d)

3 | 42 U.S.C. § 3604(a)

4 | Rule 24 of the Federal Rules of Civil Procedure

5

6

7

8

9

10

11

12

13

14

15

16

17

18

19

20

21

22

23

24

1

MEMORANDUM OF POINTS AND AUTHORITIES

2

I.   INTRODUCTION

3   Plaintiff Paula Patt filed a claim against Defendant Dan Donner for violating the Fair Housing

4   Act and the California Fair Employment and Housing Act, which prohibit discrimination in the

5   rental and sale of housing. 42 U.S.C. §§ 3604 *et seq.* (2006); Cal. Gov't. Code § 12955(d). Specifically,

6   Ms. Patt claims that Will Walters, the building manager at 1357 Telegraph Avenue, Berkeley,

7   California, discriminated against her as a prospective tenant because she has a minor child and is

8   not married, that he did so in violation of the Acts listed above, and that Mr. Donner is liable as the

9   building's owner. Amended Compl. ¶ 20. The Berkeley Association for Fair Rental Policy, Inc. ("Fair

10   Rental") has moved to intervene, claiming an interest of helping landlords when they are sued for

11   housing discrimination.

12

II. STATEMENT OF FACTS

13   Defendant Mr. Donner owns the building located at 1357 Telegraph Avenue, which is managed

14   by Mr. Walters. Affidavit of Dan Donner, ¶¶ 5, 7. Plaintiff Paula Patt is the mother of S.P., age five.

15   Am. Compl. ¶ 11. On or about August 15, Mr. Walters showed Ms. Patt an apartment that was then

16   available at 1357 Telegraph Avenue. *Id.* at ¶¶ 9–10, 13. Ms. Patt submitted an application to rent

17   the apartment but Mr. Walters rejected her application. *Id.* at ¶¶ 16–17. Ms. Patt brought a claim

18   to establish that Mr. Walters denied her the apartment because she is unmarried and has a child

19   and that in doing so he violated federal and state law. *Id.* at ¶ 20.

20   Fair Rental filed a Motion to Intervene in the case between Defendant Donner and Plaintiff

21   Patt. Fair Rental's mission is to ensure that landlords are protected against housing discrimination

22   lawsuits.

23

24

III. ARGUMENT

A. Legal Standard for Intervention

Intervention under Rule 24(a)(2) involves a four-part test, each prong of which must be satisfied. Fed. R. Civ. P. 24(a)(2); *Arakaki v. Cayetano*, 324 F. 3d 1078, 1083 (9th Cir. 2003). The four-part test requires courts to examine whether (1) the application is timely, (2) the applicant has a significantly protectable interest in the pending lawsuit, (3) disposition of the lawsuit may adversely affect applicant's interest absent intervention, and (4) the existing parties do not adequately represent the applicant's interests. *Id.* The applicant bears the burden of showing that each of the four elements is met. *Freedom from Religion Found. Inc. v Geithner*, 644 F.3d 836, 841 (9th Cir. 2011).

B. Fair Rental Should Not Be Permitted to Intervene Because It Fails to Meet Its Burden Under Rule 24(a)(2) of the Federal Rules of Civil Procedure

    a. Fair Rental Should Not Be Permitted to Intervene Because It Does Not Have a Protectable Interest of Sufficient Magnitude to Warrant Intervention

To satisfy the second prong of the four-part test, Fair Rental must show "a protectable interest of sufficient magnitude to warrant inclusion in the action." *See Smith v. Pangilian*, 651 F.2d 1320, 1324 (9th Cir. 1981). The Ninth Circuit does not require the applicant to identify a specific legal or equitable interest in the pending litigation, but the applicant must prove that it would "suffer a practical impairment of its interests as a result of the pending litigation." *California ex rel. Lockyer v. United States*, 450 F.3d 436, 411 (9th Cir. 2006).

As the putative intervenor has argued, in *Grutter v. Bollinger*, a white student claimed that the University of Michigan's Law School improperly used race as a factor in admissions. *Grutter*, 188 F.3d 396–97. A group of minority applicants, current students, and a non-profit organization

1 dedicated to preserving higher education opportunities for minorities sought to intervene. *Id.*

2 Because the intervening parties' mission of ensuring that minorities had access to institutions like

3 Michigan's Law School might be jeopardized by a change in the school's admission policy, the court

4 held that the intervening parties had a substantial interest in the action. *Id.* at 399. The intervenors'

5 interest was of sufficient magnitude because the litigation tangibly jeopardized minority access to

6 professional higher education. *Id.*

7 However, unlike the intervenors in *Grutter*, Fair Rental merely asserts that it has an interest

8 in the efficient and reliable enforcement of housing discrimination law but fails to demonstrate that

9 its interest is of sufficient magnitude to warrant intervention in the pending litigation. Everyone

10 has an interest in the efficient and reliable enforcement of housing discrimination law, but not

11 everyone is permitted to intervene as of right under Rule 24(a)(2). Accordingly, the Ninth Circuit

12 has viewed the "interest test" as a "practical guide of disposing of lawsuits by involving as many

13 apparently concerned persons as is compatible with efficiency and due process." *In re Estate of*

14 *Marcos*, 536 F.3d 980, 985 (9th Cir. 2008).

15 Fair Rental is simply a group of landlords who want to restrict the ability of plaintiffs to bring

16 housing discrimination cases. Fair Rental can attempt to reform the law through lobbying and can

17 file amicus briefs, but they have no interest in the outcome of this particular litigation at the district

18 court level because unlike the court in *Grutter* this court will not be making a policy determination

19 that affects other landlords or tenants. This court will be deciding whether the defendant violated

20 Ms. Patt's legal rights when he refused to rent her housing because she is unmarried and has a

21 child, but will not be restricting or enlarging access to housing for other single parents. The

22 plaintiff's action is solely concerned with her individual claim; there is no demand for class-wide or

23

24

1 | broad impact. Because Fair Rental fails to articulate why it has any sufficient interest in this

2 | particular case, the court should deny its motion to intervene.

3 | **b.   Fair Rental Should Not Be Permitted to Intervene Because Any Hypothetical**

4 | **Interest It Might Have in this Case Would Not Otherwise Be Impaired by Denying**

5 | **Intervention**

6 | Unlike the cases on which Fair Rental relies, Fair Rental's interest in the non-enforcement of

7 | housing discrimination law will not be impaired if it is not allowed to intervene in Ms. Patt's suit.

8 | In *Bustop v. Superior Court*, an organization representing white parents sought to intervene in

9 | the court's determination of whether a school reassignment plan formulated by the community

10 | complied with the Supreme Court's desegregation mandate. 69 Cal. App. 3d 66 (1977). The court,

11 | applying California law which runs parallel to federal law, held that the parents had an interest

12 | that could be impaired or impeded by the court's determination, since reassigning students to

13 | schools would directly impact their education, which in turn would impact their social environment,

14 | economic opportunities, and other aspects of their lives. *Id.* at 71. The court permitted the parents

15 | to intervene in the lawsuit, even though the record showed that "citizen as well as staff participation

16 | was involved" in formulating the plan. *Id.* at 68.

17 | *(Compare this case to the facts from Bustop and Grutter, above, to argue that the court order will*

18 | *have no effect on Fair Rental or its landlord members.)*

19 | **c.   Fair Rental Should Not Be Permitted to Intervene Because Existing Parties**

20 | **Adequately Represent the Interests It Asserts**

21 | Fair Rental's interest in this case is not unique because the defendant is actively representing

22 | Fair Rental's hypothetical interests. In this instance, Mr. Donner is an educated defendant who is

23 | professionally an accountant and earns over $100,000.00 in rentals from this building each year. He

24 |

1   has the resources to hire adequate representation, and he is represented by a well-regarded

2   Berkeley law firm that specializes in real property law. He has done nothing to suggest that he

3   cannot adequately defend this suit. Since he has aggressively litigated this suit through moving to

4   dismiss on various grounds, conducting discovery, and has indicated an intent to move for summary

5   judgment, it is clear he is represented by competent counsel that have offered every defense at every

6   stage of this litigation.

7   The only legitimate interests the landlords have are, first, in avoiding some precedent because

8   of sloppy lawyering on the part of the defendant, and, second, in remedying the defendant's lack of

9   representation. Here, there is no reason to believe this case will influence other cases, and the

10 defendant is well represented. Additionally, there is no difference between how Mr. Donner's

11 attorneys are handling the case and how Fair Rental would handle the case. Fair Rental's position

12 is a position that the defendant has raised himself. Fair Rental is not suggesting a defense that is

13 different and conflicting with the defendant's defense. Because Defendant Dan Donner's interests

14 align with those of Fair Rental and Fair Rental is adequately defending this suit, Fair Rental's

15 motion to intervene should be denied.

16   **IV. CONCLUSION**

17   Since Fair Rental does not have a substantial legal interest in this particular case, and since

18 any hypothetical interest would not be impeded if Ms. Patt's suit were adversely decided, and since

19 Mr. Donner shares Fair Rental's interest and thus will adequately represent it, the court should

20 deny Fair Rental's motion to intervene.

21   Respectfully submitted,

22 _____

    Sam Pellegrino
23 Date: October 9

24

STATEMENT OF NON-OPPOSITION

1 | JANE JOHNSON (State Bar No. 31415927)
Jane.Johnson@johnsonshermen.com
2 | JOHNSON & SHERMEN, LLP
10000 Shattuck Ave., Suite 3500
3 | Berkeley, California 94704
Telephone: (510) 555-3500
4 | Facsimile: (510) 555-3501

Attorney for Defendant

5

6 | UNITED STATES DISTRICT COURT
NORTHERN DISTRICT OF CALIFORNIA

7 | PAULA PATT,   Case No. C 1357 DBO

8 | Plaintiff,   **DEFENDANT'S STATEMENT OF NON-OPPOSITION TO MOTION TO INTERVENE**
      v.
9 | DAN DONNER,

10 | Defendant.
                                                   Date: October 16
11 | _____ /   Time: 12:00 p.m.
                                                   Judge: Hon. Dianne B. Osaka
12

13 | Defendant Dan Donner does not oppose the motion to intervene of proposed defendant

intervenor Berkeley Association for Fair Rental Policy, Inc.
14

Dated: October 7
15

16 | Respectfully submitted,
                                                   /s/ _____ .
17 | JANE JOHNSON
                                                   Attorney for Defendant
18

19

20

21

22

23

24

CHAPTER 6 MATERIALS

ORDER DENYING MOTION TO INTERVENE

IN THE UNITED STATES DISTRICT COURT
FOR THE NORTHERN DISTRICT OF CALIFORNIA
OAKLAND DIVISION

PAULA PATT,

        Plaintiff,

        v.

DAN DONNER,

        Defendant.

                 /

No. C 1357 DBO

ORDER DENYING MOTION TO INTERVENE

The Berkeley Association for Fair Rental Policy, Inc. ("Fair Rental") has moved to intervene in the suit between Plaintiff Paula Patt and Defendant Dan Donner. The Court holds that Fair Rental does have a substantial legal interest in ensuring the enforcement and preservation of housing discrimination law, and its interest could be impeded if Ms. Patt's suit were adversely decided, but Mr. Donner shares Fair Rental's interest and his attorneys are fully qualified; thus Mr. Donner's counsel will adequately represent Fair Rental's interest.

The Motion to Intervene is therefore DENIED.

IT IS SO ORDERED.

Dated: October 15

_____

DIANNE B. OSAKA
UNITED STATES DISTRICT JUDGE

CHAPTER 7
DISCOVERY

CHAPTER 7 MATERIALS

PAULA PATT DEPOSITION TRANSCRIPT

A video of Paula Patt's deposition can be found at
http://www.kaltura.com/tiny/2lu6e

Subject: Paula Patt Deposition
From: Matt Madison <mmadison@berkeleylegalclinic.org>
To: Sam Pellegrino <spellegrino@berkeleylegalclinic.org>
Date: October 17 10:43 AM

Professor Pellegrino,

Here are excerpts of the transcript from Ms. Patt's deposition yesterday; I included three sections that you might like to review. The first is relevant to the Motion for Protective Order, which I will begin working on.

Best,

Matt

Matt Madison
Certified Law Student
Berkeley Legal Clinic
www.berkeleylegalclinic.org

IN THE UNITES STATES DISTRICT COURT
FOR THE NORTHERN DISTRICT OF CALIFORNIA

CASE NO. CV 1357 DBO

PAULA PATT,
    Plaintiff,

vs.

DAN DONNER,
    Defendant.

VIDEOTAPED DEPOSITION OF PAULA PATT

October 16
10000 Shattuck Avenue, Suite 3500
Berkeley, California 94704

REPORTED BY:

Caren Rafael, CSR

Rafael Reporting Company

123 Grand Avenue

Oakland, California 94612

Tel.: 510-133-6745

APPEARANCES:

On behalf of the Plaintiff:
    SAM PELLEGRINO, ESQ.
    MATT MADISON, CERTIFIED LAW STUDENT
    Berkeley Legal Clinic
    2013 Center Street, Suite 310
    Berkeley, California 94704

On behalf of the Defendant:
    JANE JOHNSON, ESQ.
    Johnson & Shermen LLP
    10000 Shattuck Avenue, Suite 3500
    Berkeley, California 94704

VIDEOGRAPHER: Lesleigh Viars, Viars Legal Video

1

1   REPORTER: Good morning everyone. My name is Caren
2   Rafael, I'm a certified California court reporter. This
3   is the recorded deposition of Paula Patt by Dan
4   Donner's attorney, Jane Johnson. May I please have the
5   appearances of counsel?
6
7   MS. JOHNSON: Yes, Jane Johnson for Defendant Dan
8   Donner, conducting the deposition.
9
10   MR. PELLEGRINO: Sam Pellegrino, Berkeley Law
11   Clinic, and I will be supervising Matt Madison, a
12   Berkeley Law student who is certified under the
13   California Practice Law.
14
15   MR. MADISON: Matt Madison, certified law student,
16   representing Paula Patt.
17
18   PAULA PATT
19   the witness herein, having been duly sworn, did testify
20   as follows:
21
22   DIRECT EXAMINATION
23   by MS. JOHNSON:
24
25   Q: Please state your name for the record?
26
27   A: Paula Patt.
28
29   Q: Do you understand that the deposition is taken
30   pursuant to the Federal Rules of Civil Procedure?
31
32   A: Yes.
33
34   Q: Do you understand that you are under oath?
35
36   A: Yes.
37
38   Q: Do you understand that you are obligated to
39   tell the truth?
40
41   A: Yes I do.
42
43   Q: Do you understand that your answers may be used
44   at trial?

```
1
2        A: Yes.
3
4        Q: Are you taking any medications that may affect
5    your ability to testify today?
6
7        A: No.
8
9        Q: Are you taking any other substances that may
10   affect your ability to testify today?
11
12       A: No.
13
14       Q: Are there any reasons why we should not proceed
15   with the deposition?
16
17       A: No.
18
19       Q: Ok. Where do you live?
20
21       A: I live in Berkeley.
22
23       Q: And what is your address in Berkeley?
24
25       A: It's on Shattuck Avenue, do you need the exact
26   address?
27
28       Q: Yes.
29
30       A: It's 2457 Shattuck Avenue.
31
32       Q: Great. How long have you lived there?
33
34       A: I've lived there for about a month.
35
36       Q: Okay.  Are you a student?
37
38       A: Yes, I'm a grad student, in the Ph.D.
39   anthropology program here at Berkeley.
40
41       Q: Brilliant.  So how long have you been a student
42   here?
43
44       A: I just started, this is my first semester.
```

3

```
 1        Q: Okay.  Do you get a stipend from the school?
 2
 3        A: Yes, I do.  That's how it works when you're in
 4   the Ph.D., the doctoral program.
 5
 6        Q: How much is the stipend?
 7
 8        A: The stipend is $24,000 a year.
 9
10        Q: And what is the stipend for?
11
12        A: Well it's for living expenses while I'm a
13   student.  Right now, well, eventually I'll be teaching
14   classes when I'm a little further along in the program
15   and then it counts kind of as pay for that.
16
17        Q: Okay.  Do you have a child?
18
19        A: Yes I do.
20
21        Q: How old is your child?
22
23        A: She's five years old.
24
25        Q: Ok.  What is the child's name?
26
27        A: Her name is Sally.
28
29        Q: And how long have you lived at your current
30   address?
31
32        A: Just about four weeks.
33
34        Q: Four weeks, you mentioned a month.  And how
35   long were you at your previous address?
36
37        A: Well I moved to Berkeley from the Boston area;
38   we had lived there for I think two years.
39
40        Q: So let's turn to the facts of the case.  So did
41   you ever make an effort to rent an apartment at 1357
42   Telegraph Avenue?
43
44        A: Yes, I did.
```

4

1   Q: How did you being the process?
2
3   A: Well when I first moved to Berkeley we were
4   staying at a motel for a few days and I wanted to find
5   more permanent housing. So I contacted the grad
6   student housing office to ask, you know, how do people
7   do that here? They recommended that I look at
8   Gregslist and a couple other online sites, because
9   that's where most of the landlords would post.
10
11   Q: So you saw an ad for the apartment?
12
13   A: Yes, I looked on Gregslist and I saw an ad for
14   1357 Telegraph and it looked like it would be a perfect
15   set up for me and Sally so I contacted the number that
16   was in the ad right away.
17
18   Q: Who did you speak to on the phone?
19
20   A: I guess first I sent an email to the address
21   and then ended up speaking with Will Walters.
22
23   Q: Ok. Can you relay the conversation you had
24   with Will Walters?
25
26   A: Sure. I called- talked to Mr. Walters about
27   setting up a time for me to see the apartment; we were
28   able to set up a time for that afternoon and that was
29   the whole conversation we had.
30
31   Q: What was your understanding at the end of the
32   conversation?
33
34   A: I felt pretty positive. He seemed interested
35   in me as a renter. I had said I was a grad student and
36   he seemed to like that. And I felt pretty good we had
37   arranged a time for right after- the first day the ad
38   was up.
39
40   Q: So did you understand at that time that you
41   still needed to take additional steps to complete the
42   application for the apartment?
43
44   A: Yes.

5

```
 1       Q: And did you understand that you could be one of
 2  many applicants for the apartment?
 3
 4       A: Right.  No I've looked for apartments before so
 5  I knew I might not be the only one, but that's why I
 6  wanted to get there as soon as possible.
 7
 8       Q: So you understand that you might be rejected?
 9
10       A: Yeah.
11
12       Q: So what is the next thing that you did?
13
14       A: So later that afternoon, this was August
15  fifteenth, Sally and I went to see the apartment, we
16  went over there.
17
18       Q: And who did you meet with?
19
20       A: Mr. Walters I think; the person I had talked to
21  earlier- he answered the door at the apartment to show
22  us around.
23
24       Q: In chronological order, can you describe the
25  meeting you had with Mr. Walters?
26
27       A: Well, so I rang the doorbell and he answered.
28  At first he said "hello" and seemed very friendly and
29  then he saw Sally, who was standing next to me, and his
30  whole, his whole demeanor changed.  Everything about
31  his attitude changed.
32
33       Q: How so?
34
35       A: Well he went from being friendly, and kind of
36  interested in showing me around, to being kind of,
37  almost, rude and very cold and he asked "who is this?"
38  when I explained that it was my daughter.  And then he
39  did show us around after, but he really seemed like he
40  just wanted it to end and get me out of there.
41
42       Q: Ok.  Can you- because you said he asked you
43  that he asked you some questions- can you relay the
44  conversation you had when you toured the apartment?
```

1   A: Well first he asked- you know I wanted him to
2   see how well-behaved Sally was and she was just
3   standing quietly next to me and I said "can you say
4   hello to Mr. Walters?" and she said "hi Mr. Walters,"
5   but she was I think a little nervous about meeting
6   someone new so she was you know, kind of clinging to me
7   and a little quiet. And he was just like "who is
8   this?" and I said "my daughter" and he asked "how old
9   is she?" and I said "she's five." And he just started
10   asking a lot more questions, also about how old I was-
11   and I don't normally like to tell my age but he seemed
12   very insistent. So I said that I'm twenty-three and he
13   also didn't seem- he seemed like he didn't like that-
14   that I had a five year old daughter when I was only
15   twenty-three.
16
17   Q: Did he say that he didn't approve of Sally?
18
19   A: No, he didn't say that, but it was just the way
20   that he was- his tone was kind of dismissive, and he
21   just seemed to be giving me a look like "what are you
22   doing here with this five year old daughter when you're
23   so young."
24
25   Q: Did he say anything else or anything that might
26   have suggested that he was unwilling to rent the
27   apartment to you?
28
29   A: Well then we continued- so then we went inside
30   and he showed me around the apartment and it looked
31   great. It was a big one bedroom, carpeted so if Sally
32   was running around I wouldn't worry about her getting
33   hurt. There was space for her to be in the bedroom and
34   for me to be in the living room working. So I saw all
35   of that and I was excited. But then Mr. Donner- excuse
36   me, Mr. Walters started asking me even more questions.
37
38   Q: Like what?
39
40   A: Very invasive, personal questions that made me
41   uncomfortable. Like did I even know who Sally's father
42   was?
43
44   Q: Who is Sally's father?

```
 1        A: He- he was another student-
 2
 3        MR. MADISON: Objection.  I'm objecting to this
 4   question on the grounds that it's not relevant to any
 5   party's claim or defense.
 6
 7        MS. JOHNSON: Are you instructing your client not
 8   to answer?
 9
10        MR. MADISON: Yeah I'm instructing her not to
11   answer.
12
13        MS. JOHNSON: Ms. Patt, will you answer the
14   question?
15
16        MR. MADISON: I just instructed her not to do that.
17
18        MS. JOHNSON: I'm asking her if she will answer the
19   question.
20
21        MS. PATT: My attorney just told me not to answer.
22
23        MS. JOHNSON: Okay, but do you understand that you
24   can be called back to answer the question after the
25   judge throws out your attorney's objection?
26
27        MS. PATT: Yes.
28
29        MR. PELLEGRINO: Let's go off the record here.
30
31        COURT REPORTER: You're off the record.
32
33   (Thereupon discussion occurred off the record.)
34
35        MR. PELLEGRINO: For the record, we've had a
36   discussion off the record and we've agreed that Ms.
37   Johnson will continue with this deposition. She will be
38   moving to compel answers to the prior question, which
39   we've instructed our client, the witness, not to answer
40   and we will make a cross motion for a protective order.
41
42        Q (By MS. JOHNSON): What else did Mr. Walters ask
43   you?
44
```

1   A: Well then he was asking about other people in
2 my life, like if anyone else was going to live in the
3 apartment- it would have just been me and Sally- and
4 if- how many sexual partners I had had.
5
6   Q: How many sexual partners have you had?
7
8   MR. MADISON: Objection. Ms. Patt's sexual
9 partners are not relevant to any claim or defense in
10 this case.
11
12   MS. JOHNSON: Ok. Let's go off the record.
13
14   MR. PELLEGRINO: I'd like to stay on the record for
15 another minute counsel. I'd like your explanation for
16 why you're pursuing this line of questions.
17
18   MS. JOHNSON: Well I think Ms. Patt's sexual
19 partners are relevant in this case because we want to
20 know if there would be anyone else living with her,
21 what kind of lifestyle she's had, whether Mr. Walters
22 worries about her being an irresponsible is relevant.
23 That's why we would like to ask the question.
24
25   MR. PELLEGRINO: Well we'd seek the same
26 stipulation, that the witness will decline to answer
27 the question under instructions that you can seek an
28 order to compel and we will seek a protective order.
29
30   MS. JOHNSON: Ok.
31
32   Q: What else did you do when you visited the
33 apartment?
34
35   A: Well after we looked around I asked Mr. Walters
36 what I needed to do in order to finish the application,
37 because when I had first come, he had sent me the link
38 to like a standard online application and I had printed
39 that out at home, filled it out, and made a copy to
40 keep for myself and one for Mr. Walters- to give to Mr.
41 Walters. So I had already done that.
42
43   Q: Ok, great. I ask the reporter to mark this as
44 Exhibit 1. Ms. Patt, do you recognize Exhibit 1?

1   A: Yes, this is the application that I filled out
2 and brought with me to the apartment on the fifteenth.
3
4   Q: Ok. And did you fill out any other paperwork?
5
6   A: So this was the only paperwork I filled out,
7 but then Mr. Walters said at the end of our meeting
8 that I needed to give him a $35 check for a credit
9 check and that was the second part of the –
10
11   Q: Was it a credit check or a background check?
12
13   A: Um, he said a credit check.
14
15   Q: Ok. Are you absolutely sure it was for a
16 credit check?
17
18   A: That's what Mr. Walters said when he asked for
19 the money.
20
21   Q: I ask the reporter to mark this as Exhibit 2.
22 Ms. Patt, do you recognize Exhibit 2?
23
24   A: Uh, yes. That's what I- that's the check that
25 I gave Mr. Walters.
26
27   Q: And you understand that this check was
28 necessary to rent the apartment?
29
30   A: Yes, that it was the application and the check.
31
32   Q: So what did you do then, after you handed him
33 the application and the check?
34
35   A: Well that was pretty much the end of the visit
36 that day. And you know, I wasn't- I wasn't really sure
37 what my chances were with Mr. Walters- he seemed like
38 he wasn't really interested in me anymore, but I wanted
39 to give it every chance I had. So I gave him the
40 paperwork and the check, I told him that I was still
41 interested and that I looked forward to hearing from
42 him. And then Sally and I left.
43
44   Q: In the past, have you ever visited other

[pages 10-26 omitted]

1   and that's really the only time I lived in a building
2   with an on-site property manager who wasn't the owner.
3
4   Q: Now I want to go back and ask you about some of
5   the expressions on Mr. Walters' face, that you took to
6   be so important as to tell us what was inside his mind
7   when he saw you and Sally. So, can you- you said that
8   he kind of looked unhappy or that he had a disapproving
9   look?
10
11   A: Yes. Like at first when I walked in and he saw
12   it was me, he seemed friendly. Then when he saw Sally,
13   he kind of grimaced almost.
14
15   Q: And you didn't think it could be because of
16   back pain?
17
18   A: No, I don't think so.
19
20   Q: Have you ever seen anyone with back pain?
21
22   A: Yeah.
23
24   Q: Did he- did Mr. Walters have the same look as
25   people with back pain do?
26
27   A: It was a pained expression I guess.
28
29   Q: So did you ever ask him if he had back pain?
30
31   A: No.
32
33   Q: Even though it could have cleared things up?
34
35   MR. MADISON: Objection, it's unintelligible.
36
37   MS. JOHNSON: Did you understand the question?
38
39   MS. PATT: Um, no?
40
41   MS. JOHNSON: Did you understand the question that
42   did you ask him- you didn't ask him about the back pain
43   even though it could have cleared things up?
44

1   MS. PATT: Um, can you repeat the question that you
2   want me to-
3
4   MS. JOHNSON: Court reporter, can you re-read the
5   last question?
6
7   COURT REPORTER: Did you understand the question?
8
9   MS. JOHNSON: The question before that.
10
11   COURT REPORTER: Even though you could have cleared
12   things up?
13
14   MS. PATT: Now I'm not sure.
15
16   Q (by MS. JOHNSON): Ok, so you didn't ask Mr.
17   Walters whether he was giving you the look because he
18   had a back pain?
19
20   A: No, I didn't ask. He had that expression only
21   as soon as he saw Sally.
22
23   Q: But you didn't ask because, were you worried
24   that he might lie about it?
25
26   A: No, I didn't know, I didn't think to ask if he
27   had back pain. I just saw that he didn't- that he was
28   making a face when he saw my daughter.
29
30   Q: Okay. What I'm getting at here, Ms. Patt, is
31   did you consider other possible reasons for this facial
32   expression that you claim Mr. Walters made?
33
34   A: It seemed clear to me that he was reacting to
35   seeing my daughter.
36
37   Q: Do people frequently have pained facial   Damn
38   expressions when they see your daughter?
39
40   A: Excuse me?
41
42   Q: I'm sorry - How can you be sure that he was
43   reacting to seeing your daughter, as opposed to, say,
44   pain he felt from the physical motion of looking down

[pages 29-54 omitted]

1   said that he needed it for a credit check.
2
3   Q: Did you do anything else with the check?
4
5   A: Well eventually I ended up canceling the check.
6
7   Q: Why?
8
9   A: Because it seemed like Mr. Walters wasn't
10   interested in renting to me.
11
12   Q: But you knew you wouldn't be able to get the
13   apartment once you canceled the check?
14
15   A: Well, he hadn't really said that, he just
16   hadn't gotten- I hadn't heard from him at all so I
17   didn't know what was going on.
18
19   Q: So you believed you still had the possibility
20   of renting the apartment even though you canceled the
21   $35 check?
22
23   A: Well I thought I had a possibility until I
24   called him- Mr. Walters- a week later to find out what
25   had happened with the apartment.
26
27   Q: Right. So you still believed you had a chance
28   of renting it without Mr. Walters processing your
29   check, which was part of the application packet?
30
31   A: I guess?
32
33   Q: I don't want you to guess Ms. Patt, please say
34   yes or no.
35
36   A: I think I- I thought I still had a chance until
37   I called Mr. Walters a week later.
38
39   Q: In your experience, if you purchase an item and
40   end up returning it for a refund, do you get to keep
41   the product?
42
43   A: No.
44

56

1   Q: Did you have to apply to UC Berkeley for grad
2 school?
3
4   A: Yes, of course.
5
6   Q: Did you have to pay an application fee with
7 that process?
8
9   A: Yeah.
10
11   Q: So if you had withdrawn the application fee, do
12 you think you still would have had a chance of applying
13 to UC Berkeley?
14
15   A: I guess I never really thought about that.
16
17   Q: Ok. I have no further questions.
18
19   MR. PELLEGRINO: Very good. And we have no
20 questions.
21
22   (Thereupon the foregoing proceedings concluded at
23 11:43 a.m.)
24
25
26
27
28
29
30
31
32
33
34
35
36
37
38
39
40
41
42
43
44

CHAPTER 7 MATERIALS

WILL WALTERS DEPOSITION TRANSCRIPT

A video of Will Walters' deposition can be found at
http://www.kaltura.com/tiny/52b5g

Subject:	Will Walters Depo
From:	Jane Johnson <jane.johnson@johnsonshermen.com>
To:	Sheila Shermen <sheila.shermen@johnsonshermen.com>
Date:	October 21 7:17 PM

Sheila,

Here are the relevant excerpts of the Walters deposition today.

The fact that he may have already rented the apartment to the other candidate when he learned Paula's check was canceled is far from proof of discrimination, but it certainly doesn't help us. Same for the nature of his "background checks," his questions about her sexual history (he answered that one about as well as he could under the circumstances), and his personal views on single motherhood.

Matt, the law student, deposed him and did a reasonably good job, although he got off on a long tangent in the middle about prior work history and irrelevant details of the day of the apartment viewing, which I haven't included here. Happy to send the full version if you'd like it.

Best,

Jane

Jane Johnson
Johnson & Shermen LLP | www.johnsonshermen.com
jane.johnson@johnsonshermen.com | (510) 555-3500

This message may contain privileged attorney-client communications. If you are not the intended recipient, please delete this message immediately and notify the sender.

IN THE UNITES STATES DISTRICT COURT
FOR THE NORTHERN DISTRICT OF CALIFORNIA

CASE NO. CV 1357 DBO

PAULA PATT,
    Plaintiff,

vs.

DAN DONNER,
    Defendant.

VIDEOTAPED DEPOSITION OF WILL WALTERS

October 21
2013 Center Street, Suite 310
Berkeley, California

REPORTED BY:
Caren Rafael, CSR
Rafael Reporting Company
123 Grand Avenue
Oakland, California 94612
Tel.: 510-133-6745

APPEARANCES:

On behalf of the Plaintiff:
    SAM PELLEGRINO, ESQ.
    MATT MADISON, CERTIFIED LAW STUDENT
    Berkeley Legal Clinic
    2013 Center Street, Suite 310
    Berkeley, California 94704

On behalf of the Defendant:
    JANE JOHNSON, ESQ.
    Johnson & Shermen LLP
    10000 Shattuck Avenue, Suite 3500
    Berkeley, California 94704

VIDEOGRAPHER: Lesleigh Viars, Viars Legal Video

```
 1        REPORTER: Good afternoon. My name is Caren Rafael,
 2   certified California court reporter. This is a video
 3   recorded deposition pursuant to the Federal Rules of
 4   Civil Procedure of Will Walters by counsel for the
 5   plaintiff. May I please have appearances of counsel?
 6
 7        MR. MADISON: Matt Madison, certified law student,
 8   representing the plaintiff, and my counsel Sam
 9   Pellegrino.
10
11        MR. PELLEGRINO: Sam Pellegrino for the plaintiff.
12
13        MS. JOHNSON: Jane Johnson for the defendant.
14
15                        WILL WALTERS
16   the witness herein, having been duly sworn, did testify
17   as follows:
18
19                     DIRECT EXAMINATION
20   by MR. MADISON:
21
22        Q: Will you please state your name for the record?
23
24        A: Will Walters.
25
26        Q: Do you understand that you are under oath
27   today?
28
29        A: Yeah.
30
31        Q: Do you understand that you are obligated
32   therefore to tell the truth?
33
34        A: Yes.
35
36        Q: And you understand that the statements you make
37   today can be used in trial?
38
39        A: Yes.
40
41        Q: Ok. Are you under any substances that may
42   affect your ability to be in this deposition?
43
44        A: No.
```

```
1
2          Q: Is there any other reason why we shouldn't
3     proceed with this deposition today?
4
5          A: No.
6
7          Q: Ok. Can you tell me where you live?
8
9          A: Yeah, I live at 1357 Telegraph in Berkeley.
10
11         Q: Have you lived in Berkeley a long time, and you
12    live here now, right?
13
14         MS. JOHNSON: Objection. Compound.
15
16         MR. MADISON: I'm sorry. Withdraw that question.
17    Have you lived in Berkeley a long time?
18
19         A: I've lived in Berkeley probably six years now.
20    I went to undergrad here and now I'm at the business
21    school.
22
23         Q: And, also, what else do you do here in
24    Berkeley? Do you have a job here?
25
26         A: I'm an apartment manager. Yeah.
27
28         Q: And in that apartment managing position, what
29    do you do?
30
31         A: Mostly I just collect the rent checks each
32    month. I also process-- fill in vacancies when they
33    arise. I let people look at the apartments and choose
34    who to rent to. Sometimes small repairs - I'll change a
35    light bulb or something.
36
37         Q: Is this your first time working as a property
38    manager?
39
40         A: Yes.
41
42         Q: And have you ever had a job where you hired or
43    fired people before?
44
```

```
 1        A: No.
 2
 3        Q: And have you ever been sued for discrimination
 4   before?
 5
 6        A: No.
 7
 8        Q: Ok. I'm sorry. And just to be clear, what is
 9   your actual - what is your actual job title at the
10   place that you work?
11
12        A: Property manager.
13
14        Q: And it's at 1357 Telegraph?
15
16        A: That's correct.
17
18        Q: Ok. And you work for Dan Donner, correct?
19
20        A: That's right.
21
22        Q: Ok.  Tell me a little bit about this building.
23   So are there any other families with children in this
24   building?
25
26        A: There aren't any families with children, no.
27
28        Q: Are there any couples in the building?
29
30        A: We have two couples, yes.
31
32        Q: Are they married or unmarried?
33
34        A: One's married.
35
36        Q: Are there any specific policies for the
37   building about couples or about children?
38
39        A: No, there's no policies like that.
40
41        Q: And did you have any training in anti-
42   discrimination law before you started your job as the
43   property manager?
44
```

1   A: Well pretty soon after I started Dan sent me a
2 packet that I think he got from his insurance company.
3 I glanced at it. It might have had something about
4 discrimination. I'm not sure.
5
6   Q: Do you know who Paula Patt is?
7
8   A: She applied to rent an apartment.
9
10   Q: How did you first get in contact with Paula
11 Patt?
12
13   A: She sent me an email in response to an ad I
14 posted.
15
16   Q: And what did she say in the email?
17
18   A: She said that she was interested in the
19 apartment and we talked on the phone after that.
20
21   Q: When she contacted you how did you respond?
22 What did you send back to her?
23
24   A: Well I, uh, I'm not sure I responded to her
25 email, I think that I might have called her after that
26 and we talked on the phone and then I set up a time for
27 her to come visit the apartment. I also sent her a link
28 to the application form.
29
30   Q: What was the content of that phone
31 conversation?
32
33   A: Just the time to come meet, that she would need
34 to fill out an application.
35
36   Q: What time did you guys schedule to meet at the
37 apartment?
38
39   A: I think we said two o'clock.
40
41   Q: And that was the same day that she contacted
42 you?
43
44   A: That was the same day, yes.

```
 1
 2        Q: Ok. So when she arrived were you the one to
 3   show her the apartment?
 4
 5        A: Yes.
 6
 7        Q: When she first arrived was she alone?
 8
 9        A: No. She brought her daughter with her and she
10   hadn't mentioned to me on the phone or in the email
11   that she had a daughter.
12
13        Q: What was your response? How did you feel when
14   you saw that she had her daughter there?
15
16        A: Well I was a little bit surprised just because
17   I didn't realize that she had a daughter. She's also
18   pretty young, and the daughter was - I don't know, I
19   think she was maybe five years old. So she must have
20   had her when she was young and that sort of surprised
21   me because I didn't get the impression that she had a
22   kid when we talked on the phone.
23
24        Q: Did you have a positive impression of her when
25   you talked on the phone?
26
27        A: Of Paula?
28
29        Q: Yes.
30
31        A: I didn't really have an impression one way or
32   the other.
33
34        Q: When the - when Ms. Patt showed up with her
35   daughter, what did they say to you?
36
37        A: Just that they were here to see the apartment.
38
39        Q: And so did you show them the apartment?
40
41        A: Yeah.
42
43        Q: Ok. And did they ask any questions while they
44   were seeing the apartment?
```

PAGE 6

1
2   A: I think that she - well, I don't think the
3 daughter asked any questions, but Paula, she asked some
4 questions about rent, and you know, utilities, things
5 like that. Nothing out of the ordinary.
6
7   Q: Did the daughter say anything to you at all?
8
9   A: I think she, at her mother's urging she said hi
10 to me. And then after that, she was making a lot of
11 noise, I wouldn't say she really said anything to me
12 though.
13
14   Q: What was she doing to make noise?
15
16   A: She was just whining. She was kinda running
17 around. Um, just a noisy kid.
18
19   Q: Did you ask any questions of Ms. Patt?
20
21   A: Sure, we made conversation, yeah.
22
23   Q: Can you tell us about the content of those
24 conversations?
25
26   A: I asked her where she was from. I asked her
27 about her family I think. What she was doing in
28 Berkeley.
29
30   Q: And did she answer all of your question?
31
32   A: She... I don't remember.
33
34   Q: What happened next after you guys got done
35 looking at the apartment?
36
37   A: It took a while because she kinda had to keep
38 the kid under control. But after we were done, I said
39 that we would be in touch and she gave me the
40 application and check.
41
42   Q: What did she give you a check for?
43
44   A: That was for a background check.

PAGE 7

1
2   Q: So it was for a background check not a credit
3   check?
4
5   A: That's right, a background check.
6
7   Q: And what was the purpose of the background
8   check?
9
10   A: Well I do that for each apartment - any
11   applicants for apartments. I just want to make sure
12   we're getting responsible people in the building.
13
14   Q: And how do you conduct the background check? Do
15   you send the information out to someone else to figure
16   things out?
17
18   A: No, I do it myself.
19
20   Q: What is the content of the background checks
21   that you perform?
22
23   A: It's internet research. It's public records,
24   that sort of thing.
25
26   Q: Can you be more specific about how you research
27   the public records?
28
29   A: Well I usually start with a google search and,
30   uh, maybe facebook and if I find something that seems
31   out of the ordinary I might follow up from there.
32
33   Q: The thirty five dollar check, who was it to?
34
35   A: That's made out to me.
36
37   Q: Did you use that, or did you pass that money on
38   to Mr. Donner?
39
40   A: No, no. This is for my time doing the
41   background check.
42
43   Q: So after Paula left was there anybody else who
44   saw the apartment?

```
1
2        A: Yeah, there was another woman, a barista.
3
4        Q: How did the meeting with her go?
5
6        A: It went great. She seemed really responsible.
7   She seemed like she'd be a good tenant, and it went
8   well.
9
10       Q: Did she bring an application and pay the fee
11  for the background check?
12
13       A: Yes, she did.
14
15       Q: Did you conduct a background check on the
16  second tenant?
17
18       A: Yes.
19
20       Q: Did you conduct a background check on Ms. Patt?
21
22       A: Yes.
23
24       Q: After the barista came to the - or came to
25  visit the apartment, did you ever contact Ms. Patt
26  again about the apartment?
27
28       A: No, Ms. Patt contacted me.
29
30       Q: What was the content of your conversation with
31  Ms. Patt?
32
33       A: She -  it was later on, and she asked if the
34  apartment, what was going on with her application, and
35  I told her the apartment was rented to someone else.
36
37       Q: When you say later on, how much time passed
38  before she contacted you?
39
40       A: It was about a week.
41
42       Q: When you conducted the background check of Ms.
43  Patt, did you find anything negative?
44
```

inconsistent

```
1      A: No, not that I recall. I don't recall finding
2  very much at all.
3
4      Q: And when you did rent the apartment, did you
5  end up renting it to the other person who was in that
6  day?
7
8      A: Yes.
9
10     Q: The barista.
11
12     A: Yes that's right.
13
14     Q: Ok. Did you cash the check for Ms. Patt's
15  background check?
16
17     A: I tried to.
18
19     Q: What happened when you tried to?
20
21     A: The check - she had canceled, she had stopped
22  payment on the check.
23
24     Q: What day did you - when in the week did you try
25  to cash the check?
26
27     A: I think it was two days after she visited, so
28  it would have been the seventeenth maybe.
29
30     Q: And what day did you decide to rent the
31  apartment to the barista?
32
33     A: Um, I'm not sure. I guess I... I guess I got
34  back to her the sixteenth.
35
36     Q: When you're renting the apartments to tenants
37  do you have a policy of collecting multiple
38  applications from people or is it a policy of accepting
39  the first application that you receive?
40
41     A: Well I take the first well qualified
42  application usually. I don't have a strict policy
43  though.
44
```

weird

[pages 10-50 omitted]

1   think I came straight from class, but I don't really
2   remember.
3
4   Q: When you showed her the apartment, did you ask
5   Ms. Patt questions about her personal relationships?
6
7   A: Yes, I guess so.
8
9   Q: I don't want you to guess. Do you remember
10   asking questions about her personal relationships?
11
12   A: Yes.
13
14   Q: Why did you ask these questions?
15
16   A: I wanted to know if anyone else would be living
17   in the apartment. It's big enough for one person, maybe
18   two, but no more than that. There's a two person limit
19   in the lease.
20
21   Q: Mr. Walters, did you ever ask Ms. Patt about
22   the number of sexual partners that she'd had?
23
24   A: You know, I did, and I don't know why I asked
25   her that. And I apologized immediately. It was
26   inappropriate of me to ask.
27
28   Q: Did you ask her about, if she knew the father
29   of her child?
30
31   A: Yeah, I did. She said yes she did. I guess
32   that's what got into the sexual history thing but...
33
34   Q: Do you approve of Ms. Patt being a single
35   mother?
36
37   A: Personally? No, I don't think that's a great
38   way to raise a child, but that wasn't why I didn't rent
39   to her.
40
41   Q: Do you ever let your personal feelings affect
42   your decision about who you rent the apartments to?
43
44   A: I'm not sure how to answer that.

PAGE 52

```
 1
 2      Q: With regards to the policies for the building,
 3  do have a preference for any particular types of people
 4  in the apartments?
 5
 6      A: Well, I don't have a policy on this but I do
 7  like to rent to other grad students. I'm a grad student
 8  and they tend to be responsible and quiet.
 9
10      Q: Did you tell Ms. Patt that you had a preference
11  for graduate students?
12
13      A: I don't think so.
14
15      Q: You mentioned earlier that there's a policy of
16  your accepting the first qualified applicant. Did you
17  tell her about the policy of accepting the first
18  qualified applicant?
19
20      A: No, I don't think that I did.
21
22      Q: With regards to the background checks, did you
23  ever discuss with Mr. Donner that you were performing
24  background checks?
25
26      A: No.
27
28      Q: Did you ever discuss the possibility of doing
29  background checks in general with Mr. Donner?
30
31      A: No, he just asked me to make sure to bring in
32  good tenants and so I felt that this was the best way
33  to do that.
34
35      Q: Mr. Walters, do you experience any back pain on
36  a regular basis?
37
38      A: I do, yeah, I had a frisbee injury a few years
39  back.
40
41      MR. MADISON: Do you have any further questions?
42
43      MR. PELLEGRINO: No, I think you did a great job.
44
```

```
1       MR. MADISON: All right, we have no further
2  questions.
3
4       (Thereupon the foregoing proceedings concluded at
5  2:19 p.m.)
6
7
8
9
10
11
12
13
14
15
16
17
18
19
20
21
22
23
24
25
26
27
28
29
30
31
32
33
34
35
36
37
38
39
40
41
42
43
44
```

CHAPTER 7 SKILLS EXERCISE

MOTION TO COMPEL/MOTION FOR PROTECTIVE ORDER

These exercises require you to complete a motion to compel discovery and a motion for a protective order. Portions of the briefs in support of the motions (also referred to as the "Memorandum of Points and Authorities") have been drafted for you. In Exercise (a) you must complete Section B, specifically where it reads, *"Apply Fed. R. Civ. P. 26(b)(1) to the Defendant's Motion to Compel."* In Exercise (b), you must complete Section B, specifically where it reads, *"Apply the analysis from Vinson to the Plaintiff's privacy-based claim for a protective order."*

As you have learned in your Civil Procedure course, the Federal Rules of Civil Procedure permit a party to discover any non-privileged information that is relevant to any party's claim or defense and proportional to the needs of the case. Fed. R. Civ. P. 26(b)(1). The Federal Rules of Civil Procedure do not explicitly refer to a party's privacy, although they do allow a party to seek a protective order to avert "annoyance, embarrassment, oppression, or undue burden or expense." Fed. R. Civ. P. 26(c)(1).

In the critical portion of Exercise (a) that has been left for you to draft, you will complete section B, arguing that Paula Patt's personal history is relevant to the Defendant's theory of the case, specifically the defense that Will Walters declined to rent the apartment to Ms. Patt because she is unreliable and irresponsible. To do so, you will apply the facts and allegations set forth in the record thus far to argue that this information is relevant to a defense and proportional to the needs of the case under Fed. R. Civ. P. 26(b)(1).

In the critical portion of Exercise (b) that has been left for you to draft, you will complete the section of the motion regarding Paula Patt's right to privacy. To do so, you will apply the court's analysis in *Vinson v. Superior Court* to the facts of Paula Patt's claim. Your goal is to use the facts and allegations set forth in the case record thus far to convince the judge that Paula Patt's right to privacy and interest in avoiding "annoyance, embarrassment, oppression, or undue burden or expense" outweighs the Defendant's right to broad discovery. *See* Fed. R. Civ. P. 26(c)(1). Exercises (a) and (b) should be completed after you have studied the topic of discovery in your Civil Procedure course.

Some tips for drafting the briefs:

- Before starting, read the portions of the motion that have already been drafted. Avoid unnecessary repetition of points made earlier in the motion.

- Avoid unsupported conclusory statements. You must explain *why* the facts you use support the argument you make.

- Do not simply ignore facts that may seem more unfavorable to your party; instead, try to frame those facts in a way that supports your argument, or explain why they are not sufficient to outweigh the facts that favor your party.

- Do not introduce any facts that are not included in the declarations attached to the motion or otherwise set forth in the case record thus far.

- There is no need to add additional case law in the section you are completing. Instead, focus on the facts, with citations to the record. Most discovery motions turn on the specifics of the case at hand rather than disputed issues of law.

1   JANE JOHNSON (State Bar No. 31415927)
      Jane.Johnson@johnsonshermen.com
2   JOHNSON & SHERMEN, LLP
      10000 Shattuck Ave., Suite 3500
3   Berkeley, California 94704
      Telephone: (510) 555-3500
4   Facsimile: (510) 555-3501

5   Attorney for Defendant

6   IN THE UNITED STATES DISTRICT COURT
             FOR THE NORTHERN DISTRICT OF CALIFORNIA

7   PAULA PATT,   No. C 1357 DBO

8   Plaintiff,   **DEFENDANT DAN DONNER'S NOTICE**
        v.   **OF MOTION AND MOTION TO COMPEL**
9   DAN DONNER,   **DISCOVERY**

10   Defendant.   **MEMORANDUM OF POINTS AND**
                            /   **AUTHORITIES**
11

12   Date: November 1
                                 Time: 12:00 p.m.
13   Judge: Hon. Dianne B. Osaka

14   TO PLAINTIFF AND HER ATTORNEY OF RECORD:

15   NOTICE IS HEREBY GIVEN that on November 1, at time 12:00 p.m., or as soon thereafter as

16   the matter may be heard in Courtroom 3 of the above-entitled Court, located at 1301 Clay Street,

17   Oakland, California, Defendant Dan Donner will and hereby does move the Court, pursuant to Rule

18   37(a)(3)(B)(i) of the Federal Rules of Civil Procedure, to compel Plaintiff Paula Patt to respond to a

19   question posed at her deposition on October 16, by Defendant. This Motion is brought on the ground

20   that Plaintiff did not respond to a question that was properly posed during a deposition on behalf of

21   Defendant.

22   This Motion is based on this Notice of Motion and Motion and supporting Memorandum of

23   Points and Authorities, and on such further written and oral argument as may be presented at or

24   before the time the Court takes this Motion under submission.

TABLE OF CONTENTS

TABLE OF AUTHORITIES

Cases

Vinson v. Superior Court, 43 Cal. 3d 833 (1987)

Statutes, Rules, and Other Sources

42 U.S.C. § 2000e–5(g)(2)(B)

Rule 26 of the Federal Rules of Civil Procedure

Rule 30 of the Federal Rules of Civil Procedure

Rule 37 of the Federal Rules of Civil Procedure

1 | Fed. R. Evid. 412

2 | Cal. Civ. Proc. Code § 2036.1

3

4

5

6

7

8

9

10

11

12

13

14

15

16

17

18

19

20

21

22

23

24

DEFENDANT DAN DONNER'S NOTICE OF MOTION AND MOTION TO COMPEL DISCOVERY

3

1

MEMORANDUM OF POINTS AND AUTHORITIES

2

I.   INTRODUCTION

3   The case concerns allegations of housing discrimination by the Plaintiff, Paula Patt. *See*

4 *generally* 1st Am. Compl. Specifically, Ms. Patt claims that Will Walters, Defendant Donner's

5 property manager, declined to rent an apartment to her because she has a minor child and is not

6 married, that in doing so he violated state and federal law, and that Mr. Donner is responsible for

7 Mr. Walters' alleged conduct because he is the building's owner and Mr. Walters' employer. *See id.*

8 During a deposition by Mr. Donner's attorney, Ms. Patt refused to answer a question concerning the

9 identity of the father of her child. Patt Dep. at 6:44–7:21. Mr. Donner brings this motion to compel

10 discovery because the Federal Rules of Civil Procedure permit broad discovery as to any information

11 "relevant to any party's claim or defense and proportional to the needs of the case. *See* Fed. R. Civ.

12 P. 26(b)(1). The identity of the father of Ms. Patt's child falls within this scope, and Ms. Patt should

13 provide an answer to the pending question.

14

II.   STATEMENT OF FACTS

15   On or about August 21 of this year, Will Walters showed Plaintiff Paula Patt an apartment that

16 was then available in the building he manages for Defendant, located at 1357 Telegraph Avenue.

17 Patt Dep. at 5:14–22; Walters Dep. at 5:2–5. Ms. Patt submitted an application to rent the

18 apartment and a check to cover the cost of a background check. Patt Dep. at 9:1–40; Walters Dep.

19 at 6:37–44. Without alerting Mr. Walters, Ms. Patt then stopped payment on the check. Patt Dep.

20 at 55:5; Walters Dep. at 9:14–22. Ms. Patt's rental application was declined because she failed to

21 demonstrate that she would be a suitable tenant. Walters Dep. at 21:17–19. On or about October

22 16, Ms. Patt was deposed. *See generally* Patt Dep. Ms. Patt, on the advice of her lawyers and in

23 response to their objection, refused to provide a complete answer to a question asking for the identity

24

1   of her daughter's father.[1] *Id.* at 6:44–7:21. Ms. Patt's attorneys argued that the answers to these

2   questions were not relevant. *Id.* at 7:3–5. Ms. Patt did not at that time or at any later date answer

3   these questions. Mr. Donner files this motion to compel Ms. Patt to produce this information or to

4   confirm that it is not within her knowledge.

III. ARGUMENT

6   **A. This Court Should Grant Defendant Dan Donner's Motion to Compel Because This**

7   **Case Does Not Fall into the Narrow Exceptions to the Broad Scope of Discovery**

8   **Under the Federal Rules of Civil Procedure.**

9   A party is permitted to discover any non-privileged information that is relevant to any party's

10   claim or defense and proportional to the needs of the case. Fed. R. Civ. P. 26(b)(1). The Federal Rules

11   of Civil Procedure do not explicitly refer to a party's privacy, although they do allow a party to seek

12   a protective order to avert "annoyance, embarrassment, oppression, or undue burden or expense."

13   Fed. R. Civ. P. 26(c)(1). The rare cases permitting any exceptions to the broad scope of discovery

14   make clear that such exceptions are narrow. Where a plaintiff is allowed to make "very serious

15   allegations," a defendant should have the opportunity to put the truth of those allegations to the

16   test. *Vinson v. Superior Court*, 43 Cal. 3d 833, 842 (1987) (discussing an analogous provision under

17   California discovery law).

18   In *Vinson v. Superior Court,* a case that is not binding on this Court but may serve as a source

19   of persuasive authority, the California Supreme Court held that a plaintiff in a sexual harassment

20   case had to undergo a mental examination pursuant to the California Code of Civil Procedure

21   § 2032, although the court limited the scope of the examination. 43 Cal. 3d 833. The plaintiff had

22   alleged that she was transferred and then fired from her job because she had turned down the

23

DEFENDANT DAN DONNER'S NOTICE OF MOTION AND MOTION TO COMPEL DISCOVERY

5

24

---

[1]   Ms. Patt also failed to answer a question regarding other previous sexual partners. Patt Dep. at 8:6-28. After subsequently conferring with Plaintiff's counsel, Mr. Donner does not seek to compel an answer to this question at this time.

1   defendant's sexual advances during her initial interview. *Id.* at 837. Since her complaint alleged

2   that this harassment had caused her severe emotional distress, the defendant moved for an order

3   compelling her to undergo a mental examination. *Id.* at 838. The plaintiff argued that this would

4   violate her privacy, and the defendant countered that the information was necessary to evaluate the

5   existence or extent of any mental harm she had suffered. *Id.*

6   The California Supreme Court characterized its inquiry as balancing the "right of civil litigants

7   to discover relevant facts against the privacy interests of person subject to discovery." *Id.* at 842. It

8   stated that the plaintiff's mental condition was "directly relevant" to her claim and "essential to a

9   fair resolution of her suit" and that she had "waived her right to privacy in this respect" by making

10   her mental condition an element of her claim. *Id.* It thus granted the defendant's motion to compel

11   with respect to the mental examination. *Id.* at 841.

12   The court also stated that the defendant had failed to demonstrate why the plaintiff's sexual

13   history was relevant to the claim, and that given this failure, the plaintiff had not waived her right

14   to refrain from discussing her sexual history. *Id.* at 842. However, the court stated that the plaintiff's

15   rights in this area were "not necessarily absolute" and that in some instances "her privacy interests

16   may have to give way to her opponent's right to a fair trial." *Id.* It then went on to apply a newly

17   enacted section of the California Code of Civil Procedure specifically designed to protect plaintiffs

18   bringing sexual harassment or assault claims. *Id.* at 843 (citing then-existing Cal. Civ. Proc. Code

19   § 2036.1). That statute—not applicable to the case at hand in this Court—required that anyone

20   seeking discovery from a plaintiff in such a suit establish specific facts showing good cause for

21   discovering information concerning the plaintiff's conduct with anyone other than the defendant.

22   *Id.* Since the defendant failed to establish those facts, the court held that he had not shown good

23   cause for obtaining this information. *Id.*

24

1   The decision in *Vinson* is too narrow to include Ms. Patt's situation. Since it concerned a claim

2   for sexual harassment—an inherently personal claim and one that has historically invited

3   humiliating discovery requests from defendants—it fell within the special rules and exceptions that

4   courts make regarding such matters. *See, e.g.,* Fed. R. Evid. 412 (rendering inadmissible evidence

5   of a victim's prior sexual conduct "in a civil or criminal proceeding *involving alleged sexual*

6   *misconduct*" (emphasis added)). In addition, the defendant in *Vinson* failed to clearly demonstrate

7   that his questions about the plaintiff's sexual history were relevant to his defense. *See* 433 Cal. 3d

8   at 842. Here, in contrast, the claim is not one for sexual harassment but rather for discrimination,

9   and special rules like Rule 412 and the statute on which the *Vinson* court relied are not applicable.

10   As discussed below, information about Ms. Patt's and the father's intent regarding who would

11   live in the apartment is relevant to Mr. Donner's defense. Mr. Donner would be wholly unable to

12   conduct reasonable discovery into this matter without knowing the father's identity. Because the

13   narrow exceptions to the obligation to disclose relevant information during discovery do not apply

14   here, and based on the importance of assuring Mr. Donner a fair trial, this Court should grant Mr.

15   Donner's Motion to Compel Discovery.

16   **B.   This Court Should Grant Defendant Dan Donner's Motion to Compel Discovery**

17   **Because Plaintiff Patt's Personal History is Relevant to the Defense.**

18   This Court should grant Mr. Donner's Motion to Compel Discovery because Ms. Patt's personal

19   history is relevant to the defense that Mr. Walters declined to rent to her because she is unreliable

20   and irresponsible. *(Apply Fed. R. Civ. P. 26(b)(1) to the Defendant's Motion to Compel.)*

21   The question of whether Ms. Patt would attempt to let her daughter's father live in the

22   apartment with her is also relevant to the issue of damages. As a general principle of discrimination

23   cases, damages may be limited or unavailable if the defendant would have had a legitimate,

24

1 nondiscriminatory reason to take the same action. *Cf.* 42 U.S.C. § 2000e–5(g)(2)(B) (barring

2 damages in employment discrimination cases when the employer would have taken the same action

3 for nondiscriminatory reasons). Here, the lease for the apartment limited occupancy to two people,

4 and Mr. Walters asked Ms. Patt about the father in an effort to learn whether she would be likely

5 to violate that provision by adding another tenant besides herself and her daughter. Walters Dep.

6 at 51:16–19. If it becomes clear through discovery that the father would have moved into the

7 apartment in violation of the lease, damages for any alleged discrimination would be limited because

8 Ms. Patt would inevitably have been evicted. The father's identity is therefore relevant to damages,

9 which falls within the broad scope of "any party's claim or defense." *See* Fed. R. Civ. P. 26(b)(1).

10 **C.   This Court Should Grant Defendant Dan Donner's Motion to Compel Discovery**

11 **Because Plaintiff Patt Failed to Respond to a Proper Deposition Question.**

12 During an oral deposition, testimony is taken subject to any objection. Fed. R. Civ. P. 30(c)(2).

13 A deponent must answer a question, *even if he or she objects to it. Id.*[2] Any objections that arise are

14 noted on the record and the deponent may later object to admission of contested testimony at trial.

15 *Id.*; Fed. R. Civ. P. 30(b). Attorneys may only instruct their clients not to answer under specific,

16 enumerated circumstances not properly applicable here: "when necessary to preserve a privilege, to

17 enforce a limitation ordered by the court, or to present a motion under Rule 30(d)(3)." Fed. R. Civ.

18 P. 30(c)(2). A party may move the court to compel an answer if another party fails to respond to a

19 deposition question. Fed. R. Civ. P. 37(a)(3)(B)(i).

20 Ms. Patt's attorneys based the instruction not to answer on Rule 30(d)(3), which permits the

21 Court to terminate or limit a deposition "that it is being conducted in bad faith or in a manner that

22 unreasonably annoys, embarrasses, or oppresses the deponent or party." Fed R. Civ. P. 30(d)(3).

23 **DEFENDANT DAN DONNER'S NOTICE OF MOTION AND MOTION TO COMPEL DISCOVERY**
   8

24

---

[2] "An objection at the time of the examination—whether to evidence, to a party's conduct, to the officer's qualifications, to the manner of taking the deposition, or to any other aspect of the deposition—must be noted on the record, but the examination still proceeds; the testimony is taken subject to any objection." Fed. R. Civ. P. 30(c)(2).

1   However, the question at issue was neither unreasonable nor posed in bad faith, because as

2   discussed above it sought an answer that is properly within the scope of discovery. *See* Fed. R. Civ.

3   P. 26(b)(1).

4   The court should grant Mr. Donner's Motion to Compel Discovery because Ms. Patt did not fully

5   respond. Her lawyer voiced an objection and then instructed her that she did not have to respond,

6   which was without legal foundation, and blocked the discovery of relevant information.

7   **D. Plaintiff Paula Patt Is Liable for Defendant Dan Donner's Costs and Attorneys' Fees**

8   **Incurred to Bring This Motion.**

9   Rule 37 of the Federal Rules of Civil Procedure states that if a motion to compel is granted, "the

10   court *must* . . . require the party or deponent whose conduct necessitated the motion . . . to pay the

11   movant's reasonable expenses incurred in making the motion, including attorney's fees." Fed. R.

12   Civ. P. 37(a)(5)(A) (emphasis added). The Rule only excuses this remedy when the party bringing

13   the motion failed to confer in good faith, when the opposing party's nondisclosure was substantially

14   justified, or when circumstances would render such an award unjust. *Id.* Here, Mr. Donner's

15   attorneys have conferred with Ms. Patt's attorneys, and have demonstrated good faith by electing

16   not to pursue an answer to a second unanswered deposition question. Ms. Patt's nondisclosure was

17   not substantially justified, because the question properly sought discoverable information and, in

18   the context of deposition, a deponent must answer questions even subject to objection. *See* Fed. R.

19   Civ. P. 30(c)(2). There are no special circumstances rendering an award of fees—which, again, is

20   normally mandatory when a motion to compel is granted—unjust in the present case. Mr. Donner

21   therefore respectfully that the Court award him reasonable costs and fees for bringing this Motion,

22   in an amount to be determined after Ms. Patt provides the requested information.

23

24

1

IV. CONCLUSION

2   Mr. Donner sought discoverable information during a deposition and Ms. Patt failed to respond

3   to a proper question. Mr. Donner respectfully requests that this Court grant this Motion to Compel

4   Discovery, require Ms. Patt to pay Mr. Donner's attorneys' fees for bringing this Motion, and grant

5   any other relief it deems appropriate.

6   Respectfully submitted,

7   _____

8   Jane Johnson
                                                       On behalf of Dan Donner
9   Date: October 22

10

11

12

13

14

15

16

17

18

19

20

21

22

23

24

1	SAM PELLEGRINO (State Bar # 11235813)
	spellegrino@berkeleylegalclinic.org
2	BERKELEY LEGAL CLINIC
	2013 Center Street, Suite 310
3	Berkeley, CA 94704
	Telephone: (510) 555-5151
4	Facsimile: (510) 555-5155

Attorney for Plaintiff

IN THE UNITED STATES DISTRICT COURT

FOR THE NORTHERN DISTRICT OF CALIFORNIA

PAULA PATT,	No. C 1357 DBO
Plaintiff,	**PLAINTIFF PAULA PATT'S NOTICE OF**
v.	**MOTION AND MOTION FOR**
DAN DONNER,	**PROTECTIVE ORDER**
Defendant.	**MEMORANDUM OF POINTS AND**
	AUTHORITIES IN SUPPORT OF
	MOTION FOR PROTECTIVE ORDER
	AND IN OPPOSITION TO MOTION TO
	COMPEL DISCOVERY

Date: November 1

Time: 12:00 p.m.

Judge: Hon. Dianne B. Osaka

TO DEFENDANT AND HIS ATTORNEYS OF RECORD:

NOTICE IS HEREBY GIVEN that on November 1, at time 12:00 p.m., or as soon thereafter as the matter may be heard in Courtroom 3 of the above-entitled Court, located at 1301 Clay Street, Oakland, California, Plaintiff Paula Patt will and hereby does move the Court, pursuant to Rules 26(c)(1) and 30(d)(3) of the Federal Rules of Civil Procedure, to limit the deposition of Plaintiff Paula Patt and grant a protective order barring discovery of personal information extraneous to the case, including questions regarding Ms. Patt's sexual history posed at her October 16 deposition.

1   This Motion is based on this Notice of Motion and Motion and supporting Memorandum of

2   Points and Authorities, and on such further written and oral argument as may be presented at or

3   before the time the Court takes this Motion under submission.

4   Further, as set forth in the attached Memorandum of Points and Authorities, Ms. Patt opposes

5   Mr. Donner's Motion to Compel Discovery.

6

7

8

9

10

11

12

13

14

15

16

17

18

19

20

21

22

23

24

TABLE OF CONTENTS

TABLE OF AUTHORITIES

Cases

Eisenstadt v. Baird, 405 U.S. 438 (1972)

Griswold v. Connecticut, 381 U.S. 479 (1965)

Vinson v. Superior Court, 43 Cal. 3d 833 (1987)

Rules

Rule 26 of the Federal Rules of Civil Procedure

Rule 30 of the Federal Rules of Civil Procedure

Rule 37 of the Federal Rules of Civil Procedure

MEMORANDUM OF POINTS AND AUTHORITIES

I.   INTRODUCTION

The case arises from Defendant Dan Donner's unlawful and discriminatory refusal to rent an apartment to Plaintiff Paula Patt. *See generally* 1st Am. Compl. By the actions of his agent and employee Will Walters, Mr. Donner discriminated against Ms. Patt because she has a minor child and is not married, in violation of state and federal law civil rights law. *See id.* Recently, Mr. Donner's attorney asked inappropriate and irrelevant personal questions regarding Ms. Patt's sexual history during a deposition. Patt Dep. at 6:44, 8:6. Mr. Donner has now filed a motion to compel Ms. Patt's answer to one of these questions. Ms. Patt opposes that motion, and now hereby moves for a protective order ruling that this personal and extraneous information is outside the scope of discovery in this case.

II.   STATEMENT OF FACTS

On or about August 15 of this year, Will Walters showed Ms. Patt an apartment that was then available in the building that he managed. Patt Dep. at 5:14–22; Walters Dep. at 5:2–5. Mr. Walters reacted negatively to Ms. Patt being a single mother, asked inappropriate questions about Ms. Patt's personal life, and declined to rent the apartment to her. Patt Dep. at 5:27–6:42, 8:1–4, 27:11–13; Walters Dep. at 8:33–35; 51:4–7. Mr. Walters has since reaffirmed his disapproval of Ms. Patt's single parenthood. Walters Dep. at 51:20–21. Ms. Patt filed this action seeking damages and other relief for discrimination on the basis of marital and familial status. *See generally* 1st Am. Compl.

On or about October 16, Ms. Patt was deposed. *See generally* Patt Dep. At a deposition on October 16, Mr. Donner's lawyer asked Ms. Patt inappropriate, irrelevant, and personal questions about Ms. Patt's previous sexual partners, including asking the identity of S.P.'s father. Patt Dep. at 6:44, 8:6. Ms. Patt, on advice of counsel, refused to answer these questions but otherwise

1   permitted the deposition to continue. *Id.* at 7:3–40; 8:6–28. Although Mr. Donner is not pursuing

2   the egregious question of how many sexual partners Ms. Patt has had, he has filed a motion to

3   compel Ms. Patt to identify the father of her daughter S.P. *See generally* Mot. to Compel. Ms. Patt

4   opposes this motion, and brings a cross motion for a protective order barring Mr. Donner from

5   inquiring into irrelevant aspects of her private life. Pursuant to Rule 26(c)(1) of the Federal Rules

6   of Civil Procedure, Ms. Patt hereby certifies that the parties have conferred in good faith and have

7   been unable to resolve this dispute.

III. ARGUMENT

9   **A. This Court Should Deny Mr. Donner's Motion to Compel Discovery Because It Seeks**

10   **Irrelevant and Unreasonable Information.**

11   Under the Federal Rules of Civil Procedure, a party is entitled to discover information about

12 "any nonprivileged matter that is *relevant* to any party's claim or defense." Fed. R. Civ. P. 26(b)(1)

13 (emphasis added).

14   The identity of S.P.'s father is no more relevant to any party's claim or defense than is any other

15 aspect of Ms. Patt's sexual history. In order to prevail on her claims, Ms. Patt must show that she

16 belongs to a protected class and that she was intentionally denied the benefit of renting an

17 apartment because of her membership in that class. Thus Ms. Patt's marital and familial status and

18 Mr. Walters' knowledge of that status are relevant facts; the specific identity of S.P.'s father is not.

19 Other factors that legitimately bear on Ms. Patt's qualifications as a tenant may also be relevant,

20 but only to the extent Mr. Walters knew of such factors *at the time he refused to rent the apartment*

21 *to her.* Since her intimate past is unknown to Mr. Walters, it could not have figured into his rental

22 decision at all, even if it were somehow relevant in the abstract to evaluating a rental applicant.

23 Further, by arguing that this information is relevant to Mr. Walters' decision because it bears on

24

1   Ms. Patt's current social behavior or level of "responsibility," Mr. Donner suggests that his manager

2   has a special screening process for single mothers, whose status makes their personal lives of

3   particular interest. This is precisely the kind of generalization that the antidiscrimination laws are

4   meant to prevent.

5   Mr. Donner argues that the father's identity is relevant to the issue of damages because if,

6   contrary to all of Ms. Patt's representations, the father lived with her and S.P. in the apartment,

7   Mr. Donner would have inevitably evicted Ms. Patt for exceeding occupancy limits, thus reducing

8   her damages for his unlawful discrimination. This is an extremely tenuous argument to justify an

9   intrusive question. S.P.'s father lives in Boston, Massachusetts, Patt Decl. ¶ 9, and Mr. Donner has

10   no reason whatsoever to believe that the father would be moving into the apartment in violation of

11   the lease agreement. From a legal perspective, Mr. Donner cites no authority applying such an

12   "inevitable eviction" doctrine in housing discrimination cases. The Court should not endorse such a

13   broad and speculative fishing expedition.

14   Contrary to Mr. Donner's argument that Ms. Patt should nevertheless be required to answer

15   this inappropriate question simply because it was posed in a deposition, *see* Mot. to Compel at 9–

16   10, Ms. Patt's refusal to answer, on advice of counsel, was fully justified under the Federal Rules of

17   Civil Procedure. An attorney may properly instruct the deponent not to answer inappropriate

18   questions when necessary to bring a motion under Rule 30(d)(3) to limit the scope of the deposition.

19   Fed. R. Civ. P. 30(c)(2). The question regarding S.P.'s father was not merely irrelevant, it was also

20   unreasonably annoying, embarrassing, and oppressive to Ms. Patt. *See* Fed. R. Civ. P. 30(d)(3)(A).

21   The identity of S.P.'s father is a private and personal matter. He is not a part of S.P.'s life, and

22   S.P. is not currently aware of his identity. Patt Decl. ¶¶ 9–10. Although Ms. Patt intends to discuss

23   this matter with S.P. when she is older, it is more properly the subject of an intimate discussion

24

1 between mother and daughter than of public litigation records to which S.P. might inadvertently be

2 exposed at any time. *Id.* ¶ 10. Further, Ms. Patt fears that involving S.P.'s father in this case could

3 lead him to seek greater involvement in S.P.'s life, and that he would be a negative influence on S.P.

4 *Id.* ¶ 11. Here, Ms. Patt's attorney instructed her not to answer in order to bring a motion for a

5 protective order because the deposition was being conducted "in a manner that unreasonably

6 annoys, embarrasses, or oppresses" Ms. Patt. *See* Fed. R. Civ. P. 30(d)(3)(A); Patt Dep. at 7:10–40.

7 At that time, Ms. Patt could have terminated the deposition entirely, *see* Fed. R. Civ. P. 30(d)(3),

8 but in a gesture of good faith instead allowed it to proceed on the condition that she would not

9 answer the offensive questions unless compelled by court order. Patt Dep. at 7:35–40.

10   The unreasonableness of this deposition is reinforced by the other question Ms. Patt rightly

11 refused to answer: how many sexual partners she has had. *See* Patt Dep. at 8:6–28.[1] While Mr.

12 Donner has agreed not to pursue an answer to that question, *see* Mot. to Compel at 4 n.1, the fact

13 that it was asked at all evinces the unreasonable and improper manner in which the deposition was

14 conducted.

15   The identity of S.P.'s father is not relevant to this case and the question on that subject was

16 unreasonable. This Court should therefore deny Mr. Donner's Motion to Compel Discovery.

17 **B.   This Court Should Grant Ms. Patt's Motion for a Protective Order to Prevent an**

18   **Invasion of Her Privacy and Undue Humiliation.**

19   On a party's motion, a court may issue a protective order to guard that party from "annoyance,

20 embarrassment, oppression, or undue burden or expense." Fed. R. Civ. P. 26(c)(1). A party may also

21 move to "limit [a deposition] on the ground that it is being conducted in bad faith or in a manner

22

23 PLAINTIFF PAULA PATT'S NOTICE OF MOTION AND MOTION FOR PROTECTIVE ORDER
    7

24 ---
    [1] This question by Mr. Donner's attorney echoes one of Mr. Walters' questions that provides a strong basis to infer discriminatory intent. *See* Walters Dep. at 51:21-24. The primary difference is that while Mr. Walters knew that his question was inappropriate, *see id.* at 51:25-26, Mr. Donner's attorney argued at the deposition that this highly improper question was fair game. Patt Dep. at 8:18-23.

1   that unreasonably annoys, embarrasses, or oppresses the deponent or party." Fed. R. Civ. P.

2   30(d)(3)(A). A court may craft a protective order to entirely forbid discovery or disclosure of a

3   particular topic or to otherwise restrict dissemination or publication of discovered information. Fed.

4   R. Civ. P. 26(c)(1)(A)–(H). Such protection is particularly necessary when a party's constitutional

5   right to privacy is at stake. The United States Constitution protects the privacy of both the "marital

6   relationship . . . and the sexual lives of the unmarried." *Vinson v. Superior Court*, 43 Cal. 3d 833

7   (1987); *see also Eisenstadt v. Baird*, 405 U.S. 438 (1972); *Griswold v. Connecticut*, 381 U.S. 479

8   (1965).

9   In *Vinson v. Superior Court*, a California case cited in Defendant Donner's brief, the California

10 Supreme Court held that the scope of the mental examination to be given to the plaintiff in a sexual

11 harassment case had to be limited to exclude questions about her sexual conduct with anyone other

12 than the defendant. 43 Cal. 3d 833. The plaintiff in that case alleged that she was transferred and

13 then fired from her job because she had turned down the defendant's sexual advances during her

14 initial interview. *Id.* at 837. Since her complaint alleged that this harassment had caused her severe

15 emotional distress, the defendant moved for an order compelling her to undergo a mental

16 examination. *Id.* at 838. The plaintiff argued that this would violate her privacy and the defendant

17 countered that the information was necessary to evaluate the existence or extent of the mental harm

18 she suffered. *Id.*

19   The California Supreme Court held that the plaintiff had not waived all of her privacy rights

20 simply by bringing the suit, and that she was not required to expose "her persona to the unfettered

21 mental probing of defendants' expert." *Id.* at 841. The court would not compel the plaintiff to "discard

22 entirely her mantle of privacy" upon entering the courtroom. *Id.* at 841–42. The court also held

23 that—in contrast to her overall mental state—the plaintiff's sexual history was not relevant to the

24

PLAINTIFF PAULA PATT'S NOTICE OF MOTION AND MOTION FOR PROTECTIVE ORDER

1   claim, and thus the defendant was not entitled to discover information on that topic. *Id.* at 842. The

2   court reasoned that since the plaintiff had not alleged that the harassment was "detrimental to her

3   present sexuality . . . [h]er sexual history [was] even less relevant to her claim." *Id.* at 842.

4   Like the plaintiff in *Vinson*, Ms. Patt has not made any allegations that implicate her sexual

5   present, let alone her sexual past. *(Apply the analysis from* Vinson *to Ms. Patt's privacy-based claim*

6   *for a protective order.)*

7   **C. This Court Should Award Fees and Costs to Ms. Patt, Not to Mr. Donner.**

8   Under the Federal Rules of Civil Procedure, attorneys' fees for discovery motions are a double-

9   edged sword. Although a party moving to compel answers may in some cases recoup fees and costs

10   if the motion is granted, a court that denies such a motion "must, after giving an opportunity to be

11   heard, require the movant, the attorney filing the motion, or both to pay the party or deponent who

12   *opposed* the motion its reasonable expenses incurred in opposing the motion, including attorney's

13   fees." Fed. R. Civ. P. 37(a)(5)(B) (emphasis added). The Court should therefore award Ms. Patt her

14   reasonable costs and fees for opposing Mr. Donner's motion, in an amount to be determined after a

15   suitable protective order has been entered.

16   Under no circumstances should Ms. Patt be liable for Mr. Donner's expenses in bringing his

17   recent motion. Even when a motion to compel succeeds, the opposing party is not liable for costs and

18   fees if that party's "nondisclosure, response, or objection was substantially justified," or if "other

19   circumstances make an award of expenses unjust." Fed. R. Civ. P. 37(a)(5)(A)(ii)–(iii). Ms. Patt's

20   nondisclosure and objection were substantially justified because, as previously discussed, the

21   question at issue had no apparent connection to any defense that might be available to Mr. Donner.

22   The Court should therefore deny Mr. Donner's request for costs and attorneys' fees.

23

24

1

IV. CONCLUSION

2   The questions by Mr. Donner's attorney fall far outside of any reasonable effort to obtain

3   relevant evidence, and instead served only to humiliate and harass Ms. Patt. Ms. Patt therefore

4   respectfully requests that the Court deny Mr. Donner's Motion to Compel Discovery, grant a

5   protective order barring Mr. Donner from continuing this inappropriate inquisition, and award Ms.

6   Patt her fees and costs in this matter, as well as any other relief the Court deems appropriate.

7   Respectfully submitted,

8   _____

9   Matt Madison
                                                          Certified Law Student

10   Sam Pellegrino
                                                          Attorney for Plaintiff

11   Date: October 29

12

13

14

15

16

17

18

19

20

21

22

23

24

EXHIBIT 1

DECLARATION OF PAULA PATT IN SUPPORT OF PLAINTIFF'S

MOTION FOR A PROTECTIVE ORDER

My name is Paula Patt. I am a resident of Berkeley, California. If called upon to testify in these proceedings, I would affirm under oath and under penalty of perjury that:

1.   Will Walters, the agent and employee of Dan Donner, refused to rent an apartment to me after he became aware that I have a five-year-old daughter, S.P., and that I am unmarried.

2.   The circumstances of Mr. Walters' refusal are set forth in my September 16 declaration, filed in support of a motion for preliminary injunction. I hereby reaffirm and adopt by reference paragraphs 1 through 9 of that declaration, as if included in full herein.

3.   On August 28 of this year, I filed a lawsuit against Mr. Donner alleging housing discrimination on the basis of familial status.

4.   On October 16 of this year, Mr. Donner's attorney Jane Johnson took my deposition.

5.   Ms. Johnson asked me intrusive, personal, and irrelevant questions about my sexual history and the father of my daughter.

6.   My attorneys objected to these questions and instructed me not to answer. On advice of counsel, I did not answer the questions.

7.   Previously, when initially viewing the apartment, Mr. Walters asked me similar inappropriate questions.

8.   I know the identity of S.P.'s father. I am not currently in contact with him.

9.   S.P.'s father lives in Boston, Massachusetts. As far as I know, he currently has no plans to leave Boston. He is aware that S.P. exists but does not have a relationship with her.

DECLARATION OF PAULA PATT IN SUPPORT OF PLAINTIFF'S MOTION FOR A PROTECTIVE ORDER
1

EXHIBIT 1

10.   S.P. is not aware of her father's identity. I intend to discuss this issue with S.P. when she is older, but I am concerned that it could confuse and upset her while she is young, particularly if her father's identity becomes a matter of public record through court proceedings.

11.   I am also concerned that S.P.'s father, if contacted about this case, might attempt to insert himself into our life. I believe that he would not be a good influence on my daughter.

12.   I am not aware of any relevant information that S.P.'s father could provide to Mr. Donner for the purposes of this case.

Dated: October 28

/s/ _____

Paula Patt

ORDER RE: DISCOVERY DISPUTE

1

2   IN THE UNITED STATES DISTRICT COURT
           FOR THE NORTHERN DISTRICT OF CALIFORNIA
3   OAKLAND DIVISION

PAULA PATT,   No. C 1357 DBO
4   Plaintiff,
                                         ORDER DENYING MOTION TO COMPEL
5   v.   **DEPOSITION ANSWER AND GRANTING**
                                         MOTION FOR PROTECTIVE ORDER
   DAN DONNER,
6   Defendant.

7   /

8   This is a case of alleged housing discrimination based on marital status and familial status.

9   The motions before the Court concern a discovery dispute, specifically the scope of permissible

10   questions in a deposition. During a deposition of the Plaintiff, defense counsel asked her to identify

11   the father of her minor daughter. Patt Dep. at 6:44. Plaintiff's counsel objected and advised Plaintiff

12   not to answer the question. *Id.* at 7:3–11. After some discussion, the parties agreed to continue the

13   deposition and submit cross motions to the Court to resolve whether Plaintiff should be required to

14   disclose her child's paternity. *Id.* at 7:35–40.

15   As a general matter, the scope of civil discovery is broad. Discoverable information need not be

16   admissible in evidence, but rather merely must be "relevant to any party's claim or defense and

17   proportional to the needs of the case." Fed. R. Civ. P. 26(b)(1). Further, the Federal Rules of Civil

18   Procedure require that witnesses generally answer even those questions to which an attorney lodges

19   an objection. Fed. R. Civ. P. 30(c)(2). However, "[d]istrict courts need not condone the use of

20   discovery to engage in 'fishing expedition[s],' " and may "invoke the Federal Rules of Civil Procedure

21   when necessary to prevent [parties] from using the discovery process to engage in wholesale

22   searches for evidence." *Rivera v. NIBCO, Inc.*, 364 F.3d 1057, 1072 (9th Cir. 2004). An attorney may

23   justifiably instruct a deponent not to answer a question that "unreasonably annoys, embarrasses,

24   or oppresses the deponent." *See* Fed. R. Civ. P. 30(c)(2) (permitting an instruction not to answer in

ORDER DENYING MOTION TO COMPEL DEPOSITION ANSWER AND GRANTING MOTION FOR PROTECTIVE ORDER

1 | order to bring a 30(d)(3) motion); Fed. R. Civ. P. 30(d)(3) (stating grounds for limiting a deposition

2 | involving improper questions).

3 | The Court finds that the identity of S.P.'s father falls near the boundary of this broad definition

4 | of relevance, but is not discoverable in this case. On the one hand, the father's identity is inherently

5 | tied to Plaintiff's status as a single mother, a central aspect of the subject matter involved in the

6 | action. On the other hand, Plaintiff correctly notes that this case primarily concerns what Defendant

7 | and his agent knew about Plaintiff at the time they refused to rent her an apartment, and what

8 | their motive was in doing so—questions on which the information they now seek cannot be expected

9 | to shed any light.

10 | Defendant's argument that the father's identity could lead to relevant evidence regarding

11 | damages (because Plaintiff could have been evicted if she rented the apartment and the father

12 | moved in) is at least logically sound, but highly speculative. Defendant has presented no grounds

13 | for belief that the father would move in or that Plaintiff's sworn affidavit that the father lives in

14 | Boston with no intent to leave is false. *See* Patt Aff. ¶ 9. The Court takes judicial notice of the fact

15 | that evictions, particularly in California, tend to be difficult, time consuming, and unpredictable.

16 | Defendant has presented only the most theoretical explanation of how the father's identity could

17 | possibly be relevant to this case.

18 | Plaintiff raises significant privacy concerns, including the fact that her daughter does not

19 | currently know the identity of her father. Patt Aff. ¶ 10. Disclosing the father's identity in public

20 | judicial records would negate Plaintiff's decision as to how and when to discuss this matter with her

21 | daughter, a decision on which the Court expresses no opinion except that it is emphatically not the

22 | Court's decision to make, at least not on the motions presented here. *See Elk Grove Unified Sch.*

23 | *Dist. v. Newdow*, 524 U.S. 1, 12–13 (2004) (federal courts should avoid wading into issues of domestic

24 |

ORDER DENYING MOTION TO COMPEL DEPOSITION ANSWER AND GRANTING MOTION FOR PROTECTIVE ORDER

1   relations except in "rare instances in which it is necessary to answer a substantial federal question").

2   There is also another privacy concern at issue that is not represented by either party to this case:

3   the interest of the father, who may not wish it known that he has a daughter who is not a part of

4   his life. Finally, the Court must be mindful of the "possibility that discovery tactics such as that

5   used by defendant herein might intimidate, inhibit, or discourage [civil rights plaintiffs] from

6   pursuing their claims," an effect that would "clearly contravene the remedial effect intended by

7   Congress." *Priest v. Rotary*, 98 F.R.D. 755, 761 (N.D. Cal. 1983) (considering evidence of sexual

8   history in a workplace sexual harassment case); *see also Macklin v. Mendenhall*, 257 F.R.D. 596,

9   602 (E.D. Cal. 2009) (same, quoting *Priest*).

10   Given the speculative nature of Defendant's relevance argument, as well as Plaintiff's privacy

11   interests and the public policy concerns articulated in *Priest*, the question of the father's identity is

12   precisely the sort of "fishing expedition" that this Court need not facilitate. *See Rivera*, 364 F.3d at

13   1072. The Court finds that this question falls outside the scope of permissible discovery in this case.

14   There is also the issue of the general rule that a deponent must usually answer questions even

15   subject to objection. Fed. R. Civ. P. 30(c)(2). Defendant argues that even if the question was

16   irrelevant, Plaintiff violated the Federal Rules by refusing to answer it. On these facts, however,

17   the Court holds that Plaintiff's refusal to answer was justified. Rule 30(c)(2) authorizes an

18   instruction not to answer when necessary to bring a motion under Rule 30(d)(3) to limit a deposition

19   conducted "in a manner that unreasonably annoys, embarrasses, or oppresses the deponent or

20   party." For the reasons stated above, compelling disclosure of S.P.'s father would "unreasonably

21   annoy[ ], embarrass[ ], or oppress[ ]" Plaintiff and her daughter. Other than two questions, one of

22   which Defendant has withdrawn and the other the Court now finds impermissible, Plaintiff

23

24

ORDER DENYING MOTION TO COMPEL DEPOSITION ANSWER AND GRANTING MOTION FOR PROTECTIVE ORDER

cooperated in the deposition and answered Defendant's questions. Plaintiff's invocation of Rule 30(d)(3) was appropriate under the circumstances.

For the reasons stated above, Defendant's Motion to Compel is DENIED and Plaintiff's Motion for Protective Order is GRANTED. Defendant is hereby ordered not to seek information regarding the father's identity, and Plaintiff is not required to provide such information.

Each party has requested that the Court award costs and attorneys' fees for these motions. However, the Court finds that such an award is not warranted against either party, because both parties acted with substantial justification in filing or opposing the motions at issue and in requesting or withholding the father's identity. *See* Fed. R. Civ. P. 37(a)(5). Although the Court finds Plaintiff's subjective assessment that the questioning was abusive valid, Defendant had a non-frivolous (although ultimately unsuccessful) argument that the father's identity was relevant, and had no reason to know of the disruptive effects that disclosure could have on Plaintiff's family life.[1] The requests for costs and fees are DENIED as to both parties.

IT IS SO ORDERED.

Dated: November 3

DIANNE B. OSAKA
UNITED STATES DISTRICT JUDGE

ORDER DENYING MOTION TO COMPEL DEPOSITION ANSWER AND GRANTING MOTION FOR PROTECTIVE ORDER
4

---

[1]   Defendant's question regarding Plaintiff's sexual history is more clearly inappropriate, but is not before the Court. The Court takes Defendant's withdrawal of that question and apology to Plaintiff at the hearing into account in denying the request for fees and costs.

CHAPTER 8

SUMMARY JUDGMENT

CHAPTER 8 MATERIALS

MEMORANDUM TO FILE RE: PARTIAL SUMMARY JUDGMENT MOTION

TO: Memo to File
FROM: Jane Johnson
RE: Strategy Moving Forward

To File:

Plaintiffs have brought claims under both the federal Fair Housing Act and the California Fair Housing Law. After reviewing the legal standards, we believe a court would likely dismiss Plaintiff's federal Fair Housing Act claim because she stopped payment on the application fee and thus never made a "bona fide" offer to rent the apartment as required by the federal law.

Unfortunately, California law does not require applicants to make a "bona fide" offer to have standing under the California Fair Housing Law. Under § 12955(b), any "written or oral *inquiry* concerning the . . . marital status" of an applicant constitutes discrimination.

By moving for Partial Summary Judgment on Plaintiff's federal Fair Housing Act claim, we can narrow the case down to the California state law claims. We can then move the federal district court to dismiss the state law claims under 28 USC § 1367(c), which gives the federal court discretion over whether to exercise supplemental jurisdiction over purely state law claims. This will require Plaintiff to refile in California state court.

We believe this is in our strategic interest because, frankly, it seems to me that Judge Osaka has been a bit favorable towards Plaintiff.

Jane Johnson

CHAPTER 8 MATERIALS

DEFENDANT'S MOTION FOR SUMMARY JUDGMENT

1   JANE JOHNSON (State Bar No. 31415927)
Jane.Johnson@johnsonshermen.com

2   JOHNSON & SHERMEN, LLP
10000 Shattuck Ave., Suite 3500

3   Berkeley, California 94704
Telephone: (510) 555-3500

4   Facsimile: (510) 555-3501

    Attorney for Defendant

5

                UNITED STATES DISTRICT COURT

6   NORTHERN DISTRICT OF CALIFORNIA

7   PAULA PATT,   Case No. C 1357 DBO

           Plaintiff,

8   **MOTION FOR PARTIAL SUMMARY**
   v.   **JUDGMENT**

9   DAN DONNER,

           Defendant.   **MEMORANDUM OF POINTS AND**

10   /   **AUTHORITIES**

11   —————————————————————   Date: November 2
                                      Time: 12:00 p.m.

12   Judge: Hon. Dianne B. Osaka

13   TO PLAINTIFF AND HER ATTORNEY OF RECORD:

14   NOTICE IS HEREBY GIVEN that on November 1 at 12:00 p.m. in Courtroom 3 of the above-

15 entitled Court, located at 1301 Clay Street, Oakland, California, Defendant Dan Donner will and

16 hereby does move the Court, pursuant to Rule 56 of the Federal Rules of Civil Procedure, to grant

17 partial summary judgment in favor of Defendant. This Motion is brought on the grounds that on

18 Plaintiff's Fair Housing Act claim there is no genuine dispute as to any material fact.

19   This Motion is based on Defendant's Motion for Summary Judgment, Defendant's

20 Memorandum of Points and Authorities in Support of Motion for Partial Summary Judgment, and

21 on such further written and oral argument as may be presented at or before the time the Court

22 takes this motion under submission.

23 Dated: November 2

24

1	Respectfully submitted,
2	/s/ _____
3	JANE JOHNSON *Attorney for Defendant*
4	
5	
6	
7	
8	
9	
10	
11	
12	
13	
14	
15	
16	
17	
18	
19	
20	
21	
22	
23	
24	MOTION FOR PARTIAL SUMMARY JUDGMENT

1

TABLE OF CONTENTS

11

TABLE OF AUTHORITIES

12

Cases

13   *Celotex Corp. v. Catrett*, 477 U.S. 317 (1986)

14   *Mitchell v. Shane*, 350 F.3d 39 (2d Cir. 2003)

15   *McDonald v. Coldwell Banker*, 543 F.3d 498 (9th Cir. 2008)

16   *Petrello v. Prucka*, 484 Fed. Appx. 939 (5th Cir. 2012)

17

Statutes

18   42 U.S.C. § 3604 (1968)

19

Rules

20   Rule 56(a) of the Federal Rules of Civil Procedure

21

22

23

24

1

I.   INTRODUCTION

2   This case concerns allegations of housing discrimination by the Plaintiff, Paula Patt. *See*

3   *generally* Am. Compl. The Plaintiff is a graduate student at the University of California, Berkeley

4   who was seeking housing in the Berkeley area. *See id.* During her search, she came across a rental

5   listing for an apartment in the building located at 1357 Telegraph Avenue. *Id.* at ¶ 9. The building

6   is owned by Defendant Dan Donner. *Id.* at ¶ 18. The listing was posted by Will Walters, a graduate

7   student hired by the Defendant to manage the property. *Id.* at ¶¶ 10, 19.

8   Every applicant for 1357 Telegraph Avenue must undergo a routine background check before

9   their application will be considered, which requires a $35.00 processing fee. Walters Dep. at 7:10–

10   12. Plaintiff provided Will Walters with a check. See *id.* However, she changed her mind the

11   following day and stopped payment on the check. *Id.* at 9:19–22. Plaintiff now claims that she was

12   discriminated against on the basis of her familial status for an application she never bothered to

13   complete. *See generally* Am. Compl.

14   Plaintiff alleges that Mr. Donner, through his property manager, Will Walters, rejected her

15   rental application because of her familial status, in violation of the federal Fair Housing Act of 1968

16   ("FHA"). Id. at ¶ 3. However, Plaintiff fails to disclose that she chose to stop payment on her check

17   for the processing fee, effectively withdrawing her application. Walters Dep. at 7:10–12; Patt Dep.

18   at 55:3–5. Mr. Donner, through his property manager, decided to rent the apartment to a qualified

19   applicant. Walters Dep. at 9:4–12. Defendant chose a qualified applicant who completed her

20   application, over an applicant who never completed her application. *See id.* This was not a decision

21   based on, or in any way related to, Plaintiff's familial status.

22   Plaintiff does not dispute that she stopped payment on her check—effectively withdrawing her

23   application from consideration—and thus does not present a genuine dispute as to any material fact

24

1   under § 3604. Patt Dep. at 55:3–5; *see generally* Am. Compl. Accordingly, Mr. Donner moves for

2   summary judgment on Plaintiff's claim of discrimination in violation of the federal FHA.

II.   STATEMENT OF FACTS

4   Defendant Dan Donner owns the apartment complex located at 1357 Telegraph Avenue.

5   Donner Aff. (Ex.1) ¶ 5. Mr. Donner has never visited the property or been to the State of California.

6   Donner Aff. ¶ 4. In January 2018, Mr. Donner hired Will Walters to manage the property. Donner

7   Aff. ¶ 6. Mr. Walters is responsible for collecting rent and for basic maintenance and repairs. Donner

8   Aff. ¶ 6. Further, Mr. Walters is solely responsible for interviewing and selecting new tenants.

9   Donner Aff. ¶ 8. Mr. Walters is a business student at the University of California, Berkeley, and

10   suffers from back pain on a regular basis. Walters Dep. at 2:20–21; 52:38–39.

11   Mr. Walters posted an ad on Gregslist on August 15th for a one-bedroom apartment in the

12   apartment complex. Gregslist Advertisement (Ex. 2); Walters Dep. at 4:13–14. Mr. Walters spoke

13   with Ms. Patt that day and set up an appointment for Ms. Patt to view the apartment the same

14   afternoon. Patt Dep. at 4:26–29. At the time of their phone call, Ms. Patt understood that to rent

15   the apartment, she was required to submit both a paper application and a check for $35.00. Patt

16   Dep. at 9:30. The $35.00 payment was a processing fee for a required background check. Walters

17   Dep. at 7:10–12. On August 15, Ms. Patt and her five-year-old daughter, S.P., arrived at the

18   apartment for their scheduled appointment. Walters Dep. at 5:39–41. Ms. Patt noticed that Mr.

19   Walters had a "pained expression" when she initially met him. Patt Dep. at 27:27. Ms. Patt

20   interpreted Mr. Walters' expression as disapproval of her status as a single mother. Am. Compl.

21   ¶ 15. However, it is well-documented that Mr. Walters suffers from chronic back pain resulting from

22   a sports injury several years prior. Walters Dep. at 52:38–39. While Mr. Walters asked Ms. Patt

23

24

1   various personal questions during her visit, he did not intend to make her uncomfortable, and

2   apologized as soon as he realized he had done so. Walters Dep. at 51:21–39.

3   After the tour, Ms. Patt gave Mr. Walters a completed application and $35.00 for a background

4   check Walters Dep. at 6:39–44. Mr. Walters conducts a background check for all applicants as a way

5   of ensuring he secures responsible tenants for the building. Walters Dep. at 7:10–11. This $35.00

6   payment is a required element of the rental application for an apartment at 1357 Telegraph Avenue.

7   Patt Dep. at 9:27–30. After Ms. Patt left that afternoon, Mr. Walters showed the unit to another

8   prospective tenant. Walters Dep. at 7:43–44. This prospective tenant also submitted a completed

9   paper application and a $35.00 payment for the required background check. Walters Dep. at 8:10–

10 13.

11   After visiting the apartment, Ms. Patt stopped payment on her check for $35.00, which she

12 knew was required in order to rent the apartment. Walters Dep. at 9:21–22; Patt Dep. at 9:30. On

13 August 21, Ms. Patt called Mr. Walters to follow up on her application, and Mr. Walters informed

14 her that the apartment was no longer available, as he had rented to a qualified applicant. Walters

15 Dep. at 8:33–35; 9:4–10. Ms. Patt then brought a claim alleging familial discrimination under

16 federal and state law, accusing Mr. Walters of refusing to rent to her because she is an unmarried

17 mother. Am. Compl. ¶ 20.

18   **III. ARGUMENT**

19 **A.   Legal Standard for Summary Judgment.**

20   Defendant moves for partial summary judgment on Plaintiff's federal housing discrimination

21 claim pursuant to Federal Rule of Civil Procedure 56. A court shall grant summary judgment where,

22 as here, "there is no genuine dispute as to any material fact and the movant is entitled to judgment

23 as a matter of law." Fed. R. Civ. P. 56(a). If the movant shows that the record reveals no "genuine

24

                                MOTION FOR PARTIAL SUMMARY JUDGMENT

1   dispute," the burden shifts to the non-moving party to demonstrate the existence of a genuine

2   dispute. *Celotex Corp. v. Catrett*, 477 U.S. 317, 324 (1986). If the non-moving party fails to do so, the

3   movant is entitled to judgment as a matter of law.

4   **B.   Defendant Dan Donner is Entitled to Summary Judgment Because Plaintiff Paula**

5   **Patt Withdrew Her Application to Rent the Apartment When She Stopped Payment**

6   **on the Processing Fee, and is Therefore Not Protected by the Fair Housing Act.**

7   The federal FHA provides relief for an individual who is discriminated against on the basis of

8   her familial status. 42 U.S.C. § 3604(a). The protections of the FHA are limited to cabining

9   discriminatory practices faced by actual housing applicants, not by hypothetical plaintiffs, or those

10   who considered but did not actually apply for housing. This is made clear by the plain language of

11   the statute, which makes it unlawful to "refuse to sell or rent *after the making of a bona fide offer*

12   . . . a dwelling to any person because of . . . familial status." § 3604(a) (emphasis added). The making

13   of a "bona fide offer" requires the prospective tenant to be qualified, which includes meeting the

14   required terms of the landlord. *See McDonald v. Coldwell Banker*, 543 F.3d 498, 504–05 (9th Cir.

15   2008) (holding that a prospective buyer who failed to meet the terms of the seller could not be

16   considered "qualified" for the purposes of establishing discrimination in violation of the FHA). A

17   prospective tenant/buyer who fails to meet a required term of the seller/landlord, and therefore has

18   failed to make a bona fide offer on the property, cannot be considered to be "similarly situated" to

19   another prospective tenant/buyer who does meet those terms. *See id.* A long string of authority

20   supports the proposition that a prospective tenant who fails to make a qualified offer is not entitled

21   to the protections of the FHA. *See, e.g., Petrello v. Prucka*, 484 Fed. Appx. 939, 942 (5th Cir. 2012)

22   (holding a prospective buyer not entitled to protection by the FHA where his oral offer did not satisfy

23   the statute of frauds).

24

1   Here, Plaintiff's claim does not reach even the basic threshold that qualifies an applicant for

2 federal FHA protection. By choosing to stop payment on her application fee, Plaintiff intentionally

3 failed to satisfy the requirements of the application, and effectively withdrew her application from

4 consideration. In so doing, Plaintiff rendered herself unqualified to rent the apartment, and

5 sufficiently dissimilar from the tenant Will Walters ultimately rented to. Patt Dep. at 56:1–15; *see*

6 *Petrello*, 484 Fed. Appx. at 942. As Plaintiff did not make a "bona fide offer" for rental of the

7 apartment within the plain meaning of the FHA, she is not entitled to its protections.

8   Just as Plaintiff knew that had she stopped payment on her graduate school application fee she

9 could not have been accepted, here, Plaintiff could not have been accepted as the tenant in an

10 apartment she did not apply for. Patt Dep. at 56:1–15. This is a fact so obvious it requires no citation

11 to authority. Plaintiff unilaterally negated the steps she had taken to rent the apartment at 1357

12 Telegraph Avenue and, in so doing, withdrew her application. *See id.* The federal FHA does not

13 allow a hypothetical plaintiff—one who never completed her application for consideration—to seek

14 damages in federal court for discrimination.

15   **IV. CONCLUSION**

16   When Plaintiff Paula Patt stopped payment on her check for the required $35.00 processing fee

17 for her rental application, she withdrew her application from consideration. Because the Fair

18 Housing Act only protects those who actually applied for housing, Plaintiff's federal housing

19 discrimination claim must fail. As there is no genuine dispute as to any material fact, Defendant

20 Donner respectfully requests that this court grant his motion for partial summary judgment.

21 Dated: November 2

22

23

24

1

2

3

4

5

6

7

8

9

10

11

12

13

14

15

16

17

18

19

20

21

22

23

24

Respectfully submitted,

/s/ _____

Jane Johnson
Attorney for Defendant, Dan Donner

CHAPTER 8 MATERIALS

EMAIL MEMO RE: MOTION FOR SUMMARY JUDGMENT

To: Sam Pellegrino
From: Matt Madison
Re: Legal Research on the Doctrine of Futility

Hi Sam,

As we discussed, the Defendant has moved for summary judgment on grounds that Paula Patt stopped payment on her application fee, and therefore withdrew her application. You asked me to research whether Paula Patt's claim under the Fair Housing Act ("FHA") is precluded because she failed to submit a completed application. Based on my research, I believe that Paula Patt's claim is not precluded where, as here, it would have been a "futile gesture" for her to apply.

In housing and employment cases, courts have recognized that defendants may either directly or indirectly deter plaintiffs from submitting an application based on discriminatory grounds. In these situations, courts apply the "doctrine of futility" to ensure that victims of discrimination do not have to go through the motions of submitting an application they have reason to believe will be rejected. *See, e.g., Int'l Bros. of Teamsters v. United States*, 431 U.S. 324, 365–66 (1977); *Pinchback v. Armistead Homes Corp.*, 689 F. Supp. 541 (D. Md. 1988), judgment aff'd in part, vacated in part on other grounds, 907 F.2d 1447 (4th Cir. 1990).

In *Pinchback v. Armistead Homes Corp.*, the court held that the "doctrine of futility" applies to claims under the FHA. *See* 689 F. Supp. at 551. Defendant's agent told a prospective plaintiff that African-Americans were not allowed in the housing cooperative. *Id.* at 541. Plaintiff, who was shocked by the comment, decided not to purchase a home. *Id.* Defendant then moved for summary judgment on grounds that plaintiff had never actually applied to purchase the house and was therefore not protected under the FHA. *Id.* In rejecting this argument, the court held that the failure to submit an application did not preclude plaintiff's FHA claim where the evidence showed that plaintiff was deterred by defendant's discriminatory practices. *Id.* at 551.

Here, a court will likely find that Paula Patt was deterred by Will Walter's inappropriate and intrusive line of questioning, and that he was never going to rent to her based on her familial status. Thus, even though Paula Patt stopped payment on her application fee, her FHA claim is not precluded under the futile gesture doctrine.

Please let me know if I should look into anything further as we prepare for our Opposition to Summary Judgment.

Thank you,

Matt Madison
J.D. Candidate

CHAPTER 8 SKILLS EXERCISE

OPPOSITION TO MOTION FOR SUMMARY JUDGMENT

This exercise requires you to complete the opposition to a Rule 56 motion for partial summary judgment. The motion has been largely drafted for you, but you must complete the section where it reads, *"Apply the facts from the record to argue that Defendant is not entitled to summary judgment, because a reasonable jury could find that he discriminated against Plaintiff prior to her stopping payment on her check."*

As you have learned in your Civil Procedure course, a party is entitled to summary judgment where "there is no genuine dispute as to any material fact." Fed. R. Civ. P. 56(a). The Defendant has moved for partial summary judgment, arguing that Plaintiff is not protected by the federal Fair Housing Act because, by stopping payment on her application fee, she never submitted an application for the apartment located at 1357 Telegraph Avenue. This exercise asks you to complete Plaintiff's opposition to Defendant's motion. In the critical portion that has been left for you to draft, you will apply the facts in the record thus far to argue that Defendant's behavior **demonstrates an intention to not rent to Paula Patt based on her familial status in violation of the Fair Housing Act prior to her stopping payment on the check.** This exercise should be completed after you have studied the cases on summary judgment in your Civil Procedure course.

Some tips for drafting the briefs:

- Before starting, read the portions of the motion that have already been drafted. Avoid unnecessary repetition of points made earlier in the motion.

- Avoid unsupported conclusory statements. You must explain *why* the facts you use support the argument you make.

- Do not simply ignore facts that may seem more unfavorable to your party; instead, try to frame those facts in a way that supports your argument.

- Do not introduce any facts that are not included in the motion or set forth in the case record thus far.

- There is no need to add additional case law in the section you are completing. Instead, focus on the facts, with citations to the record.

1 | SAM PELLEGRINO (State Bar No. 11235813)
spellegrino@berkeleylegalclinic.org
2 | MATT MADISON (Certified Law Student)
BERKELEY LEGAL CLINIC
3 | 2013 Center Street, Suite 310
Telephone: (510) 555-5151
4 | Facsimile: (510) 555-5155

Attorney for Plaintiff
5 |
                UNITED STATES DISTRICT COURT
6 | NORTHERN DISTRICT OF CALIFORNIA
7 | OAKLAND DIVISION

8 | PAULA PATT,   Case No. C 1357 DBO
                    Plaintiff,
9 | v.   **OPPOSITION TO MOTION FOR**
                                             PARTIAL SUMMARY JUDGMENT
10 | DAN DONNER,
                    Defendant.   **MEMORANDUM OF POINTS AND**
11 | **AUTHORITIES**
                                         /
12 | _____

      TO DEFENDANT AND HIS ATTORNEY OF RECORD:
13 |
      Pursuant to Rule 56 of the Federal Rules for Civil Procedure, Plaintiff Paula Patt ("Plaintiff"
14 |
or "Ms. Patt") through her counsel of record, presents this opposition to Defendant Dan Donner's
15 |
("Defendant" or "Mr. Donner") Motion for Summary Judgment. As there a genuine dispute as to
16 |
material facts, the Defendant's Motion must be denied.
17 |
Dated: November 8
18 |
                                         Respectfully submitted,
19 | /s/ _____

20 | MATT MADISON
                                         Certified Law Student
21 | Supervised by SAM PELLEGRINO
                                         Attorney for Plaintiff
22 |

23 |

24 |
                                 OPPOSITION TO MOTION FOR PARTIAL SUMMARY JUDGMENT
                                                    1

1

TABLE OF CONTENTS

16

TABLE OF AUTHORITIES

17

<u>Cases</u>

18

Adickes v. S. H. Kress & Co., 398 U.S. 144 (1970)

19

Anderson v. Liberty Lobby, 477 U.S. 242 (1986)

20

Celotex Corp. v. Catrett, 477 U.S. 317 (1986)

21

International Bros. of Teamsters v. United States, 431 U.S. 324 (1977)

22

McLaughlin v. Liu, 849 F.2d 1205 (9th Cir. 1988)

23

Pinchback v. Armistead Homes Corp., 907 F.2d 1447 (4th Cir. 1990)

24

1 | *Swierkiewicz v. Sorema N.A.*, 534 U.S. 506 (2002)

2 | <u>Statutes</u>

3 | 42 U.S.C § 3604 (1968)

4 | <u>Rules</u>

5 | Rule 56 of the Federal Rules of Civil Procedure

6 | <u>Memoranda</u>

7 | U.S. Department of Housing and Urban Development Memorandum on the Elements of Proof Aug.

8 | 13, 2014

9

10

11

12

13

14

15

16

17

18

19

20

21

22

23

24

I.   INTRODUCTION

Plaintiff Paula Patt, a graduate student at the University of California, Berkeley, was seeking housing in Berkeley, CA when she came across a listing for Defendant Dan Donner's rental property located at 1357 Telegraph Avenue in Berkeley, CA. The listing was posted by Defendant's property manager and agent, Will Walters. Ms. Patt contacted Mr. Walters to schedule a showing, who expressed his preference to rent to graduate students and scheduled a showing later that day.

Upon Ms. Patt's arrival, Mr. Walter seemed pleased to see her. However, his demeanor changed when Mr. Walters realized that Ms. Patt is a single-mother to her five-year-old daughter, S.P. For the remainder of the showing, Mr. Walters asked Ms. Patt intrusive and harassing questions regarding her marital status, number of sexual partners, and the identity of S.P.'s father. While Ms. Patt submitted her application after the showing, it became clear to her that Mr. Walters had already made up his mind. Deciding there was no point in paying $35 for a credit check when it was clear she would not be considered for the apartment, Ms. Patt stopped payment on her check.

The Fair Housing Act of 1968 ("FHA") was adopted in order to prevent discrimination in the sale or rental of property. Defendants characterize Ms. Patt as a "hypothetical plaintiff" because she stopped payment on her $35 check. Under the futile gesture doctrine, however, plaintiffs do not have to go through the motions of paying for, completing or submitting an application that is certain to be rejected. By the end of the showing, it became clear to Ms. Patt that Mr. Walters would not rent to her because she is a single mother.

Based on Mr. Walters' intrusive questions and demeanor, a reasonable jury could find that requiring Ms. Patt to pay the fee for a background check would have been a futile gesture. Thus, the court should deny Defendant's Motion for Summary Judgment.

II. STATEMENT OF FACTS

Paula Patt is a 23-year-old graduate student studying anthropology at the University of California Berkeley. Patt Dep. 2:38–39, 6:12. In August, Ms. Patt and her five-year-old daughter, S.P., moved to Berkeley and began looking for housing. Patt Dep. 4:3–9. On August 15th, Ms. Patt saw an advertisement for the apartment at 1357 Telegraph Avenue, which is owned by Defendant Dan Donner. Patt Dep. 4:13–16; Walters Dep. 3:12–20. That same day, Ms. Patt contacted Will Walters, the Defendant's property manager, and scheduled a showing of the apartment for that afternoon. Patt Dep. 4:26–29. Over the phone, Mr. Walters was enthusiastic about showing the apartment to Ms. Patt, especially after hearing that she was a graduate student. Patt Dep. 4:43–48.

Upon arrival, Mr. Walters saw S.P. and his demeanor immediately changed from enthusiastic to hostile. Patt Dep. 5:27–40. During the showing, S.P. was clinging to Ms. Patt quietly because she was nervous around Mr. Walters. Patt Dep. 6:1–15. Mr. Walters asked Ms. Patt a number of invasive questions about Ms. Patt's marital status, past sexual partners, and her relationship with and the identity of S.P.'s father. Patt Dep. 4:35–42, 8:1–4; Walters Dep. 51:21–26. Mr. Walters' demeanor and line of questioning were not a result of S.P.'s behavior, but a reflection of his open disapproval of young single mothers like Ms. Patt. Patt Dep. 6:19–23; Walters Dep. 51:34–39.

Despite Mr. Walters' rude behavior, Ms. Patt gave him the completed rental application and a check for $35 that Mr. Walters said he would use to run a credit check. Patt Dep. 9:8–19. After the showing, however, Ms. Patt realized that Mr. Walters had no intention of renting her the apartment. Patt Dep. 9:35–41, 55:9–10. Thus, Ms. Patt decided to stop payment on her check. Patt Dep. 55:5. Moreover, Mr. Walters admitted in his deposition that he had no intention of ever running a credit check on Ms. Patt. Walters Dep. 6:38–7:5.

1   On August 21, Ms. Patt called Mr. Walters to see whether her application was still under

2   consideration. Patt Dep. 55:36–37. Mr. Walters informed her that the apartment was no longer

3   available, as he had rented to another applicant. Walters Dep. at 8:33–35; 9:4–10.

4   **III. ARGUMENT**

5   **A. The Legal Standard for Summary Judgment Requires the Moving Party to Show**

6   **There is No Genuine Dispute as to Any Material Fact.**

7   The Defendant, Dan Donner, moves for partial summary judgment on Plaintiff's federal claim

8   of housing discrimination pursuant to Federal Rule of Civil Procedure 56. To succeed on a motion

9   for summary judgment, the movant must show that "there is no genuine dispute as to any material

10   fact and the movant is entitled to judgment as a matter of law." Fed. R. Civ. P. 56(a). Thus, the

11   Defendant in this case has the burden of proving "the absence of any genuine issue of fact" in order

12   to be entitled to summary judgment. *See Adickes v. S. H. Kress & Co.*, 398 U.S. 144, 153 (1970); *see*

13   *also Celotex Corp. v. Catrett,* 477 U.S. 317, 324 (1986). If a reasonable jury could find in favor of the

14   non-moving party, with all inferences being viewed in the light most favorable to the non-moving

15   party, then the motion must be denied. *See Adickes,* 398 U.S. at 158–59; *see also Anderson v. Liberty*

16   *Lobby*, 477 U.S. 242, 248 (1986).

17   **B. A Reasonable Jury Could Find That the Facts Disclosed in the Depositions**

18   **Demonstrate That Will Walters Discriminated Against Paula Patt Well Before She**

19   **Stopped Payment on Her Application Fee Check.**

20   Defendant argues that because Paula Patt stopped payment on the $35.00 check for the

21   mandatory credit check fee, she did not make a bona fide offer to rent the apartment, and therefore

22   is not entitled to the protections of the Fair Housing Act (FHA). *See* Mot. for Partial Summary

23   Judgment at 4. However, the record demonstrates that Will Walters engaged in discriminatory

24

1 conduct toward Paula Patt before she submitted her rental application. Thus, Will Walter's conduct

2 demonstrates a "refus[al] to negotiate" for the sale or rental of the apartment, and constitutes

3 discrimination under the FHA regardless of whether the applicant made a bona fide offer. 42 U.S.C.

4 3604 § 804 provides that "it shall be unlawful to refuse to sell or rent after the making of a bona fide

5 offer, *or* to refuse to negotiate for the sale or rental of, *or* to otherwise make unavailable or deny, a

6 dwelling to any person because of . . . familial status." (emphasis added).

7 *(Apply the facts from the record to argue that Defendant is not entitled to summary judgment,*

8 *because a reasonable jury could find that he intended not to rent to Plaintiff prior to her stopping*

9 *payment on her check.)*

10 Although the Defendant asserts alternative justifications for Mr. Walters's questioning and

11 behavior, at the summary judgment stage determinations of which explanation may more plausible

12 are inappropriate. *See McLaughlin v. Liu,* 849 F.2d 1205, 1209 (9th Cir. 1988). Rather, all inferences

13 must be drawn in the light most favorable to the nonmoving party. *Adickes,* 398 U.S. at 157. In

14 doing so here, the court should conclude that a reasonable jury could find that Mr. Walter's

15 questioning manifested an intention not to rent to Ms. Patt due to her marital and familial status.

16 *Anderson,* 477 U.S. at 248. Thus, there is a genuine dispute of material fact as to how Mr. Walter's

17 inappropriate questioning influenced Ms. Patt's application. The extent to which these questions

18 influenced her application is an issue which must be afforded a full trial on the merits.

1   **C. A Reasonable Jury Could Find That Ms. Patt's Decision to Stop Payment on Her**

2   **Application Fee Check Does Not Preclude Her Claim of Discrimination Because Any**

3   **Further Act to Pursue Her Application Would Have Been a Futile Gesture Under the**

4   **Futile Gesture Doctrine.**

5   Even if this court were to find that Ms. Patt must establish that she made a bona fide offer to

6   rent the apartment, and further finds that no reasonable jury could find that she did make a bona

7   fide offer, the court must nonetheless deny the motion for summary judgment under the futile

8   gesture doctrine.

9   The Fourth Circuit adopted this employment discrimination law doctrine in prior housing

10   discrimination decisions to avoid requiring a victim of discrimination to "press on meaninglessly" in

11   an application process when they know that their efforts will be futile. *Pinchback v. Armistead*

12   *Homes Corp.*, 907 F.2d 1447, 1452 (4th Cir. 1990). Here, as a result of Mr. Walters's inappropriate

13   and intrusive questions and behavior, Ms. Patt reasonably concluded that he would refuse to rent

14   the apartment to her. Patt Dep. 9:35–41, 55:9–10. Thus, she was not obligated to go through the

15   motions of submitting an application she knew would prove to be a waste of her money. *See*

16   *International Bros. of Teamsters v. United States*, 431 U.S. 324, 365–66 (1977) (holding that, in the

17   employment law context, an application is not a prerequisite in circumstances when "a person's

18   desire for a job is not translated into a formal application solely because of [their] unwillingness to

19   engage in a futile gesture.") The court should apply the futile gesture doctrine here because

20   requiring a victim of discrimination to go through the added humiliation and effort of submitting a

21   pointless application is antithetical to the purpose of the federal Fair Housing Act. Moreover, the

22   requirements of the prima facie case of discrimination were "never intended to be rigid, mechanized,

23   or ritualistic," and should not be used to defeat an otherwise valid claim of discrimination.

24

1   *Swierkiewicz v. Sorema N.A.*, 534 U.S. 506, 512 (2002). Rather, the question is simply whether a

2   reasonable jury could conclude that the housing decision was made "under circumstances giving rise

3   to an inference of unlawful discrimination." (U.S. Department of Housing and Urban Development

4   Memorandum on the Elements of Proof, pg. 4 (Aug. 13, 2014)). Here, there is sufficient evidence for

5   a reasonable jury to conclude that taking further steps to apply for the apartment would have been

6   a futile gesture, because Mr. Walters had already made his decision for discriminatory reasons.

IV. CONCLUSION

8   Since Ms. Patt has established that there remain genuine disputes as to material facts, the

9   Defendant's motion for partial summary judgment must be denied. Ms. Patt and Mr. Donner

10   fundamentally disagree as to whether Mr. Walters made his decision to rent the apartment based

11   on discriminatory reasons or permissible ones. By refusing to afford Ms. Patt a fair opportunity to

12   compete for the apartment, Mr. Walter's violated the plain language of the FHA. Plaintiffs are not

13   required to go through the motion of submitting an application that is certain to be rejected for

14   discriminatory reasons. A reasonable jury could find that Ms. Patt's payment of the application fee

15   would have been a futile gesture because Defendant, through his agent Will Walters, made it clear

16   to Ms. Patt that her application would not be considered because of her familial status. Thus, these

17   questions must be submitted to the jury, and the court should deny the Defendant's motion for

18   summary judgment.

19   Respectfully submitted,

20   _____

     Sam Pellegrino
21   On behalf of Ms. Paula Patt

22

23

24

ORDER DENYING DEFENDANT'S MOTION FOR PARTIAL SUMMARY JUDGMENT

IN THE UNITED STATES DISTRICT COURT
FOR THE NORTHERN DISTRICT OF CALIFORNIA
OAKLAND DIVISION

PAULA PATT,

        Plaintiff,

    v.

DAN DONNER,

        Defendant.

No. C 1357 DBO

**ORDER DENYING MOTION FOR
PARTIAL SUMMARY JUDGMENT**

/

This matter comes before the Court on Defendant Dan Donner's Motion for Partial Summary Judgment on Plaintiff Paula Patt's federal Fair Housing Act (FHA) claim. *See* FRCP Rule 56(a); 42 U.S.C. § 3604. Based on the record, with all inferences viewed in the light most favorable to the non-moving party, the Court finds a genuine dispute of material fact regarding whether discrimination occurred before Plaintiff Paula Patt stopped payment on her application check to rent the apartment. *See Adickes,* 398 U.S. at 158–59; *see also Anderson v. Liberty Lobby,* 477 U.S. 242, 248 (1986). Specifically, a reasonable jury could find that agent Will Walters' intrusive line of questioning regarding Plaintiff Paula Patt's marital status, the identity of her daughter's father, and her past sexual partners amounted to discrimination based on Plaintiff's familial status. *See* Patt Dep. 4:35–42, 8:1–4; Walters Dep. 51:21–26.

For the foregoing reasons, Defendant's Motion for Partial Summary Judgment on Plaintiff's federal FHA claim is denied.

IT IS SO ORDERED.

Dated: November 12

_____
DIANNE B. OSAKA
UNITED STATES DISTRICT JUDGE

CHAPTER 9

NEGOTIATING A SETTLEMENT

SETTLEMENT CORRESPONDENCE

The time has come to either settle this case or take it to trial. Both sides have agreed to meet and discuss the possibility of a settlement. The process was initiated by the correspondence on the following pages.

After the correspondence you will find a record of relevant settlements and jury verdicts, chosen to provide guidance for your negotiations. Use these materials to frame your goals and set the parameters of the discussion. There is also a copy of a consent decree for the *Workman Living Trust* case included in the documents. (A consent decree is an order by a court, drafted by the parties, setting forth the terms of their settlement in the form of a court approved order.) The *Workman Living Trust* consent decree is a good illustration of how the terms of a settlement are put into writing, but you are not being asked to draft a full settlement agreement or consent decree.

In addition to the written correspondence and attached materials, your professor will provide you with confidential memoranda for each party. Consult only the materials addressed to your party; do not access material intended for others. Your professor will further instruct you regarding the process by which you should meet and attempt to negotiate a settlement.

If your group is able to agree on a settlement, you will report your results on the brief Settlement Form found at the end of this document. Only <u>one</u> form should be submitted for each group negotiation. All counsel for both the plaintiff and defendant must therefore consent to the terms and should nominate one representative to submit the form for the group as whole. If you are unable to reach a settlement, your group must prepare a Joint Pretrial Statement in accordance with the instructions found at the end of this document. Only <u>one</u> statement should be submitted for each group. Be advised that this option will require your group to prepare a lengthy document outlining the key facts, claims, and procedural history of this lawsuit. You will therefore save considerable time and effort if your group is able to negotiate a settlement.

In addition to either the Settlement Form or the Joint Pretrial Statement, each participant must also independently write two brief reflections. One should be written before, while the other should be written after, the settlement negotiation meeting(s). Your reflections should address your individual thoughts, assumptions and strategies going into the negotiation as well as your perspective on the process after it wraps up. Each paper should be no more than a paragraph or two and must be submitted individually by each student.

Please save and submit your reflection as: **PvD_Reflection_LastName**

(this should include both the pre- and post-negotiation
reflection in one document)

Berkeley Legal Clinic
2013 Center Street, Suite 310
Berkeley, CA 94704

November 9

Jane Johnson, Attorney at Law
Johnson & Shermen, LLP
10000 Shattuck Ave., Suite 3500
Berkeley, California, 94704

RE: PATT v. DONNER (Civ. #1357)

Dear Ms. Johnson,

As you know, our Legal Clinic represents Ms. Paula Patt in her action against your client Dan Donner for housing discrimination. Given the evidence that Mr. Walters changed his behavior toward Ms. Patt after learning she has a child, his discriminatory questions about her marital status, and his admission during his deposition that he accepted a later applicant **before** he attempted to deposit Ms. Patt's credit screening check, not to mention the questionable purposes for which those funds were intended, a jury will have little trouble determining that he discriminated against Ms. Patt, and holding your client liable. As a trial date has been set for next month, we would like to provide your client with a final opportunity to settle this matter on terms amenable to both parties. Below please find an assessment of the damages sustained by our client, and a proposal for settlement.

OUT-OF-POCKET COSTS: When Ms. Patt was denied the apartment at 1357 Telegraph Avenue because of her marital and familial status, she was forced to remain in a hotel for an additional fourteen nights at a cost of $100 per night. During that time, in addition to attending courses in her graduate program at Berkeley, she spent between three and five hours per day searching for an apartment. This time was spent looking through apartment listings on the Internet and in local newspapers, traveling to and from apartment viewings, and compiling the information for apartment applications. Her transportation costs totaled $35. Her printing costs were $15. The fees she paid for credit checks (which she assumes were more legitimate than your client's web surfing) totaled $150. Had she not been busy with these tasks, she would have been able to spend an additional twenty hours conducting research for her advisor, for which she would have been paid $15 per hour. The monthly rent of the apartment that she finally found is $2,000, or $200 more than she would have paid at 1357 Telegraph Avenue. This is a cost that she will have to pay every month for as long as she remains in the apartment; however, she is only seeking compensation for the first year. Thus her out-of-pocket costs total $4,300.

EMOTIONAL DISTRESS: Mr. Walters' discriminatory act caused Ms. Patt significant embarrassment and emotional distress. The questions he asked during the apartment viewing were humiliating and degrading, especially given the presence of Sally. Nearly three months after the visit, Ms. Patt continues to be despondent when she thinks about your client's discrimination. Given the size of judgments in similar cases,[1] we believe that Ms. Patt would receive at least $50,000 for her emotional distress at trial.

PUNITIVE DAMAGES: The laws of the state of California and of our nation specifically seek the eradication of housing discrimination. Since discrimination is hard to detect and hard to police, it should be harshly met wherever it is found so there can be no doubt in the minds of those who might discriminate that their actions will not be tolerated. Given the size of judgments in similar cases, we believe that Ms. Patt would receive a minimum of $100,000 in punitive damages at trial. Therefore we request $100,000 in punitive damages.

ATTORNEYS' FEES AND LEGAL EXPENSES: Our supervising attorney has spent 50 hours on this case at a fee of $500 per hour ($25,000), and our students have spent 200 hours at a fee of $250 per hour ($50,000). We have also expended $3,000 in filing fees and other legal costs. Thus our total legal expenses are $78,000.

TOTAL: In sum, a conservative estimate of the total recoverable costs in this case is $232,300.

INJUNCTIVE RELIEF: The harm caused by Mr. Donner and his agent Mr. Walters was not solely monetary: the act of discrimination offended Ms. Patt's dignity and deprived her of a tangible benefit to which she had a right. Thus she seeks an apology, to be published in the Daily Californian and the New York Times, for which we will provide the wording. She also seeks to rent the next available apartment located at 1357 Telegraph Avenue, free of rent for the first six months of her occupancy. Finally, she seeks a commitment from your client not to engage in any sort of discrimination against future applicants.

Thank you for your courtesy in this matter.

Sincerely,

Matt Madison
Certified Law Student
Berkeley Legal Clinic

Attorneys for Plaintiff

---

[1]   See, e.g., *Timus v. William J. Davis, Inc.* ($2.4 million jury verdict for housing discrimination against families with children).

November 14

Matt Madison, Certified Law Student
Berkeley Legal Clinic
2013 Center Street, Suite 310
Berkeley, California, 94704

CONFIDENTIAL SETTLEMENT LETTER—INADMISSIBLE FOR ANY PURPOSE

RE: PATT v. DONNER (C 1357 DBO)

Dear Matt:

I received your so-called "settlement offer"—if it can be called that—dated November 9. I have to say, I was frankly astonished by the sums you are seeking. It left me wondering if you have been assigned to this case simply to learn something about the law of housing discrimination, and to that end I will endeavor to explain a few things to you.

Your client does not have any hope of being able to prove her claims in court, and any reasonable jury would be shocked at the magnitude of her demands. Seeking damages because your client had to conduct a standard search for an apartment—something that everyone must do from time to time—is ludicrous.

I would further remind you that by rights your client should be paying damages to us for the fraud she perpetrated in bouncing her check for the background investigation.

As you should know, attorneys' fees under the FHA are a two way street. You may be entitled to fees if you prevail, but Mr. Donner is entitled to his attorneys' fees if the court determines that your lawsuit was frivolous. Should your client move forward with this action, she will almost surely lose and find herself responsible for paying not only her own legal expenses but also those of my client, totaling perhaps $125,000 to date, and growing.

However, if she steps forward to apologize for the nuisance she has caused, we are willing to walk away from the matter without moving for attorneys' fees. While I believe our position on this is clear, we are amenable to a conference if you feel that is necessary.

Thank you for your cooperation.

                                                  Sincerely,

                                                  Jane Johnson, Attorney at Law

Berkeley Legal Clinic
2013 Center Street, Suite 310
Berkeley, CA 94704

November 17

Jane Johnson, Attorney at Law
Johnson & Shermen, LLP
10000 Shattuck Ave., Suite 3500
Berkeley, California, 97404

RE: PATT v. DONNER (Civ. #1357)

Dear Ms. Johnson,

I appreciate your prompt response to our November 9th letter, and in light of the doubts you expressed, I thought I would bring some recent case law on the subject of housing discrimination to your attention. I have attached to this letter a number of recent reports on housing discrimination settlements. These cases affirm the validity of our position as well as the reasonableness of Ms. Patt's claims.

We are looking forward to proceeding with the settlement discussion.

Thank you for careful attention.

Sincerely,

Matt Madison
Certified Law Student
Berkeley Legal Clinic

Attorneys for Plaintiff

Jury Verdict Report
KARL S. REMINGSON v. ASHTON A. LILYHAMMER
No.7:09–cv–55575–DBO

DATE OF VERDICT: August 16

TOPIC: HOUSING DISCRIMINATION—RACE—FAMILIAL STATUS—CIVIL RIGHTS—FAIR HOUSING ACT

SUMMARY:

RESULT: Verdict-Plaintiff

AWARD: $180,000 (incl. $100,000 in punitive damages)

The jury found that Lilyhammer intentionally rejected Remingson's housing application based on his race and familial status, and awarded him $180,000 in damages, including $80,000 in compensatory damages and $100,000 in punitive damages.

ATTORNEYS:

Plaintiffs: Kevin Augustus Walker III—West Bay Community Law Center

Defendants: Jane Johnson—Johnson & Shermen, LLP

JUDGE: Hon. Dianne B. Osaka

SETTLEMENT OFFER RANGE AMOUNT: $50,000–$275,000

STATE: California

COUNTY: Alameda

COURT: United States District Court, N.D. of California

INJURIES: Remingson sought damages to compensate for discrimination on the basis of race and familial status, as well as severe emotional distress and psychic pain.

FACTS:

Plaintiff Karl Remingson is a thirty-two-year-old African-American male. From 2004 to 2010, Mr. Remingson was married to Kristen Leavensworth, a thirty-three-year-old Caucasian female. He is currently the sole legal guardian of his daughter Kalie (seven) and his son Alex (five), though Ms. Leavensworth is attempting to regain custody and proceedings are still pending in court.

On the morning of September 18th, 2011, Karl Remingson responded to a newspaper ad in the *Oakland Sentinel* listing an apartment for rent in the Crocker Highlands, near Crocker Park. The ad was also posted on the *Sentinel's* website and uploaded to Gregslist an hour after the *Sentinel's* print edition hit newsstands. The ad is reprinted below in its entirety:

1

APARTMENT FOR RENT!!!! CALL NOW!!!!

Gorgeous two-bedroom art deco apartment nestled in the Crocker Highlands. Short walk to Crocker Highlands Elementary, and a short drive to Oakland-area restaurants and attractions. Landlord wishes to rent quickly, so price is COMPETITIVE. The first ten callers will receive an EXCLUSIVE tour by appointment and have a right of first offer. Landlord reserves the right to refuse a showing for any reason.

Call (510) 672-xxxx to reserve your spot NOW!

On noticing the ad, Mr. Remingson immediately called the listed number. Defendant Ashton Lilyhammer, the landlord, answered. Mr. Remingson asked if the apartment was still available, and Mr. Lilyhammer enthusiastically confirmed it was. "Congratulations, you're the seventh caller!" exclaimed Mr. Lilyhammer. "When would you like to visit my place?" Mr. Remingson scheduled an appointment for later that afternoon.

When Mr. Remingson arrived, Mr. Lilyhammer gave him a brief tour of the apartment. According to Mr. Remingson, the two engaged in warm, personal conversation during the tour. Mr. Lilyhammer mentioned his upcoming move to Spain, and explained he wanted to be closer to his longtime girlfriend who lived in Barcelona. Mr. Remingson made a comment on the vagaries of love, followed by a brief reference to his divorce and the ongoing child custody proceedings. According to Mr. Remingson, Mr. Lilyhammer was visibly startled to learn Mr. Remingson had children. He inquired their names and ages, and Mr. Remingson noted that he seemed "perturbed." Mr. Lilyhammer's demeanor became "colder, more distant," and conversation soon languished.

Mr. Remingson, still intent on renting the apartment, repeatedly expressed his pleasure with the place and asked for an application. Mr. Lilyhammer was reluctant to furnish one, but finally provided Mr. Remingson with a two-page rental application of his own design. Mr. Remingson promptly filled out the document, indicating (among other things) his current address and his phone number, and pledging to immediately accept the apartment if offered to him.

That same night, around seven o'clock, Mr. Remingson received a phone call from a blocked number. When he answered, the caller identified himself as Mr. Lilyhammer. Speaking in a heavy, slurred manner, Mr. Lilyhammer informed Mr. Remingson he could not rent the apartment. Bewildered by the call and the abrupt refusal, Mr. Remingson requested an explanation. At this point, Mr. Lilyhammer began to verbally abuse Mr. Remingson, injecting a liberal dose of racial slurs, insulting his children and stating he would "never rent to you and your family." He then hung up.

A week later, Mr. Remingson filed suit against Mr. Lilyhammer, alleging discrimination on the basis of race and familial status.

During preliminary proceedings, the defendant moved for summary judgment, which Judge Osaka denied.

At trial, the defendant argued that Mr. Remingson's allegation of discrimination on the basis of familial status was "entirely manufactured based on internal perception" and urged the jury to discount "the feelings of an overly sensitive man eager to play the victim." Any odd behavior on the part of Mr. Lilyhammer could be chalked up to "his anxieties about his impending move and embarking on a level of sustained commitment with his girlfriend." Mr. Lilyhammer denied making any phone call to Mr. Remingson. Several of Mr. Lilyhammer's friends testified to the strength of his character, and claimed he had never spoken violently or insultingly of anyone.

2

The jury found Mr. Lilyhammer liable for discrimination on the basis of race and familial status, and awarding Mr. Remingson $180,000 in damages, including $100,000 in punitive damages.

The plaintiffs made a motion for an award of legal costs which is still pending.

Jury Verdict Report
MARIA A. SNYDER v. WILLIAM M. BOGGS AND JACOB L. REIDY
No. 2:02–cv–08867–BMT

DATE OF VERDICT/SETTLEMENT: August 16

TOPIC: DISCRIMINATION—FAIR HOUSING ACT—CIVIL RIGHTS—SEXUAL HARASSMENT

SUMMARY:

AWARD: $60,000

RESULT: Verdict-Plaintiff

The jury found that Boggs intentionally rejected Snyder's housing application based on her sex. The panel awarded her $60,000 in compensatory damages.

ATTORNEYS:

Plaintiff: Elizabeth S. Bosnian—Richardson, Young, DeCastro and Myers, LLP

Defendant: Jamal Washington—Roberts & Peralta, LLP; Marjorie N. Slivikoff—Roberts & Peralta, LLP

JUDGE: Braulio M. Torelli

SETTLEMENT OFFER RANGE AMOUNT: $25,000–$180,000

STATE: Pennsylvania

COUNTY: Not Applicable

COURT: United States District Court, E.D. Pennsylvania

INJURIES: Snyder sought damages to compensate for humiliation, embarrassment, and pain resulting from her experience.

BACKGROUND:

Plaintiff Maria Snyder, formerly Mario Snyder, has lived as a woman for the past 8 years. Four years ago, she had gender reassignment surgery and legally changed her name.

FACTS:

On June 3, plaintiff Maria Snyder, a sign language interpreter, responded to a newspaper ad for a rental condominium in an up-and-coming neighborhood near the Philadelphia waterfront.

Jacob Reidy, the rental agent, showed Ms. Snyder the condo on June 7.

Snyder claims that during the showing Reidy asked her why she had moved to Philadelphia. Snyder responded that she had secured a job as an interpreter in the area, and was hoping to get involved with a renowned non-profit organization in the area that works on the rights of transgender persons. When Reidy inquired further into her interest in that organization, Snyder revealed her personal connection to the issue, responding "I used to be a man."

1

Snyder states that Reidy did not seem to react negatively to the response at the time, but claims that Reidy refused to shake her hand when she left, and that Reidy made her uncomfortable by the way he looked at her. Still, before leaving, Snyder arranged for another appointment with Reidy on June 9 to sign the lease.

The next morning, Reidy called Ms. Snyder and told her that Mr. Boggs, the landlord, had changed his mind and would not rent the condo to her. Maria Snyder asked if his decision had anything to do with her sex or gender, and Boggs said that Reidy merely decided he wanted an applicant with a "quieter lifestyle," according to Snyder.

Snyder sued Boggs and Reidy for sexual harassment, and discrimination under the federal Fair Housing Act.

The plaintiff argued that when she first looked at the condo, she was extremely interested. She began filling out the rental application but Reidy said he had to leave immediately for a medical appointment and scheduled a time two days later when Snyder could come to the rental office to sign the lease.

The defendants presented a very different view of events.

Reidy claimed that he rescheduled the lease signing because Snyder was only able to produce a personal check, not a cashier's check. Reidy acknowledged that he asked Snyder about her social life, but he claimed the subject came up naturally in conversation as they spoke about things to do in the area, as Snyder was a new resident.

Settlement Report
MARTINEZ v. MILLER et al.

DATE OF SETTLEMENT: August 31

TOPIC:

Synopsis: Housing discrimination claims lead to settlement

Case Type: Civil Rights & Constitutional Law; Discrimination; Landlord/Tenant; Eviction; Lease-Residential

DOCKET NUMBER: 09CV02738(LJO)

STATE: California

ATTORNEYS:

Plaintiffs: Jeremy O'Brian—O'Brian and O'Brian; Lisa A. Mendez—O'Brian and O'Brian

Defendants: Michael T. Bass—Schiller & White; Bruno S. Barsakis—Jensen, Jensen, Crawford and Chu, LLP

JUDGE: Lawrence J. Black

SUMMARY:

Verdict/Judgment: Settlement

Settlement Amount: $140,000

Defendant Robert B. Miller and Pine Tree Village's insurer agreed to pay plaintiff $140,000. Defendants also agreed not to employ defendant Christopher A. Tailor as a manager of Pine Tree Village. Defendants were ordered to comply with all federal and state housing discrimination laws and to distribute a notice to current tenants that all tenants, including children are permitted to use the common areas. Defendants were also ordered to pay for attending fair housing training for all employees and agents of Pine Tree Village apartments.

FACTS/CONTENTIONS:

According to court records:

Plaintiff Cristina Martinez moved into the Pine Tree Village apartments with her two minor children in February. Plaintiff claimed that the day they moved in the apartment manager, defendant Mendez, told them that children were not allowed to play outside. Martinez said Tailor threatened to evict them if the children misbehaved.

According to Martinez, in June, Tailor told Martinez that she would have to leave upon the birth of her third child.

Plaintiff Martinez alleged violation of the Fair Housing Act, 42 U.S.C. § 3601, violation of the California Fair Employment and Housing Act, Cal. Gov't Code § 12955 et seq., negligence, violation of quiet use and enjoyment, defamation, wrongful eviction, and violation of the Unruh Civil Rights Act, Cal. Civ. Code § 51 et seq. against defendants Tailor, Miller (Tailor's supervisor), and Pine Tree Village Inc., the owner of the property.

November 19

Matt Madison, Certified Law Student
Berkeley Legal Clinic
2013 Center Street, Suite 310
Berkeley, CA 94704

Dear Mr. Madison,

Thank you for your willingness to continue settlement negotiations on behalf of your client Paula Patt and for at least expressing your willingness to find a more reasonable figure. Notwithstanding our confidence in our ability to obtain a verdict for Mr. Donner at trial, our client remains open to settlement.

However, the verdicts and settlements you have picked are entirely unrepresentative of what Paula's case is worth at settlement. You seem to have cherry-picked irrelevant, inapplicable cases just because you saw large amounts of money.

Accordingly, I have taken the liberty of conducting more thorough research to help inform both parties. Please review the attached reports of jury verdicts and settlement agreements in cases involving similar allegations. These reports will help set much more reasonable parameters as we prepare for future discussions.

I look forward to hearing back after you have read the reports.

Sincerely,

Jane Johnson

(State Bar No. 31415927)
Jane.Johnson@johnsonshermen.com
Johnson & Shermen, LLP
10000 Shattuck Ave., Suite 3500
Berkeley, California 94704
Telephone: (510) 555-3500
Facsimile: (510) 555-3501

Jury Verdict Report
CECIL G. ABERNATHY v. BENJAMIN R. BLACKSWORTH
No. 1:07–cc27084–BSC

DATE OF VERDICT: July 18th

TOPIC: DISCRIMINATION—FAIR HOUSING ACT—FAMILIAL STATUS

SUMMARY:

AWARD: $5,000

RESULT: Verdict-Plaintiff

The jury found that Blacksworth intentionally rejected Abernathy's housing application based on her familial status and awarded her $5,000 compensatory damages and no punitive damages.

ATTORNEYS:

Plaintiff: Angela DeMarco—Ginsburg, Kerouac, Burroughs, Carr & Huncke, LLP

Defendant: Susan Sharondon—Pynchon, Wallace, Salinger & Percy, LLP

JUDGE: Benedict S. Cumberhouse

SETTLEMENT OFFER RANGE AMOUNT: $1,000–$35,000

STATE: New York

COUNTY: Not Applicable

COURT: United States District Court, S.D. New York

INJURIES: Abernathy sought damages to compensate for embarrassment and lost opportunity.

FACTS:

Plaintiff Cecil D. Abernathy is a twenty-seven-year-old female and a doctoral student in anthropology at NYU. She has a daughter, Ashley (seven). In the fall, Ms. Abernathy began searching for a new apartment, looking for a place closer to NYU "with a bit more space for Ashley."

Defendant Benjamin R. Blacksworth is a successful New York businessman who owns a string of properties all across Manhattan. He is a family friend of Ms. Abernathy's parents and an acquaintance of Ms. Abernathy herself. He helped Ms. Abernathy relocate to New York from Iowa City when she began her studies at NYU. He keeps in semi-regular touch with Ms. Abernathy, and occasionally takes her and her daughter out to dinner.

Soon after she began her housing search, Ms. Abernathy contacted Mr. Blacksworth and asked for his assistance in locating a suitable rental property for her and Ashley. Mr. Blacksworth readily agreed, and suggested she take a look at a small one-bedroom apartment he owned a few blocks off of Washington Square. On February 7th, Mr. Blacksworth met Ms. Abernathy and her daughter and gave them a tour of his apartment. According to Ms. Abernathy, he was initially very warm to both of them, inquiring after Ms. Abernathy's studies and asking Ashley how she enjoyed her school. Ashley, according to her mother, was in a "sulky mood" and "behaved badly" during the apartment

1

tour. However, Ms. Abernathy claimed Mr. Blacksworth did not seemed bothered by this, laughing it off and making gentle remarks.

Ms. Abernathy "fell in love" with the apartment and immediately asked Mr. Blacksworth if she could sign a rental agreement. Mr. Blacksworth assented, though he did not have the documents with him at the time. He promised to send a copy of the rental agreement to Ms. Abernathy later that day, stating "the apartment's yours for the taking."

While they were preparing to leave, Ms. Abernathy asked Ashley to retrieve a stuffed animal she'd left lying in the family room. Instead, Ashley walked over to the dining table and pushed a vase of flowers. The vase shattered on the floor. Ms. Abernathy hurriedly rushed her daughter out the door, apologizing profusely to Mr. Blacksworth. Mr. Blacksworth did not respond. According to Ms. Abernathy, he "just stared at the mess, looking bewildered."

Later that day, Ms. Abernathy received a brief e-mail from Mr. Blacksworth. In it, he stated he'd decided not to rent the apartment after all, making a passing reference to some unforeseen business complications that left him "unable to act as a landlord for the time being." Distressed, Ms. Abernathy sent Mr. Blacksworth a number of e-mails questioning his decision and asking him to reconsider. He did not respond.

A few days later, Ms. Abernathy called Mr. Blacksworth on the phone. According to her, their conversation was "brief and terse." Mr. Blacksworth reiterated his refusal to rent her the apartment, and raised the issue of "business complications" as a justification. Frustrated, Ms. Abernathy asked Mr. Blacksworth directly if he'd reneged on his decision because of Ashley's actions. Mr. Blacksworth was "silent for a bit." He then stated that he wasn't so sure "that the apartment was a great fit for Ashley," and hung up.

Ms. Abernathy filed suit against Mr. Blacksworth, accusing him of discrimination on the basis of familial status in violation of the Fair Housing Act. She sought compensatory and punitive damages.

At trial, the jury returned a verdict for the plaintiff and awarded Ms. Abernathy $5,000 in compensatory damages. However, they denied her request for punitive damages.

2

Jury Verdict Report
LAZIZA KARIMOV AND FARHOD KARIMOV v. ROGER BROOKS
CV051156SLC

DATE OF VERDICT/SETTLEMENT: December 20

TOPIC:
Synopsis: Plaintiffs allege housing discrimination

SUMMARY:
Result: Verdict—Defendant

ATTORNEY:
Plaintiffs: Luis M. DelMonte—Specter & Torres, LLP
Defendants: Brenda R. Tokoyama—Little, McCormick, and Freston, LLP

JUDGE: Hon. Selina L. Carusso

SETTLEMENT OFFER RANGE AMOUNT: $15,000–$20,000
Trial Type: Jury
Trial Length: 3 days
Trial Deliberations: 1 day
Jury Poll: Unanimous

STATE: Ohio
COUNTY: Montgomery County

FACTS/CONTENTIONS

Laziza and Farhod Karimov emigrated from Uzbekistan to the United States with their infant son.
The Karimovs came to the U.S. without official records of their marriage. They moved to Ohio in July for Mr. Karimov's work and sought permanent housing while staying with a family friend.

Laziza Karimov sent an email to Roger Brooks on August 3 inquiring into an advertisement published two weeks prior in the *Dayton Daily*. Mr. Brooks replied that the two-bedroom home was still available for rent and the parties scheduled a viewing for the morning of August 7.

The Karimovs and their son went to the house at 1102 Glendale Avenue and met with Mr. Brooks. Later the same afternoon Mrs. Karimov called Mr. Brooks to let him know that they would like to bring the deposit check and a completed rental application over the next morning. Mr. Brooks then informed them that the house had been rented by a married couple that dropped off their deposit check just an hour earlier.

Laziza Karimov and Farhod Karimov brought suit against Roger Brooks for discrimination under the Fair Housing Act.

The Karimovs claim that Mr. Brooks discriminated against them as an unmarried couple because neither Laziza nor Farhod wear wedding bands, and that Mr. Brooks indicated a preference to rent

1

to couples without children. They also claim that Mr. Brooks, in inquiring into their immigration status, discriminated against them for not being American-born.

COMMENTS

According to Defendant: Plaintiffs made a motion for a new trial, which was denied. Defendants' motion for attorney fees was denied.

Settlement Report
ASTERLANE v. WATTS
No. 4:72–rl77251–LEF

DATE OF SETTLEMENT: April 1st

TOPIC:

Synopsis: Fair Housing claims alleging discrimination on the basis of race were settled between the parties for a lump sum.

Case Type: Housing Discrimination, Federal and State Fair Housing Laws, Discrimination on the Basis of Race

STATE: California

ATTORNEYS:

Plaintiff: Albert Ayler—Coleman, Remmings, Scott, Davis & Coltrane LLP

Defendant: Zade Reynolds—Kant, Hegel, Hume, Descartes & Rosseau, LLP

JUDGE: Hon. Leslie E. Foucault

SUMMARY

Verdict/Judgment: Settlement

Settlement Amount: $15,000

Settlement Details: Defendant William Watts agreed to pay Plaintiff Huma Asterlane $15,000 to settle claims of housing discrimination. Additionally, he promised to provide her with an apartment in his complex, at a reduced monthly rate.

Facts/Contentions:

According to court records:

Plaintiff Huma Asterlane, a twenty-five-year-old female, rented an apartment in Carmel-By-The-Sea from Defendant William Watts for a period of seven months, between August and February. The parties initially signed a year-long lease in January, with provisions allowing for the termination of the lease on the part of either party given a three-month notice period.

According to Ms. Asterlane, her relationship with Mr. Watts was cordial at first. Mr. Watts "seemed a little awkward around me, but I didn't really think about it. . .overall, he was a nice man and a fair landlord." Neither party alleged any personal conflicts prior to the events of December and January.

Over the holidays, Ms. Asterlane's boyfriend (who lives in Tokyo, Japan), stayed with her for a period of two weeks. Ms. Asterlane informed Mr. Watts of her boyfriend's visit beforehand. According to her, Mr. Watts "seemed fine with it." After her boyfriend arrived, however, Mr. Watts' attitude changed. Ms. Asterlane stated that he "glowered at us" and often "muttered things under his breath when we walked by." On one occasion, Mr. Watts asked Ms. Asterlane if she and her boyfriend "planned to get married anytime soon, or are you just going to keep sleeping with each other whenever you want?" Ms. Asterlane upbraided Mr. Watts for his offensive comment, and Mr. Watts immediately apologized.

Around the second week of January, Mr. Watts approached Ms. Asterlane and asked her to renegotiate the lease, moving from a year-long format to a month-to-month structure. He pegged his request to "business reasons," stating he "needed to restructure all my leases" in order to "adjust for market shifts." To sweeten the deal, Mr. Watts offered Ms. Asterlane a reduced monthly rate. Although she was "surprised and a little suspicious," Ms. Asterlane assented to the change in order to save some extra money. The new lease provided for termination by any party at any time, for any reason.

The new lease began on February 1st. On February 23rd, Mr. Watts terminated the lease. He informed Ms. Asterlane she was an "undesirable tenant" because she was "too young for the neighborhood" and kept "unconventional company and unconventional hours." Referencing her boyfriend, Mr. Watts advised her to "commit or quit." He gave her a week to vacate the premises.

The next week, Ms. Asterlane sued Mr. Watts for discrimination on the basis of familial status, claiming remedies under federal and state fair housing laws. She sought compensatory and punitive damages in the amount of $75,000, as well as an apartment in the same complex.

CONSENT DECREE

Case5:09-cv-01856-JF   Document30   Filed03/04/10   Page1 of 14

THOMAS E. PEREZ   **E-Filed 3/4/2010**
Assistant Attorney General
Civil Rights Division
STEVEN H. ROSENBAUM
Chief, Housing and Civil Enforcement Section
JON M. SEWARD
Deputy Chief, Housing and Civil Enforcement Section
HARVEY L. HANDLEY (VA Bar #42105)
Attorney, Housing and Civil Enforcement Section
United States Department of Justice
950 Pennsylvania Avenue, N.W.
Northwestern Building, 7th Floor
Washington, D.C. 20530
Phone: (202) 514-4756
Fax: (202) 514-1116
Email: harvey.l.handley@usdoj.gov

Attorneys for Plaintiff United States of America

IN THE UNITED STATES DISTRICT COURT FOR THE
NORTHERN DISTRICT OF CALIFORNIA

UNITED STATES OF AMERICA,)	
)	
Plaintiff; and)	
)	
KIMBERLIE LEBLANC and PROJECT)	C.A. No. 09cv1856
SENTINEL,)	
)	
Plaintiff-intervenors,)	
)	
v.)	
)	
WORKMAN LIVING TRUST, TERRY)	
STULTZ, and TONI STULTZ,)	
)	
Defendants.)	

CONSENT ORDER   1

Case5:09-cv-01856-JF   Document30   Filed03/04/10   Page2 of 14

CONSENT ORDER

PARTIES

Plaintiff, United States of America, initiated this Action on behalf of Kimberlie LeBlanc

and Project Sentinel ("Plaintiff-Intervenors"), pursuant to Section 812(o) of the Fair Housing

Act, 42 U.S.C. § 3612(o) by filing a Complaint with this Court on or about April 29, 2009

("Complaint"). Plaintiff-Intervenors were granted leave to intervene in this Action on October 5,

2009, and their Complaint in Intervention was filed as of that date ("Complaint in Intervention").

Defendant Workman Living Trust owns and manages rental residential property,

including an apartment complex located at 760-780 Northrup Street in San Jose, California ("the

Northrup Street Complex"). Defendant Toni Stultz is employed by the Workman Living Trust as

the on-site manager at the Northrup Street Complex. Defendant Terry Stultz resides at the

Northrup Street Complex with his wife, Defendant Toni Stultz.

Collectively, the United States of America, Kimberlie LeBlanc, Project Sentinel and each

of the Defendants are referred to herein as "the Parties."

ALLEGATIONS

The United States' Complaint, based upon an investigation by the Department of Housing

and Urban Development (HUD), alleges that on or about May 8, 2006, Kimberlie LeBlanc

visited the Northrup Street Complex, and was allegedly told by Defendant Toni Stultz that the

apartments were not set up for children, and the owners had a policy of not renting to children,

although Ms. Stultz showed Ms. LeBlanc an apartment and provided her with an application for

rent. Ms. LeBlanc reported the incident to Project Sentinel, a non-profit corporation organized

under the laws of the State of California, which promotes fair housing practices for housing providers and consumers. Project Sentinel claims to have sent two testers to the Northrup Street Complex, one of whom allegedly represented herself as a woman living with another adult, while the other allegedly represented herself as a woman with a child. Defendant Terry Stultz is alleged to have told the tester who stated that she had a child that apartments at the Northrup Street Complex "were not set up for children," or words to that effect.

Each of the Defendants deny making any discriminatory statements alleged in the Complaint, the Complaint in Intervention or otherwise and adamantly assert they do not discriminate in housing on the basis of any protected classification. Further, Defendants contend they have rented to families with children both at the Northrup Street Complex as well as at other properties owned by the Trust and that both the Complaint and the Complaint in Intervention are without merit.

Ms. LeBlanc and Project Sentinel filed a complaint of discrimination with HUD on September 18, 2006. Following an investigation, on October 16, 2008, the Secretary issued a Charge of Discrimination pursuant to 42 U.S.C. § 3610(g)(2)(A), charging Defendants with engaging in discriminatory housing practices in violation of the Act. On October 29, 2008, Defendants elected to have the Charge resolved in a civil action in federal district court, pursuant to 42 U.S.C. § 3612(a). The filing of this action followed on April 29, 2009, pursuant to 42 U.S.C. § 3612(o). The United States' Complaint alleges that the Defendants made statements with respect to the rental of a dwelling that indicate a preference, limitation, or discrimination, or an intent to make such a preference, limitation or discrimination, based on familial status, in violation of 42 U.S.C. § 3604(c).

In an effort to avoid costly litigation, the Parties have voluntarily agreed to resolve all

CONSENT ORDER   3

claims which have been or could have been alleged in the Complaint and/or in the Plaintiff-Intervenor's Complaint in Intervention without the necessity of a trial and without the admission of any liability by any of the Defendants. Therefore, the Parties have agreed to the entry of this Consent Order and the exchange of other consideration referenced herein, as indicated by the signatures below.

JURISDICTION OF CONSENT ORDER

1.   The Parties have consented to the entry of this Order. To this end, the Parties stipulate and the Court finds that this Court has subject matter jurisdiction over this action pursuant to 28 U.S.C. §§ 1331, 1345 and 42 U.S.C. §§ 3612(o).

GENERAL INJUNCTION

2.   The Defendants, their officers, agents, employees, successors and all persons in active concert or participation with them are enjoined, with respect to the rental of dwelling units at the apartment complexes located at the Northrup Street Complex, from making, printing, or publishing, or causing to be made, printed, or published any notice, statement, or advertisement, with respect to the rental of a dwelling that indicates any preference, limitation, or discrimination based on familial status, or an intention to make any such preference, limitation, or discrimination.

NOTICE OF DEFENDANTS' NON-DISCRIMINATION POLICY

3.   Within ten (10) days of the date of entry of this Consent Order, Defendants shall post and prominently display in a suitable public area of the Northrup Street Complex, a sign no smaller than 10 by 14 inches indicating that Defendants comply with the nondiscrimination provisions of the Fair Housing Act. A poster that comports with 24 C.F.R. Part 110 will satisfy

this requirement.

4.   For the duration of this Consent Order, in all future advertising in newspapers, and on pamphlets, brochures and other promotional literature, and electronic media regarding the Northrup Street Complex, they shall place, in a conspicuous location, the statement "Equal Housing Opportunity" or the Fair Housing Logo.

MANDATORY EDUCATION AND TRAINING

5.   Within 30 days of the entry of this Decree, each employee who is involved in showing or renting apartments at the Northrup Street Complex (presently, only Defendant Toni Stultz) as well as her husband, Defendant Terry Stultz, shall sign a statement acknowledging that he or she has received and read the Order, and had an opportunity to have questions about the Order answered. This statement shall be substantially in the form of Appendix A.

6.   Within ninety (90) days of the date of entry of this Consent Order, Defendants Toni Stultz and Terry Stultz shall undergo training on the Fair Housing Act, with particular emphasis on the provisions prohibiting discrimination on the basis of familial status. Defendants represent and warrant that Defendant Toni Stultz is the only employee currently involved in showing or renting apartments at the Northrup Street Complex. The training shall be conducted by the California Apartment Association, Tri-County Division, and any expenses associated with this training shall be borne by Defendants. The United States has satisfied itself that the CAA-Tri-County Division is an appropriate training provider.

7.   Each person who undergoes training in accordance with the preceding paragraph shall execute a certificate of attendance in the form set out in Appendix B. Within ten (10) days of the date on which such person undergoes training, Defendant Workman Living Trust shall

send a copy of that certificate to counsel for Plaintiff.

PAYMENT OF MONETARY DAMAGES TO PLAINTIFF-INTERVENORS

8.   Defendants and the Plaintff-Intervenors in this matter have reached an agreement pursuant to which Defendants will make a monetary payment of $8,250 to the Plaintiff-Intervenors in the form of a check made payable jointly to Kimberlie LeBlanc and Project Sentinel. Payment shall be sent to counsel for the Plaintiff-Intervenors who shall hold such payment in trust until such time as the Plaintiff-Intervenors each have executed a Release of all claims, legal or equitable, that Plaintiff-Intervenors might have against any of the Defendants relating to the claims asserted in this Complaint and/or the Complaint in Intervention. (Appendix C). Plaintiff-Intervenors represent that they have a separate agreement dividing the proceeds of the settlement among them and that this separate agreement provides that each of them will receive from these proceeds a monetary amount which amount each Plaintiff-Intervenor independently and voluntarily agrees constitutes, individually and collectively, full and fair consideration for the dismissal of all claims against all Defendants, the release to be executed by Plaintiff-Intervenors pursuant to this Agreement, and the other obligations to which they have agreed herein.

PROCESSING RENTAL APPLICATIONS, RECORD KEEPING AND REPORTING

9.   Defendant Workman Living Trust shall maintain, with respect to dwellings rented by them, their agents or employees, objective, uniform, non-discriminatory standards and procedures for the processing of applications.   Such standards and procedures have been submitted to the United States, which has satisfied itself that the standards and procedures are not discriminatory under the Fair Housing Act.

10.   Within four (4) months of the date of entry of this Consent Order, Defendants shall furnish to counsel for the United States documentation that Defendants have complied with the obligations of paragraphs 3-9. Six (6) months after the entry of this Decree, and every six months thereafter for the period in which the Order is in effect, Defendants shall deliver to counsel for the United States, a report stating whether (1) any new employees have been hired to show or rent apartments at the Norhtrup Street Complex; and (2) the rental procedures and standards have changed. If neither of these events have occurred, the statement "Negative Report" shall suffice.

11.   During the term of this Order, Defendant Workman Living Trust shall advise counsel for the United States in writing within fifteen (15) days of receipt of any written complaint against the Defendant Workman Living Trust regarding discrimination on the basis of familial status, and a description of the resolution of such complaint. Defendant Workman Living Trust shall provide a copy of it with the notice. The notice shall include the full details of the complaint, including the complainant's name, address, and telephone number, if such information is available to Defendant Workman Living Trust. The Defendant Workman Living Trust shall promptly provide the United States all information it may request concerning any

such complaint. Within fifteen (15) days of the resolution of any such complaints, Defendants shall advise counsel for the United States of such resolution.

DURATION OF CONSENT ORDER AND TERMINATION OF LEGAL ACTION

12.   This Consent Order shall remain in effect for two (2) years after the date of its entry. By consenting to entry of this Order, the United States and Defendants agree that in the event that Defendants are found by a court of law to have engaged in any future violation(s) of the Fair Housing Act, such violation(s) shall constitute a subsequent violation pursuant to 42 U.S.C. § 3614(d)(1)(C)(ii).

13.   The Court shall retain jurisdiction for the duration of this Consent Decree to enforce the terms of the Decree, after which time the case shall be dismissed with prejudice. Plaintiff may move the Court to extend the duration of the Decree in the interests of justice. In the meantime, once this agreement has been approved by the Court, the Court at its discretion may place this matter on its Deferred List.

14.   The Parties to this Consent Order shall endeavor in good faith to resolve informally any differences regarding interpretation of and compliance with this Order prior to bringing such matters to the Court for resolution. However, in the event of a failure by the Parties to perform, in a timely manner, any act required by this Order or otherwise to fail to act in conformance with any provision thereof, any Party may move this Court to impose any remedy authorized by law or equity, including, but not limited to, an order requiring performance of such act or deeming such act to have been performed, and an award of any damages, costs, and reasonable attorney's fees which may have been occasioned by the violation or failure to perform.

15.   The Parties agree that full implementation of this Order will provide a fair and

reasonable resolution of the allegations of the United States and the Plaintiff-Intervenors and that neither the United States nor the Plaintiff-Intervenors shall take any additional action against any of the Defendants for any of the claims that were raised or could have been raised in the Complaint or in the Complaint in Intervention so long as Defendants comply with this Order.

TIME FOR PERFORMANCE

16.   Any time limits for performance imposed by this Consent Order may be extended by mutual written agreement of the parties.

COST OF LITIGATION

17.   Each party to this litigation will bear its own costs and attorney fees associated with this litigation.

ORDERED this ___3rd___ day of _____February_____, ~~2009.~~ 2010

_____
UNITED STATES DISTRICT COURT

Agreed to by the parties as indicated by the signatures of counsel below.

FOR THE PLAINTIFFS:

DATED: December 30, 2009

THOMAS E. PEREZ
Assistant Attorney General
Civil Rights Division

STEVEN H. ROSENBAUM
Chief, Housing and Civil Enforcement Section

___s/ Harvey L. Handley, Signatory___
JON M. SEWARD, Deputy Chief
HARVEY L. HANDLEY, Trial Attorney
U.S. Department of Justice
Civil Rights Division
Housing and Civil Enforcement Section

FOR PLAINTIFF-INTERVENORS:

DATED: January 25, 2010   _____/s_____
                                                           Kimberlie LeBlanc

DATED: January 28, 2010   Project Sentinel

                                          By: Amika Stevens_____

                                          Its: Director of Fair Housing_____

Approved as to Form and Content:

DATED: January 28, 2010   FAIR HOUSING LAW PROJECT

                                                           _____/s_____
                                                           Annette Kirkham
                                                           152 N. 3d Street, 3rd Floor
                                                           San Jose, CA 95112
                                                           Counsel for Plaintiff Intervenors

Case5:09-cv-01856-JF   Document30   Filed03/04/10   Page11 of 14

FOR THE DEFENDANTS:

DATED: January 10, 2010   _____/s_____
                                            Toni Stultz

DATED: January 10, 2010   _____/s_____
                                            Terry Stultz

DATED: January 10, 1010   Workman Living Trust

                                            By: _____/s_____
                                            Les Workman, Trustee

Approved as to Form and Content:

DATED: January 4, 2010   PAHL & McCAY
                                           A Professional Corporation

                                     -     _____/s_____
                                           Karen K. McCay
                                           225 W. Santa Clara, Suite 1500
                                           San Jose, CA 95113
                                           Attorneys for Defendants

APPENDIX A

EMPLOYEE ACKNOWLEDGMENT

       I acknowledge that on _____ _____, 20__, I received a copy of the Consent Decree entered by the Court in *United States v. Workman Living Trust et al.*, Civil Action No.09cv1856. I have read and understand the Consent Decree, and have had my questions about this document answered. I understand my legal responsibilities and shall comply with those responsibilities.

_____
Signature

_____
Print Name

_____
Job Title

_____
Date

APPENDIX B

TRAINING CERTIFICATION

       I certify that on _____ _____, 20____, I received training with respect to my responsibilities under the Consent Decree entered by the Court in *United States v. Workman Living Trust et al.*, Civil Action No.09cv1856, and the federal, state and local fair housing laws. I understand my legal responsibilities and shall comply with those responsibilities.

_____

Signature

_____

Print Name

_____

Job Title

_____

Date

APPENDIX C
FULL AND FINAL RELEASE OF CLAIMS

Kimberlie LeBlanc and Project Sentinel on behalf of themselves, their family members, if any, their agents, heirs, executors, administrators, successors, employees and assigns, pursuant to the terms, provisions, and conditions of the Consent Order approved by the United States District Court for the Northern District of California in the case of *United States v. Workman Living Trust et al.*, Civil Action No.09cv1856 ("the lawsuit") and in consideration of the payment and other terms and conditions set forth in the Consent Order do fully, finally and forever release, discharge, and hold harmless Workman Living Trust, Toni Stultz and Terry Stultz (hereinafter "the Defendants"), along with their attorneys, related companies, principals, predecessors, successors, assigns, affiliates, partners, directors, officers, agents, employers, shareholders, subsidiaries, employees, former employees, heirs, executors, and administrators and any persons acting under their respective direction or control (hereinafter "Releasees"), from any and all claims set forth, or which could have been set forth, in the Complaint and/or the Complaint in Intervention in this lawsuit that they may have against Defendants or any of the Releasees for any of Defendants' actions or statements related to those claims through the date of this Consent Order, including claims for damages, costs, fines and attorneys' fees.

The undersigned affirm that the only consideration for signing this Full and Final Release of Claims are the terms stated in the Consent Order signed by the parties. The undersigned have accepted the terms of this Release and the Consent Order because they believe them to be a fair and reasonable settlement and for no other reason. This Release and the Consent Order contain and constitute the entire understanding and agreement between the parties to this Release.

DATED: December ___, 2009   _____
                                   Kimberlie LeBlanc

DATED: December ___, 2009   Project Sentinel

                                   By:_____

                                   Its:_____

CHAPTER 9 SKILLS EXERCISE

SETTLEMENT AGREEMENT

SETTLEMENT AGREEMENT FORM

If your group was able to negotiate a settlement, draft this document with your opposing counsel. This agreement should reflect the terms to which both parties have consented. Counsel for both the plaintiff and the defendant must sign their names (electronic signatures are sufficient), and must select one representative to submit the document on behalf of both parties.

Please save and submit this document as:

PvD_SettlementForm_W-X-Y-Z

(W-X-Y-Z representing the last names of each
student in alphabetical order)

CASE: Patt v. Donner (C 1357 DBO)

This Settlement Agreement is by and between Paula Patt ("Plaintiff") and Dan Donner ("Defendant") to settle all claims related to alleged violations of the Fair Housing Act and the California Fair Housing and Employment Act. In exchange for the satisfactory completion of the terms of this agreement, Plaintiff agrees to dismiss with prejudice all claims against Defendant, including claims not made that could have been made, as of the signing of this Agreement.

This Settlement Agreement constitutes the entire agreement between the parties on the matters raised herein, and no other statement, promise, or agreement, either written or oral, made by either party or agents of either party that is not contained in this Settlement Agreement will be enforceable under its provisions.

SETTLEMENT TERMS:

Defendant agrees to pay Plaintiff a <u>total</u> of $_____ as full settlement of all claims made and unmade.

The Parties also agree to the following <u>non-monetary relief</u>:

By their signatures below, the parties, by and through counsel, indicate their consent to the terms and conditions set forth above.

COUNSEL FOR THE PLAINTIFF

Name: _____   Date: _____

Name: _____   Date: _____

COUNSEL FOR THE DEFENSE

Name: _____   Date: _____

Name: _____   Date: _____

2

JOINT PRETRIAL STATEMENT INSTRUCTIONS

If your group was unable to negotiate a settlement, you must draft a Joint Pretrial Statement containing the information outlined below. Counsel for both the plaintiff and the defendant must sign their names on the document (electronic signatures are sufficient), and must select one representative to submit the document on behalf of both parties.

Please save and submit this document as:
PvD_PretrialStatement_W-X-Y-Z

(W-X-Y-Z representing the last names of
each student in alphabetical order)

Required Information

1. **The Action**
   a. **Substance of the Action.** A brief description of the substance of claims and defenses which remain to be decided, including a list of the claims and defenses to be tried. In addition, each party shall attach to the Statement the elements of proof for any claim and/or defense which they assert and a summary of the evidence anticipated to prove the same.

   b. **Relief Prayed.** A detailed statement of all the relief claimed, particularly itemizing all elements of damages claimed as well as witnesses, documents or other evidentiary material to be presented concerning the amount of those damages.

2. **The Factual Basis of the Action**
   a. **Undisputed Facts.** A plain and concise statement of all relevant facts not in dispute, as well as all facts the parties will stipulate for admission into the trial record without the necessity of supporting testimony or exhibits.

   b. **Disputed Factual Issues.** A plain and concise statement of all disputed factual elements of a claim which remain to be decided.

   c. **Agreed Statement.** A statement assessing whether all or part of the action may be presented upon an agreed statement of facts.

   d. **Stipulations.** A statement of stipulations requested or proposed for pretrial or trial purposes.

3. **Disputed Legal Issues**
   a. **Points of Law.** Without extended legal argument, a concise statement of each disputed point of law concerning liability or relief, citing supporting statutes and decisions setting forth the nature of each party's contentions concerning each disputed point of law, including procedural and evidentiary issues. Supporting statutes and decisions and the parties' contentions regarding the same shall be brief and provided in an outline or bullet-point format.

   b. **Further Discovery or Motions.** A statement of any remaining discovery and why the same was not completed by the cutoff dates and/or pending motions.

   c. **Estimate of Trial Time.** An estimate of the number of court days requested for the presentation of each party's case, indicating possible reductions in time through proposed

1

stipulations, agreed statements of facts, or expedited means of presenting testimony and exhibits.

4.   Trial Alternatives and Options

a.   **Settlement Discussions.** A statement summarizing the status of settlement negotiations and indicating whether further negotiations are likely to be productive.

b.   **Amendments, Dismissals.** A statement of requested or proposed amendments to pleadings or dismissals of parties, claims or defenses and any objections thereto.